Praise for Karen Ma's
China's Millennial Digital Generation

"Karen Ma's new book is a fascinating look at a relatively unknown group of Chinese filmmakers… many of whom have worked independently from directly state-sponsored institutions. Deftly balancing considerations around production, distribution, exhibition, and financing in the Chinese and global marketplace, Ma usefully details the specific contexts that shaped the movement and the work of a number of its key figures, who tell their own stories through interviews that comprise much of the book. *China's Millennial Digital Generation* takes readers on an eye-opening voyage of discovery, revealing a compelling new vision of Chinese cinema that still remains largely unseen in the West."

—**Matthew Solomon**, author of *Disappearing Tricks: Silent Film, Houdini, and the New Magic of the Twentieth Century.*

"Karen Ma's interviews with seven independent film directors who were born in the 1980s in rural China and focus on the rural society they know so well provide a wonderful guide to what is really happening in Chinese society at the grassroots level. It will be warmly welcomed not just by those interested in Chinese film, but anyone interested in Chinese society more generally."

—**Stanley Rosen**, co-editor of *Soft Power with Chinese Characteristics: China's Campaign for Hearts and Minds*

"Over the past decade, independent Chinese cinema has found it increasingly difficult to find its place between the dominating power of commercial cinema and the encroaching shadow of the political. In *China's Millennial Digital Generation*, Karen Ma shines a light on seven indie filmmakers who continue to push the boundaries of art and politics. Engaging and informative, what emerges through these conversations are a series of rich and nuanced portraits of some of the most innovative filmmakers working in China today."

—**Michael Berry**, author of *Jia Zhangke on Jia Zhangke*

CHINA'S MILLENNIAL DIGITAL GENERATION

Conversations with Balinghou (Post-1980s) Indie Filmmakers

Karen Ma

LONG RIVER PRESS

San Francisco

Published in the United States of America by
Long River Press
360 Swift Ave., #48
South San Francisco, CA

ISBN 978-1-59265-248-8

Printed in the USA

TABLE OF CONTENTS

PREFACE

The idea of writing a book about Chinese independent film never occurred to me until I returned to Beijing in early 2013, where I remained until the end of 2017. In retrospect, it was a time when the Chinese indie film movement was already on the wane. Nevertheless, I was fortunate enough to get close to several indie filmmakers and a few staff members working behind the scene on grassroots film festivals, which opened a whole new world for me. Over the course of the five years, I learned a great deal about the inner workings of Chinese indie film, its background and where it might be headed. I soon realized there wasn't a lot written in the West about this corner of China and the light it shone on a country increasingly affecting the rest of the world, for better or for worse. After some thought, I decided to try and share what I learned about this world. This feeling became even stronger when I started teaching a film-related course.

I've always been a film lover, especially of Chinese film. As an overseas Chinese who lived in Japan and later, the US, I relied on Chinese film to stay in touch with my parents' home and culture. In Tokyo in the 1990s, I used to go to Iwanami Hall in Tokyo's Jinbocho neighborhood to soak up early features by Chen Kaige and Zhang Yimou. This eased my homesickness as someone who felt like a stranger no matter where I was. Later, when I started freelancing for English-language newspapers in Japan, reviewing Chinese films became one of my specialties, an excuse to see as many Chinese movies as possible.

In the early 2000s, I moved to Beijing for the first time with my husband and two children. At the time, I was doing research for a novel, *Excess Baggage*, a fictionalized account of my family's rather tumultuous experience living in Japan. On landing, I started researching recent Chinese history to fill in some of the gaps I felt were missing from my manuscript. As part of that, I started visiting cinemas, film archives, smaller film houses and cafes that held regular screenings on the weekends. That was when I discovered Cherry Lane on Liangmaqiao Road.

The movies screened there were very different from what I was used to. Two of the first movies I watched at Cherry Lane were Li Yang's *Blind Shaft* and Jia Zhangke's *Xiao Wu*. They jolted me, opening my eyes to a different side of China than I'd seen before—migrant workers, corruption fueled by sudden wealth and China's headlong embrace of modernity, the hankering to "make it big" in backwater towns no matter what it took. These films, I later learned, were independently produced "underground" productions that managed to bypass China's powerful film bureau, which explained why they are so raw, bold and compelling.

During my second stint in Beijing after a five-year hiatus in India, I explored more films, which eventually led me to watch Zhao Liang's *Behemoth* at Dongsi's *Camera Stylo*, and to see Li Ruijun's *Fly with the Crane* at Sanlitun's Italian Culture Center. These confirmed my long-held suspicion—that the glitzy commercial films at regular Chinese cinemas didn't tell half of the story of modern China's rise. I couldn't believe how much I had missed, and how much others who were keenly interested in China were missing as well.

In 2015, when I started teaching a Chinese culture and film course at The Beijing Center for Chinese Studies, I had to research the scholarship on Chinese indie films to provide background for my students. I was disappointed that most English-language sources didn't go much beyond the millennium. This is especially the case with feature films.

Where was this lost decade and what had changed since early underground days? That inspired me to write this book about millennial directors doing independent narrative productions. The project would ultimately take several years and include extended interviews with filmmakers who spoke at length about their craft, cinematic ambitions, views on the genre, and what drew them to filmmaking.

I dove into research in earnest, attending film lectures, exhibitions and training camps to find experts who might guide me. Armed with introductions, I sought out young filmmakers who had come of age in the last decade or so. I then narrowed my scope to indie filmmakers born in the 1980s (known as the *balinghou*) who had made at least two feature films with something important to say about Chinese society.

I interviewed some 20 young directors with an eye to any commonalities that connected them as a group, in the process uncovering a few trends that weren't fully acknowledged in Western scholarship. For one, a lot of *balinghou* filmmakers are grassroots artists from smaller towns or rural China not formally trained at film academies. In addition, these younger directors are amongst the first generation to have benefited hugely from new technology, including affordable DV cameras, digital videos and the Internet, which significantly lowered the barriers for artists entering the industry. The Internet, in particular, had made it possible for them to watch movies and learn about filmmaking techniques independently, allowing them to turn their passion into a profession.

More importantly, most of their stories can be traced back to their rural hometowns, bringing a fresh repertoire to Chinese independent film. While rural themes are hardly new in Chinese film history, (both the 4th and 5th generations of filmmakers plumbed these before), these tended in the past to be told mostly from a top-down, urban-elite perspective. The rural narratives of *balinghou* filmmakers, on the other hand, tend to be based on people from their neighborhoods. This lends a much more grassroots perspective, giving audience when it is done well a sense of intimacy not often felt before. These discoveries helped fuel this journey.

Organizing a book is always something of an artificial construct, and that also meant I had to exclude some filmmakers whose works didn't quite fit with the book's overall focus. Some of the filmmakers I interviewed were born in the 1970s, for instance, leaving them slightly outside the *balinghou* age bracket I'd envisioned. Others had barely started their careers, with only one film under their belt. Two female directors focused mainly on urban stories, which are incompatible with the rural themes I was keen to examine.

I tried to include some *balinghou* directors who lived in other parts of China and even abroad, including Bi Gan and Zhang Dalei. But the distance and their busy schedules made their inclusion all but impossible. My move to the US in late 2017, and the 2020 outbreak of Covid-19 further complicated attempts to follow up.

In the end, I settled on six regional filmmakers whose age, cinematic themes and paths to filmmaking fit in with the book's overall objective. Li Ruijun, Huang Ji, Xin Yukun, Yang Jin, Hao Jie and Zhai Yixiang each represent a particular region of China. They all produce independent auteur films, share a rural background, are millennial *balinghou* artists born in the 1980s, and focus on rural society as a lens into China's larger social problems.

While talking to these directors, I was struck by how their personal journeys from wide-eyed adolescents to camera commanders-in-chief were often as compelling as their films. "Bad students like me would never have made it to college before," Hao Jie told me, adding that he was initially very embarrassed by his modest upbringing in a remote northeastern village. Riding the wave of China's education reform and a booming movie industry, however, he made the leap and moved to Beijing. In classic fashion, he slept on a barbershop floor rent-free while studying filmmaking, and realized his director dream a few years later. My hope is that stories like Hao's and the visceral themes these directors cover will give readers insight into the massive jigsaw puzzle that is China's rise in the 21st century.

Although I sought to include more women directors in the book, ultimately, I was only successful in highlighting Huang Ji. This wasn't by design, but is unfortunately a reflection of a persistent gender imbalance in China's film industry, mirroring a situation that is equally prevalent in Hollywood and other international film industries. Huang's inclusion is also important because of her unwavering commitment to independent, socially aware films despite the lure of big money in commercial productions.

With each interview, I've included a short biographical sketch about the filmmaker, filmography, detailed interviews in Q&A format, a "case study" of one of the filmmaker's features and "the director's take." The interviews include things the filmmakers wanted to share about their path to filmmaking, early cinematic influences, film aesthetics, funding and their working relationship with collaborators. I asked each of them similar questions, including: 1) where they were brought up; 2) why they wanted to become a director; 3) what messages they want to convey in their films; 4) their views on the current climate for filmmaking, and 5) challenges they have encountered in the course of their filmmaking.

The case studies are meant to explore the aesthetics and storytelling of individual film-makers, while "the director's take" is a shortcut meant to highlight the filmmakers' artistic vision, favorite films and definition of a truly independent film. About half of the case studies are focused on their directorial debuts, the rest their second films. Almost all the movies featured in the case studies were produced after 2010 and received some kind of local or international recognition or awards, even though a couple of them were regarded as "underground" films.

In addition to the six chapters, I've included a seventh chapter with an interview of millennial film expert Wang Fei—a film festival curator and director in his own right. Wang provides meaningful perspective and analysis on the overall body of work produced by the selected directors. To update the many changes and the impact of Covid-19 on China's film industry, and given that some readers may not be familiar with China's film history, I also included an "Afterword" and "A Guide to Seven Generations of Chinese Filmmakers" in the appendix.

In writing this book I took inspiration from Michael Berry's *Speaking in Images*, Sheila Cornelius' *New Chinese Cinema*, Xu Jinjing's *Interviews About Chinese Independent Films* and Josh Horowitz's *The Mind of the Modern Moviemaker*. I hope this book provides some insight for those interested in learning about Chinese independent film and the larger social and political environment that has helped shape the industry over the last two decades. I'd feel even more rewarded if this modest project helped inspire additional scholarship and dialogue in English or other foreign languages about young Chinese independent filmmakers and their works.

The book took me two years to plan and three years to complete, with some fits and starts accentuated by Covid-19. It would not have been possible without the generous help and support of many people. I'd like first and foremost to thank the many *balinghou* filmmakers who not only endured lengthy interviews and follow-up email exchanges, but also kindly granted permission to use some of their images. The participation of Li Ruijun, Huang Ji, Hao Jie, Yang Jin, Xin Yukun and Zhai Yixiang has been invaluable. I'm also grateful to a dozen other filmmakers and movie experts who graciously gave their time and important insights, but for various reasons could not be included in this book, particularly Xing Jian, Yang Zhengfan, Zhang Dalei, De Gena, Liu Jiayin, Wang Xuebo, Geng Jun, Wang Zijian, Zhang Ping, Sun Yao, Marie Ruggieri and Qin Yan.

I'm also deeply indebted to Professor Zhang Xianmin, who has added tremendously to my understanding over countless cups of tea, dinners and meetings about the history of China's grassroots film festivals and key issues shaping the development of Chinese indies. I am humbled by Zhang's patience and steadfast love for Chinese independent film.

Similarly, I want to extend my sincere thanks to Wang Fei, whose early introductions to several key filmmakers and tireless explanations about the industry's inner workings were invaluable. My deepest appreciation also goes to Professor Matthew Solomon, Paul Bach

Jr. and Helen Wing for generously taking the time to read my manuscript at various stages, and for their invaluable suggestions. Likewise, a heartfelt thank you to Professor Stanley Rosen, who graciously took my interviews and provided me with many key insights.

I also want to thank Chris Robyn, my publisher, for seeing the potential in this book. His steadfast belief in the project kept me going, particularly when our spirits sank during the darkest days of the Coronavirus pandemic.

Lastly, I want to extend a big thank you to Mark Magnier, my long-suffering husband, who has provided me with copious support and editing help over the years through thick and thin. Without his understanding and encouragement, I'd never have been able to finish the book.

*   All Chinese names in this book appear family name first, given name second in keeping with
       Chinese tradition except in the case when an English first name is used.

INTRODUCTION

The term *balinghou*, which literally means "post-80s", refers to those born in the decade after 1979. This generation came of age around the millennium, when China experienced rapid change and fast economic growth. The term came into wider use after 2010 when an influx of new indie directors who were not only from urban centers, but also smaller towns and provincial China exploded onto the scene.

The *balinghou* filmmakers were among the first from their villages to embrace cell phones, the Internet and other modern technology. This enabled them to quietly but deliberately question with thought-provoking art-house narratives the singular, official image of a glorious urban China. The Internet helped changed the way the generation watches films, exposing youngsters from remote regions for the first time to film produced in China and well beyond.

Later, as video became cheaper and more widespread, many fans have been inspired to make their own movies. In this way, the Internet has become an unintentional equalizer in Chinese filmmaking, bringing in new themes and stories audiences might not otherwise be exposed to on the silver screen.

▷ Why is the *balinghou* indie cinema relevant now?

Empowered by the digital revolution, this new cohort of regional filmmakers has chosen to be "independent" in order to claim full ownership of their films and continue to shed light on Chinese society. The term "independent film" has taken on new meanings in the post-millennium era in the Chinese context. In the 1990s, the term referred to a film lacking an official screening permit, which made it an underground film, helping to safeguard the filmmaker's freedom of expression.

In recent years, however, it has also been used to mean any non-mainstream, smaller-budget or self-funded film characterized by its artistry and/or social discourse. Increasingly, these films have a screening license. (See a more detailed discussion on this topic in the section "What is Independent Cinema in the Chinese Context" below.)

Instead of focusing their lenses on urban subjects, as did many of their immediate predecessors, (e.g., the 6th and 7th generations of filmmakers—see appendix, "A Guide to Seven Generations of Chinese Filmmakers" for a detailed explanation) many younger directors have deliberately zoomed in on current rural concerns and the lives of those often overlooked as China sheds its image as a developing nation and emerges as a capitalist powerhouse. The rapid shift has seen farmers, the elderly and disenfranchised children left behind in backwater towns while young adults leave for better jobs. With vacated farmhouses in ruins, entire communities are reduced to ghost towns. Despite accounting for some 50 percent of China's population, farmers too often remain on the economic and political fringes of society, paying the heaviest price for China's glittering lights and economic miracle. Understanding this hopefully will provide a more honest and complete look at the development of contemporary Chinese society.

One of the most interesting phenomena to emerge around the turn of the century was the rise of Chinese style independent film, once dubbed the "underground" cinema of the 1990s. Interestingly, there has been more discussion about Chinese indie films in English-language academic writing than Chinese-language scholarship, particularly involving documentaries. Paul G. Pickowicz and Yingjin Zhang's *From Underground to Independent*, and Zhang Zhen's *The Urban Generation: Chinese Cinema and Society at the Turn of the Twenty-First Century* are some of the best-known examples. However, this discussion is largely confined to the works of early, better established indie filmmakers and doesn't go much beyond the advent of the millennium. *China's Millennial Digital Generation* hopes to fill this gap by examining independent films from the past ten to 15 years through interviews, available scholarship and news sources (both in English and Chinese).

Most academic and popular English literature on contemporary Chinese cinema also tends to focus on commercial hits produced by famous or established directors. Unfortunately, these don't tell us much about what is happening elsewhere in Chinese society, or the real-life experiences of the *laobaixing* (ordinary folks). Zhang Yimou and Chen Kaige, pillars of the 5th Generation of filmmakers, (see appendix, "A Guide to Seven Generations of Chinese Filmmakers" for a detailed explanation) jointly put Chinese cinema on the world map in the 1980s with their mesmerizing aesthetics and bold questioning of the party line. But they are now producing expensive and politically-correct period dramas such as *The Great Wall* and *Legend of the Demon Cat* that avoid meaningful social discourse.

Even the likes of Zhang Yuan (*Beijing Bastards*), Wang Chao (*The Orphan of Anyang*) and Zhang Ming (*Rain Clouds Over Wushan*) have moved on. These once defiant, first-generation independent filmmakers made their name as part of a critical, underground cohort in the 90s that championed the idea of "bearing witness" to the grim realities of a fast-changing China. Most now are either engaged in non-film projects or have bowed to the pressure of ever-tightening censorship by making non-controversial comedies or TV productions that play to the recreational needs of the public.

The true value of indies is that they are not only fertile ground for creativity but also examine and reflect the reality of everyday life. Renowned 6th Generation (see appendix, "A Guide to Seven Generations of Chinese Filmmakers") filmmaker Jia Zhangke, a leader in the indie film movement, once related in a memoir: "We pay attention to the condition of people and the condition of society...we are true to the facts, and we are true to ourselves. We promise ourselves—we will not modify." [1]

Although many established filmmakers have turned their backs on indie films, the *balinghou* art-house filmmakers are poised to fill the gap. Born in the 1980s and coming of age at the height of China's digital era around 2000, these younger filmmakers grew up gorging on Chinese and foreign films through pirated DVDs and affordable downloading previously out of reach. This has not only transformed how this younger generation communicates and connects with one another, it also made it possible for many newcomers from extremely diverse backgrounds to engage in social and political discourse as they produced independent films previously monopolized by a few mostly urban-based elites.

More passionate than their predecessors, they are often more willing to take risks. Among the themes tackled by this younger generation, sometimes called the "grassroots directors" or the "roots-seeking generation," include migrant workers who cannot go home, sexual abuse of left-behind children in Chinese villages, rural bachelors unable to find wives, and the hollowing out of villages and townships as farmers migrate en masse to grim urban factories. Often, these themes are tackled with a more balanced and fresher perspective. These filmmakers have chronicled this history just as smaller villages, towns and rural culture are disappearing from the Chinese landscape, giving them something of a role as historical preservationists.

Xie Fei, a renowned Beijing Film Academy (BFA) professor and director from the 4th Generation, famously said "the best body of work by a filmmaker will come from the decade between his/her 30s and 40s—a peak production time." [2] Today, the 5th Generation filmmakers are well in their 60s while the 6th Generation filmmakers are moving into their 50s. Born during in 1980s, most of the *balinghou* filmmakers are at the top of their game. Less focused on turning a profit and more committed to making a statement, they are coming into their own. This group of artists deserves our attention.

Through extended conversations with individual fiction filmmakers about their backgrounds, film styles, thematic and aesthetic views, the book will look at their works as a collection of art products produced at a specific time. It will also examine how this younger cohort of filmmakers try and bring about their vision amid constant tightening censorship and the government's renewed efforts to crack down on electronic communication. By examining the bigger social and historical backdrop, I also hope to shed light on the individual creators' journeys to filmmaking. Attention in the introduction is also given to broader social-political and economic changes since 2000 that shaped the millennial filmmakers, and how their works, in turn, help illuminate our understanding of Chinese society and today's film trends.

The introduction is divided into three sections. The first two map out the history and developments of Chinese indie cinema starting from the early 1990s. The third takes a look at the rise of "roots-seeking" or "hometown" filmmakers roughly a decade after the arrival of the 21st century, and how the directors included in the book fit into the larger canvas of cinematic trends and contexts. We'll start with a look at censorship, which has a decisive impact on how Chinese films are shaped and made.

▷ Chinese Film Censorship

China does not have an explicit film code or rating system. Like many other communist countries, China views cinema as a powerful medium for "education," given its unique ability to disseminate ideology in an easily comprehensible manner to "the masses." This is in part why film content is tightly controlled by the government's powerful censorship bureau, with censors expected to ensure films don't run counter to government policy. Under this system, all films must be submitted to the authorities for scrutiny and approval before receiving a permit for public viewing. While depiction of nudity, graphic violence, sex acts, superstition and other obscenity and vulgar content are restricted, other issues are at least as important to censors. These include sensitive historical topics, religion, war, diplomatic relations or adverse social conditions that can be interpreted as critical of government policy.

Before 2017, scripts had to be submitted for review prior to shooting. Beginning in March 2017, those producing non-sensitive films are only required to provide an outline of their screenplay for evaluation before filming. Those making special-themed films involving particularly delicate topics (including past wars, diplomatic relations and adversities in recent history), however, must still send in full scripts before shooting begins. (See chapter 7, interview with Wang Fei, for a more detailed discussion on the changes of the new film law enacted in 2017).

Tough restrictions can result in tense standoffs between filmmakers and the authorities. For a while in the 1980s, an increasingly relaxed political and social environment saw cinema with diversified subject matter flourish. But controls quickly tightened after the Tian'anmen Square crackdown in 1989. Control can be rigorous and extensive. Beyond wholesale cuts to finished films, filmmakers also face home distribution or export bans and long delays when censors demand months of re-shooting. At times, films are delayed until the subject matter seems outdated or no longer controversial, effectively eroding what was once an edgy production.

As the Party has grappled with changing media and technology, an increasingly complex society and its own internal dynamics, its censorship apparatus and approach have also changed. Initially, oversight was handled by the Administrative Department of Radio, Film and Television (ADRFT). In the 1990s, when ADRFT was in charge of handling film inspection, the process was particularly laborious for filmmakers. They had to submit their screenplays for approval before shooting. Once the film was finished, the director then re-submitted it for both a "content permit" (commonly known as the "dragon logo", or *longbiao* in Chinese) and a "technical permit" (a paper document signifying the filmmaker has fulfilled all technical requirements) before a public screening permit could be granted. With the "dragon logo" (also known as the "head" of the license because it appears at the opening of a film) and the "technical permit" (i.e., the "tail" since it appears at the end close to the film credits) in hand, the filmmaker could then hope to gain a screening license, essentially subjecting a film to two separate censorship processes.

In 1998, ADRFT was renamed the State Administration of Radio, Film and Television, or SARFT. In 2013, it saw another rebranding when it became the State Administration of Press, Publication, Radio, Film and Television, or SAPPRFT. A new law was enacted in 2017, with control assumed directly by the Communist Party's propaganda department in March 2018. Before the 2017 law, artists could show their films overseas with their "dragon logo." With China increasingly concerned about controlling its image abroad, the new law makes it illegal and punishable to exhibit at an international film festival without the "technical permit" as well.

The granting of a full screening permit can take anywhere from a few months to several years depending on content, political timing and the whims of censors. Usually, the "technical permit," the last hurdle for a director in gaining a theatrical release, is harder to come by than the "dragon logo." And underscoring the opaque nature of the process, an approval can be revoked even after it is granted. In 2012, Lou Ye got the go ahead to screen his crime film *Mystery* after a grueling five-month script revision. Weeks before the release, however, he received word that he had to make more changes, to his extreme frustration.[3]

Since the Communist Party's propaganda department took over the role of regulating film and television, last minute cancellations of previously approved film releases have increased sharply, notes Stanley Rosen, a political science professor at the University of Southern California who specializes in Chinese politics and cinema. (see "Afterword" for greater details of the discussion). In general, Chinese censors tend to get much tougher when an important national anniversary is looming.

▷ What is "Independent Cinema" in the Chinese Context?

It is important to define the word "independence" in the modern Chinese context given that the term often has a very different connotation in the West, creating some confusion among foreign scholars and writers. In the U.S., for example, the category of "independent film" is usually defined in contrast to the big Hollywood studios. In China, however, it can mean many things. As *Variety* writer Rebecca Davis wrote: "Does independence lie in the lack of an official 'dragon logo,' or purely in a film's mode of financing, or in its content and style, its interest in artistry or in non-mainstream stories?"[4]

The short answer is: all of the above. The truth is, the word "independent" has morphed several times in recent Chinese history, mirroring the vagaries of the industry itself. To better understand Chinese usage, we might factor in recent film history and the outsized role censorship has played.

For some of the 6th Generation filmmakers who emerged in the early 1990s, side-stepping the censor content review, screening permit and commercial release process sometimes was their only hope, a last resort in making a film without getting lost in the labyrinth of bureaucracy. During the early 1980s, coinciding with China's period of reform and opening-up, the so-called 5th Generation filmmakers newly graduated from the prestigious BFA were able to enjoy financial support and artistic freedom while working for state-owned studios. The likes of Chen Kaige and Zhang Yimou benefited with their, in retrospect, perfectly timed directorial debuts. By the 1990s, however, the industry was weathering reforms and policy changes that significantly reduced opportunities and leeway for the new generation of directors. That often left younger moviemakers waiting five to ten years in the increasingly rigid, seniority-based system to make their first films.[5]

Wang Xiaoshuai, a key figure among 6th Generation directors—BFA graduates of the late 1980s who started churning out films in the early 1990s, worked at state-owned Fujian Film Studio starting in 1991. He wrote half a dozen screenplays within two years but was told he would have to wait five years before making his own films. Frustrated, Wang left Fujian for Beijing looking for alternative opportunities.[6]

Wang used his own money to make his first film, *The Days* (1993), using equipment borrowed from Beijing Film Studio. On returning to Fujian, print in hand, expecting some appreciation for having saved the studio money, he was instead told he'd made a grave mistake. Wang eventually took it overseas, where film festival attendees lauded him as a major new voice. Apparently irked at his bypassing the system, Chinese authorities in 1994 included Wang and six other filmmakers in a sweeping ban for showing their films internationally without a *longbiao*. As one Beijing film critic noted, Wang's naiveté underscored how the forerunners of China's early "independent film" movement started out mostly clueless about the larger political climate.[7]

These misunderstandings were more characteristic of early indie filmmakers. Some also chose to work outside the censorship system or remain "underground" (a preferred term of the American scholar Paul Pickowicz—see "The Emergence of China's Underground Film" below for a more detailed discussion) because of their displeasure over the inflexible state film regime of the early 1990s and the uninteresting, banal mainstream films of their times. Jia Zhangke once said he decided to shoot *Xiao Wu* (aka *Artisan Pickpocket*) because he felt "there is a life story representing a lot of people's real-life experience that is not being told." [8]

In some cases, filmmakers may start out applying for a *longbiao* in order to secure a wider release only to reverse course, frustrated by repeated editing demands by censors that become unbearable. That can compel filmmakers to go the "illegal" route to stay true to their vision. Jia Zhangke's *A Touch of Sin*—a 2014 crime drama about real events in contemporary China—is a case in point. Although the film was well received at Cannes, it never cleared Chinese censors despite Jia's repeated attempts. Film scholar Wang Xiaolu outlined this shadow play: "A film is an independent film if it's shot honestly. But then it will be sidelined, becoming an isolated movie, and eventually banned." [9]

Although some may truly want to maintain their cinematic independence, an increasing number of young moviemakers are working outside the studio system as a calculated strategy, critics note, hoping to replicate the success of early indie filmmakers the West regarded as "dissident" directors. The likes of Zhang Yuan and Jia Zhangke, for example, won numerous prizes at major European film festivals. Well known film scholar Dai Jinhua views many latter-day "underground" filmmakers as little more than "copycats" hoping to catch the attention of Westerners eager to frame Chinese indie film as little more than an anti-authoritarian confrontation against the censors. "If the 'Zhang Yimou model' has become a narrow door for Chinese movies to 'go out into the world,' then independent productions are a shortcut for newcomers to 'contend' in Western film circles" as competition intensifies, she said. [10]

With the advent of digital video cameras in the early 2000s, more private firms and individuals got involved in smaller film projects. Scholars say social commentary once associated with the term "independent" has lost much of its original meaning and is now more about individual expression, though these gradations can be a bit wobbly. Even the likes of Zhang Yuan, Duan Jinchuan and Wu Wenguang, the first indie filmmakers to emerge in the 1990s, are now distancing themselves from the "independent filmmaker" label—a loaded term they feel places them too much in opposition to the "mainstream" state. Many instead prefer to call themselves creators of "individualized" works. And, perhaps unsurprisingly, many are now a part of the mainstream film industry. [11]

Since the mid-2000s, with more private financing and production options available to smaller projects, and a younger generation of filmmakers more eager to reach large audiences than make political statements, a growing number of art-house films have screening permits these days. Increasingly, the term "independent film," or *duli pian*, is synonymous with smaller-budget, non-mainstream, non-government-backed films heavy on artistry and light on commercial elements, also known as *wenyi pian* (art films).[12]

At the same time, independent cinema is enjoying growing popularity among young moviegoers bombarded with too many big-budget production films that are glitzy but artistically banal. That's seen some gravitate to experimental cinema with a stronger storyline. A case in point is Xin Yukun's *The Coffin in the Mountain*, a suspense drama with a very distinctive auteur-style that received rave reviews on its release in 2014 (see chapter 5 for more details). Thus "independent film" is increasingly a selling point—a far cry from its original connection to illegality and taboo subjects, and now closer to its connotation in the West.

▷ The Emergence of China's Underground Film (1989 to 1997)

Chinese independent cinema expanded in the early 1990s, initially pushing back against the dominance of 5th Generation filmmaking and a system that put newcomers at a disadvantage. Some scholars also cite Tian'anmen as a catalyst that coalesced disgruntled moviemakers. "How could such a thing occur?" Lu Xinyu expresses the shock over Tian'anmen some filmmakers felt at the time. "They discovered that they understood little about what China actually was…During the 1980s [filmmakers] had examined China from on high. Now they felt the need to go to the grassroots, and to understand China's changes and their causes from this other vantage point," Lu observed.[13]

Film critic Cao Kai believes pressure was also building as young filmmakers bridled against the status quo. The first underground filmmakers were predominately from TV companies who resented having to serve the propaganda machine. Making documentaries outside the state-sanctioned system allowed them to express their individuality. This group includes Wu Wenguang from Yunnan TV Channel and Duan Jinchuan from China Tibet Broadcasting, both only produced documentaries.[14]

Included in this first underground group, according to Yingjin Zhang, were also the 6th Generation Filmmakers. Among them were Zhang Yuan, Wang Xiaoshuai, Lou Ye, He Jianjun and later, Jia Zhangke. Some of these early "dissident" filmmakers had a sense of mission in discovering the "truth." They turned their cameras to the disenfranchised, alienated or otherwise forgotten. This focus and their recurring themes on politically sensitive subjects often made their films controversial and targets of censorship, precluding mainstream distribution.[15]

When these early filmmakers realized that unofficial screenings were the only way to reach domestic audiences, (usually at alternative spaces such as bars or cafes) many turned to international film festivals, often without official permission. This came to a head in 1994, when several filmmakers, including Zhang Yuan, Wang Xiaoshuai and He Jianjun, saw their passports confiscated and future films banned for "illegally" shipping their films abroad.[16]

The Naming of China's First "Independent" Film

Many scholars cite Wu Wenguang and Zhang Yuan as key figures in the Chinese independent film movement. Wu's documentary *Bumming in Beijing: The Last Dreamers* (流浪北京 , 1990) and Zhang's feature film *Mama* (妈妈 , 1990) are the seminal films of Chinese independent cinema, according to Fan Bei and Mathew D. Johnson.[17]

Wu's *Bumming in Beijing* follows five drifting artists who chased their dreams to the capital and eked out a threadbare existence by freelancing. Although much of it relies on talking heads, the stripped-down aesthetic and long-takes heavily influenced later Chinese independent documentaries and fiction films. Zhang's *Mama*—considered a pioneering film for the 6th Generation—is about a mother and her developmentally-delayed grown son. The feature, shot on a shoestring budget inside Zhang's apartment, focuses on the mother's struggle to make ends meet in modern-day Beijing while dealing with an absent and unresponsive husband. Originally written to end on the mother euthanizing her son, Zhang eventually opted for a less dour, more open-ended and ambiguous conclusion.[18]

In a 2011 interview with film scholar and curator Wang Xiaolu, Zhang Yuan said the concept of an "independent film" did not really exist in China in 1990. Only after he took *Mama* to France's Festival of the Three Continents in Nantes did Zhang hear the term used, he said, adding that the encounter left him quite surprised at the time.[19]

Similarly, Fan Bei points to a conversation at Zhang Yuan's house in 1991 between Zhang and Wu on the definition and concept of "independent films" in the Chinese context.[20] The two main points that came out of that discussion were that independent film 1) "must be produced with independent thought and 2) be operated independently. "The ideas I want to express must be free of interference, so you shouldn't take other people's money," Zhang said. Fan cites this meeting as the first of its kind in China.

Paul Pickowicz, however, cautions in an article that China's use of the term "independent film," refers to "independence from the Chinese state rather than independence from the sort of powerful private conglomerates that have dominated Hollywood."[21] Pickowicz argues that "underground," though not without its problems, better captures the "unofficial nature of the work and clear intention of these young artists to resist state control." Most of their earlier films were, in fact, "illegal," he adds.

Critic Valerie Jaffee, meanwhile, points out that making an underground film is, for some, less a statement than a strategy for the "entry of aspiring filmmakers," given that a newbie filmmaker's work is more likely to attract attention at festivals if it is not "under the ominous-sounding auspices of the China Film Corporation, but as a work that is 'banned in China'."[22] She cites the comparison between Zhang Yuan's banned *Beijing Bastards* and Guan Hu's *Dirt*, which received a "dragon logo." Both are BFA graduates from the 6th Generation cohort. Both films are about disaffected youth and Beijing rock and roll, and both were financed "independently" outside of a state-run studio. Jaffee argues that while Zhang was playing to the foreign crowd, his classmate Guan Hu made a similarly controversial feature about equally edgy social issues within the system just a year later. Guan Hu submitted his film to the censors, who approved it, which Zhang could easily have done if he wanted to.[23]

20

Characteristics of China's early underground films of the 1990s:

Regardless of motive, early underground films share some identifiable, common, distinguishing characteristics. These include:

a) An Elite Nature

Zhang Xianmin, a BFA professor, producer and Chinese independent film advocate, cites the strong "elite" nature of works by early underground filmmakers, especially when it comes to feature films. Zhang believes this relates to technological challenges, given that video cameras were still largely unavailable in China in the early 1990s. As a result, production was only possible for workers with connections at state-owned film studios or for broadcasters able to borrow cameras from their employers.[24]

Predictably, the subjects of these early, alternative films were semi-biographical, focused on characters with backgrounds similar to those of the filmmakers. In Wu Wenguang's *Bumming in Beijing*, for example, the five artists who the filmmaker focuses on were painters and playwrights. The characters dared to leave their *danwei*, or assigned work units, and struck out on their own, mirroring what Wu was doing with his filmmaking at the time. Similarly, *The Days*, the 1993 directorial debut of Wang Xiaoshuai, follows the life of two married artists recently graduated from the elite BFA. This focus on the well-connected is also seen in Zhang Yuan's second feature, *Beijing Bastards*, about the lives of a group of musicians and freelance artists struggling to find their feet in fast-changing Beijing. The focus on the educated and privileged continued into the mid-90s until Jia Zhangke's 1997 debut film *Xiao Wu* (aka *Artisan Pickpocket*).

b) An Urban Focus

Another trademark of Chinese alternative cinema is its urban orientation, which is why this early cohort is sometimes referred to as the "Urban Generation"—a term coined by film scholar Zhang Zhen.[25] Zhang believes the new urban cinema is an obvious response to China's rapid urbanization and globalization as it rushed to make up for decades of relative isolation. Their subjects tend to be a motley collection of "troubled people on the margins of the age of transformation" ranging from aimless bohemians, petty thieves, bar hostesses, prostitutes and postmen to local cops, taxi drivers, alcoholics, homosexuals, the disabled and migrant workers. These people "form a group of floating new urban subjects," and their collective portrayal became "one of the defining features of the new urban cinema." [26]

Some of the feature films Zhang listed in this category include Wang Xiaoshuai's *So Close to Paradise* (1997) and *Beijing Bicycle* (2001), Ning Ying's *On the Beat* (1995), and Jia Zhangke's *Xiao Wu* (1997). Li Hong's *Back to Phoenix Bridge* (1997) and Wu Wenguang's *Jiang Hu: On the Road* (1999) were included for documentaries. [27]

c) A Documentary's Approach to Truth

In his book *Chinese National Cinema*, Yingjin Zhang says the underground filmmakers' alternative approach was, in part, a reaction to the lavish, full-scale dramatization of historical events by 5th Generation filmmakers, including Chen Kaige, Zhang Yimou and Tian Zhuangzhuang. The young directors insisted on "personal perspective" and commitment to a new vision of 'truth' or 'objectivity' that they felt was missing in their predecessors' films, and conscientiously sought to "distinguish themselves from their immediate predecessors."[28] Whereas the previous generation leaned on rural landscapes, grand epics, historical reflection and allegorical framework, younger filmmakers are more associated with an urban milieu, modern sensitivity, documentary effects and subjectivity. "Their films are definitely more 'truthful' to reality than the 5th Generation's glamorization of ethnicity, sexuality and history," Zhang observes.[29]

To enhance the "truth" of their films, many younger filmmakers adopted a "documentary aesthetic" heralded by the likes of Wu Wenguang and Jiang Yue whose "decade-long new documentary movement has run a parallel course alongside the experimental narrative film," Zhang Zhen notes. She cites Wang Xiaoshuai's *The Days* (1993) and Zhang Yuan's *Beijing Bastards* (1993) as examples, adding that both directors had embraced "inter-textual links" to Wu's Bumming in Beijing (1990) by shooting their fiction films in the same way as Wu approached his documentary.[30]

Given the hand this generation was dealt—marginalized by the studios, with limited access to expensive studio filming, lacking the resources available to younger generations, including video cameras, digital video and editing software increasingly available around the millennium—the filmmakers' early films tend to be low-budget productions shot on the street and in private apartments well beyond the confines of the system.[31]

▷ Jia Zhangke and the Rise of "Amateur" Filmmakers (since 1998)

The independent spirit that characterizes the early cinema of the 6th Generation would take on a new look and energy with the arrival of Jia Zhangke's *Xiao Wu* (1997) and *Platform* (2000), critics observe, heralding a different phase in the independent movement. Both Zhang Zhen and Lin Xudong note that Jia is remarkably different from other directors from the 6th Generation cohort. Born in 1970 rather than the 60s, Jia was "a product of the reform era of the 1980s," Lin once remarked.[32] Furthermore, Jia was not an elite from Beijing. In fact, the young Shanxi native is a self-described "ordinary director who comes from the lower ranks of Chinese society," Lin added.[33]

Jia's rural upbringing informed his aesthetics. In 1995, Jia created the Beijing Film Academy Young Experimental Film Workshop and began the practice of "amateur cinema" (*yeyu dianying*) or "unofficial cinema" (*minjian dianying*) with this group, Zhang Zhen notes.[34] They soon found a following among emerging filmmakers working mostly outside the elite academy, and later joined forces with an emerging digital video (DV) movement. A desire by Jia and his followers to make their own films, and their distaste for overly academic filmmaking fostered at BFA, saw them make extremely low-budget film projects, she observes.[35]

Jia cut his teeth with a traveling troupe from Shanxi—among China's poorest provinces—then migrated to Beijing as a non-matriculated BFA student. He had a "desire to reclaim cinema as a communicative tool for the ordinary Chinese citizen," said Zhang Zhen.[36] That followed, she added, because at the time of Jia's graduation in 1997, with China swept up by urbanization and socioeconomic transformation, Jia felt compelled "to place the 'migrant-artisan' at the center stage of his cinema" instead of the haughty urban bohemians that dominated the early underground films.[37]

Jia's "amateur director" dream very much overlapped with China's debut of DV camera and the ensuing DV revolution, said film critic Wei Xin. Wei noted that 1995 was the year when Jia made his first student film *Xiao Shan Going Home* with a video camera he'd borrowed from a friend, the year when DV cameras were introduced to China.[38]

In 1998, enraptured by the technology, sense of possibility and promise of more broad-based access to moving images, Jia made his famous proclamation in *Southern Weekly:* "The Age of Amateur Cinema Will Soon Arrive." This made him among the first to herald the DV movement and among its earliest successful practitioner. In 2002, his third feature, *Unknown Pleasures*, would become the first Asian digital film screened at the Cannes Film Festival. Jia's success, Wei adds, proved that filmmaking was morphing from an elite privilege to an activity increasingly available to ambitious film enthusiasts.[39]

Jia's early "amateur cinema" is informed by a raw realism and real-world shooting. It also embraces improvisation, with most of his films lacking a complete storyline. Some of the techniques and film language Jia and his group adopted included the use of video, more pronounced long takes and a "on the spot" filming often without the scripts that 6th Generation filmmakers relied on. He also pioneered the use of unknown, non-professional actors, and he showcased local dialects rather than Mandarin that is standard in most films. *Xiao Wu* (aka *Artisan Pickpocket*), for example, about a drifting pickpocket in Fengyang city of Shanxi and his encounters in the village, is played entirely by non-professional actors. In one scene, a long-take shot lasts six minutes.[40]

D-Buff Community, the Proliferation of Film Clubs and Festivals

After Jia Zhangke's 1998 "Age of Amateur Cinema" proclamation, many scholars noted a turning point. The appearance of affordable digital equipment helped empower a second wave of independent filmmakers who focused on the margins of society and vulnerable groups, (the *diceng*, or bottom strata of society). In addition to Jia, others included Zhao Liang, Du Haibin, Wang Chao and Wang Bing.[41] This focus on the ordinary and vulnerable would greatly influence younger filmmakers who came of age a decade after the millennium.

Cao Kai sees 1998-2003 as a period of heady growth as more independent filmmakers, emboldened by the proliferation of film clubs and festivals, poured in with creative products.[42] This period was also significant because censors hadn't fully grasped the impact of the new technology, allowing artists to enjoy greater freedom of expression during these early years, Cao said.[43]

Jia Zhangke notes that the establishment of the first unofficial Chinese film group "Office 101" emerged in Shanghai around 1997.[44] The group inspired others elsewhere, with the more famous ones including Guangzhou's "Southern Film Forum" and later, Beijing's "Practice Society," with the latter screening films in a bar near Tsinghua University. These clubs not only offered a grassroots platform for film screenings and discussions, they also provided a venue to watch European and American classics, banned Chinese movies or newly available films. Before this, it was virtually impossible for ordinary Chinese city dwellers to see the likes of Godard's *Breathless*, Tarkovsky's *The Mirror*, or popular US films such as *The Godfather* or *Taxi Driver*, with viewing of Western films strictly limited to a handful officials and elite intellectuals.

The proliferation of pirated VCDs, DVDs and inexpensive VCD players after 1995 certainly played a role in fueling the popularity of these groups. Film scholar Jinying Li, however, also believes the emergence of a subculture of devoted consumers of pirated material having played a role. These aficionados not only self-identified as "disc buffs" (*die-you*) or simply "D-buffs" (*D-you*), with "D" referring to both "disc" (*die*) and "piracy" (*daoban*), but their leisure time was largely shaped by the culture of piracy.[45]

Discussions within the film clubs ranged from criticism of Western films to reflections on Chinese cinema, Jia said. "Independent unauthorized Chinese films that had been shot since the 1990s but never released drew attention. Zhang Yuan's *Sons*, Wang Xiaoshuai's *The Days*, He Jianjun's *The*

Postman, and Lou Ye's *Weekend Lover*—all these dust-covered films started to appear on film group program lists." [46] Jia believes the free viewing provided by these film clubs "instilled in more young people, including students, workers, office employees, writers or poets, an interest in shooting films," adding that "the technical limitations that their amateur background imposed on them were not that great because this was the vibrant era of digital video." [47]

Film scholar Zhang Zhen, meanwhile, views this alternative, "unofficial" cinema extended by the new breed of not-for-profit cinephile community, which was often hosted at university campuses, as an antidote to the isolation of the individual in the Internet age. She also sees it as pushback against the contrived film culture dominated by Hollywood blockbusters and state-sponsored melody film. [48]

▷ China's Grassroots Film Festivals Surface Above Ground (2001 to 2011)

Critics say China's first grassroots film festivals were set up precisely because there was a large collective mass of film clubs and film buffs by the turn of the millennium. In 2001, for example, Beijing's "*Practice Society*" co-organized the "*First Independent Film Festival*" (首屆獨立影像節) with the help of *Southern Weekly*. This was the "first public film event not sponsored by a state entity, which represented a significant institutionalization of the alternative and public spaces that had begun to emerge after 1989, originally in artist villages or as loose film clubs or associations." [49]

In 2003, similar film festivals popped up nationwide, including the biennial Yunnan Multicultural Visual Festival (YunFest) in Kunming—a program that only screened indie documentaries; and the China Independent Film Festival (CIFF) in Nanjing, which for a long time was the only platform to showcase independent fiction films. Three years later, the Beijing Independent Film Festival (BIFF) started in the eastern Beijing suburbs of Songzhuang (BIFF was formerly known as Chinese Documentary Exchange Week, which was also started in 2003). BFA professor Zhang Xianmin writes in an article that these festivals not only helped preserve the creativity and the independent spirit of filmmakers, they also served as a valuable chronicler of events. [50]

In the same article, Wang Fei, a CIFF co-curator, referred to YunFest, CIFF and BIFF as the "Big Three" festivals, adding that they had the greatest impact on the development of China's indie films. Amongst the three, CIFF had the longest history. (The annual event was held for 14 consecutive years until January 2020, when it announced a permanent halt.) Wang says CIFF was an important platform for documentary and narrative filmmakers during their early days. It also helped them reach their targeted Chinese audience—a privilege not available to pioneering 6th Generation indie directors. In fact, some of the entries for the 2004 edition of CIFF included established directors such as Wang Anchuan (*The Story of Ermei*), Ning Hao (*Incense*) and Wang Xiaoshuai (*Drifters*).[51]

Other Contributing Factors

In addition to domestic film clubs and festivals, or "forums," as they're sometimes more delicately called, a few other social and industry-related factors also spurred the rise of indie film festivals and "amateur" cinema in the first decade of the millennium.

One of these was a crisis in the domestic film market at the beginning of the millennium created by technological advancements in home entertainment and intensified competition from international films. With television bursting onto China's popular culture scene, people were able to enjoy a variety of shows and TV entertainment in the comfort of their homes. This greatly challenged China's domestic film industry, which, as pointed out by Kevin Lathan, was already feeling intense pressure from Hollywood after China joined the World Trade Organization (WTO) in 2001. As part of WTO membership, China was required to increase its quota of foreign films to 20 a year.[52]

When authorities decided to mount an all-out defense against Hollywood's challenge with mega-hits such as Feng Xiaogang's *Cell Phone* or *Big Shot's Funeral* and Zhang Yimou's *Hero*, "the Chinese film producers were pushed into two very distinctive paths, according to Yu Yaqin, an independent critic with *Beijing News*. These were: 1) make multi-million-dollar, Hollywood-like commercial flicks centered on Chinese stories in order to win the lion's share of the domestic film market by appealing to the masses; or 2) produce low-budget, more independent-minded art films with greater emphasis on individual expression."[53]

In the past, low-budget, more personalized films relied on international film festivals for recognition and foreign distribution. After these started gaining wider appeal amongst mature movie-goers tired of the banality of big-budget films, however, a whole new generation of indie filmmakers, whether formally trained or not, were encouraged to try their luck at making films. As we will explore in greater depth later, Li Ruijun (chapter 1) and Xin Yukun (chapter 5), both from humble backgrounds without formal academic training in filmmaking, gained popularity around 2010 by making smaller-budget but more thought-provoking films that satisfied the changing taste of the Chinese audience.

The second factor relates to China's higher education reform that started around 1998 during the administration of Premier Zhu Rongji. By the end of the 20th century, the authorities realized that China's low education levels would undercut the Socialist Market-oriented Economy that they had envisioned.[54] This led the government to expand college enrollment and the development of world-class universities. By restructuring, consolidation, mergers and oversight reform, they sought to address the problems of insufficient capacity and low efficiency.[55]

According to *Time Magazine*, over the next decade, the number of colleges in China "has doubled and the number of students quintupled, going from 1 million in 1997 to 5.5 million in 2007." The expansion was unprecedented, with China building the largest higher-education sector in the world in 10 years.[56]

Before the higher education reform, there were only three to four Chinese universities that offered cinematic education or film majors, according to BFA professor Zhang Xianmin. By 2003, some 120 universities or colleges offered film courses. This exponential expansion, coupled with the emerging digital revolution in cinema, saw a rapid growth of grassroots filmmakers, a field previously monopolized by Chinese elites.[57]

Hao Jie, featured in chapter 3, readily epitomized Zhang's observation. Originally from a remote village in Zhangjiakou in Northeast China, Hao was able to take advantage of these changes. "Youngsters like me in the past wouldn't have been able to break into an elite field such as the film business," he said. (See chapter 3)

Another factor has been the rise of online and grassroots training centers. Since 2000, the Ministry of Education (MOE) has allowed 68 higher education institutions to establish pilot distance education colleges, online and continuing education colleges.[58] Similarly, a few private training schools also took advantage of rising interest in acquiring filmmaking skills to offer short-term courses. Zhou's Experimental Film School, founded first as an online forum in 2000 by retired BFA professor Zhou Chuanji, is one example. The school eventually established a physical presence in Yunnan in 2009 and started offering regular three-week concentrated training camps. After Zhou passed away, his assistants continued to offer training through the school.[59]

Like Zhou's Experimental Film School, the Li Xianting Film School set up in Beijing's artist village of Songzhuang is another noted indie film training ground that has provided courses in directing, producing and film editing since 2008. The school, which offers one-week workshops and a month-and-a-half intense summer courses, prides itself on offering an open environment that encourages students to explore filmmaking as a tool to articulate their attitudes towards society. Courses delivered by such grassroots film schools are not accredited, allowing anyone to sign up for them. Schools like these lower the bar further for many hoping to enter the industry regardless of backgrounds. Filmmaker Zhai Yixiang, featured in chapter 6, graduated from the Academy of Arts of Southwestern University in Chongqing. The young design major made a career switch into cinema, with his only training a 40-day intensive boot camp at Li Xianting Film School. This proved enough for him to go on and make two feature films.

▷ Commercialization of China's New Indie Cinema (since early 2000s)

For some indie filmmakers who were not formally trained, changing market conditions and new government policies at the dawn of the 21st century allowed them to take advantage of new initiatives and supportive programs that promoted and financed young auteur directors, bringing them into the "mainstream" from the amateur sidelines.

China's state studio system suffered a rapid decline after the 1990s. Following deregulation in the late 1990s, Beijing decided in 2001 to let the private sector make productions, provided that applicants received state filmmaking qualification first.[60] This significantly bolstered the environment for independent cinema. Since 2008, close to 30 young director support programs have been announced in China, according to one news report, with fund in excess of 2 billion RMB. Of these, 40 percent came from private film studios, the largest source of financing.[61]

The Rise of Private Studios and Film Initiatives

This greatly helped young filmmakers because independent studios tended to focus on making smaller-budget indie films more marketable, increasing the chances they would be picked up by a theater chain. Early independent companies included XStream Pictures（西河星汇, formed in 2003 by Jia Zhangke, Yu Li and producer Zhou Qiang), which produced many of Jia's films and those of other newcomers. Another one was Laurel Films（劳雷影业, formed in 2000 by Producer Fang Li), which produced many creative productions by Wang Chao, Lou Ye and Li Yu.

Heaven Pictures（天画画天）and Blackfin Productions（黑鳍）, formed in 2010 and 2014 respectively, funded or otherwise helped *balinghou* directors. While lacking in professional credentials, many of these filmmakers were imbued with a distinct regional flavor. Notable Heaven Pictures talent include Hao Jie, Li Ruijun, Yang Jin and Tibetan filmmaker Pema Tseden, while Bi Gan, Geng Jun and Zhai Yixiang, among others, received production support from Blackfin.[62]

As online media expands rapidly amid growing demand for content, some of the *balinghou* directors saw their films released on the Internet through new distribution channels with the help of Heaven Pictures. While Hao Jie's debut feature *Single Man* was not released in theaters, for instance, Heaven Pictures managed to sell a four-year copyright to Tudou—a video-hosting website largely reliant on user uploads for revenue. This was Tudou's first purchase of an original independent film, an unprecedented move in the industry, according to Yang Cheng, Heaven Pictures' then manager. (Yang later left to form his own company, Nezha Brothers Pictures.) Yang said while the payment wasn't high, the site's large traffic base made the cumulative effect quite considerable.[63]

A program similar to Heaven Pictures is Jia Zhangke's Tianyi Project (添翼计划), launched in 2010 to support and raise the visibility of young indie directors. This was joined in 2015 by Alibaba Pictures' "A plans" (阿里影业 A 计划), providing rich financial support and other resources to identify and cultivate top talent. The program benefited such young directors as Han Jie, Song Fang and Quan Ting, who went on to win various awards at the Shanghai, Locarno and Berlin film festivals. In one notable example, Song Fang's debut film *Memories Look at Me* won best first feature at Locarno in 2012.[64]

The Changing Roles of Film Festivals

Despite the support of homegrown private studios, however, recognition at international film festivals remains a crucial way for newcomers to gain invaluable name recognition. According to a 2017 survey of 60 Chinese film directors born between 1974 and 1994, 75 percent said they took part in film festivals to showcase their early films.[65] The word-of-mouth publicity and prestige of a nominated or prize-winning film at a foreign festival can significantly help its marketability in the domestic market. Festivals also serve a project incubation role, affording a way to meet benefactors, win prize money, even land overseas distribution rights that help fund future projects.

Although the top three European film festivals (Cannes, Berlin and Venice) helped a lot in launching the careers of Chinese filmmakers during the 1990s and early 2000s, including some early underground moviemakers like Wang Xiaoshuai, Zhang Yuan and Jia Zhangke, the bar for entry subsequently rose, making it much harder for newcomers to get their big break.[66] This convinced many to seek out less prestigious festivals, including Rotterdam, Locarno, Toronto, Hong Kong and Busan.

Among these, Rotterdam and Locarno have remained steadfast supporters of Chinese indie cinema. Chinese directors who have won Rotterdam's top Tiger Award include Han Jie (*Walking on the Wild Side*, 2006), Huang Ji (*Egg and Stone*, 2012) and Cai Chengjie (*The Widowed Witch*, 2018); while those who have garnered Locarno's Golden Leopard Prize include Bi Gan (*Kaili Blues*, 2015) and Wang Bing (*Madame Fang*, 2017).[67]

Young indie filmmakers fortunate enough to receive help from private studios found a faster, easier path to entry at these festivals. And those who won prizes often attracted bigger investors on subsequent projects, as with Hao Jie and Bi Gan. Hao Jie (chapter 3) convinced Wanda Pictures (Qingdao), among China's largest film production companies, and other studios to finance *My Original Dream* (2015), a romantic comedy, after only making two small-budget indie films with support from Heaven Pictures. Similarly, Bi Gan managed to attract $2.8 million dollars in investment from several international film companies for his surreal art-house hit movie *Long Day's Journey into Night* (2018). This came after a single directorial role on *Kaili Blues*—a film supported by several independent film companies, including Heaven Pictures and Blackfin Productions.[68]

Others without initial support from not-for-profit studios have relied on savings and money borrowed from friends or family to produce their early films. Completed film in hand, they would then approach film festivals hoping to attract publicity, seed capital or prize money from international funds. Some of the more famous international funds include the Rotterdam Hubert Bals Fund, the Southern Fund of France, the South Korean Busan PPP Fund, and the Hong Kong-Asia Film Financing Forum (HAF Award).

Li Ruijun (chapter 1), for one, initially borrowed from his parents and friends the equivalent of US$50,000 while working as a TV director in order to raise enough seed money for his first film *Summer Solstice*. In 2010, Li won a 20,000-euro post-production award from the Rotterdam Hubert Bals Fund for *The Old Donkey*, which allowed him to pay off debts and start his third film. Similarly, in 2005, Yang Jin (chapter 4) won US$5,000 from Switzerland's Fribourg International Film Festival for his directorial debut, *The Black and White Milk Cow*,[69] which he invested in his second feature *Er Dong*.

Huang Ji (chapter 2) was also able to finish her second feature *The Foolish Bird* with a post-production award from the HAF in 2015, after winning several international prizes for her directorial debut *Egg and Stone*. She also won 10,000 euros from the Hubert Bals Fund for her third feature, *Stonewalling*. The three films are all part of her hometown trilogy.

Huang, the only female director featured in this book, is unique in the sense that she self-funds and produces her films with financial and production support from her cinematographer and producer husband Ryuji Otsuka, who works professionally as a TV director. The two teamed up to create their own company—Yellow Green Pi—to handle Huang's pre-production work. They will then typically take the project to various international film festivals hoping to attract post-production money and related resources. This, she says, helps her maintain her vision and autonomy in a market that is overly hyped and commercialized. (See chapter 2 for more details.)

Needless to say, the three main domestic grassroots film festivals (YunFest, CIFF and BIFF) have also provided a platform for novice filmmakers to showcase their craft. Beginning in 2012, however, local festivals and forums started facing growing state pressure to shut down, which severely undercut their ability to operate. BIFF, for example, had its power cut during a 2012 screening and a few attendees detained. A year later, the biennial YunFest was also shut down. And CIFF was driven underground after its 2012 festival was canceled. CIFF organizers switched location several times in subsequent years hoping to survive, before finally announcing in January 2020 that it also would shut down permanently. BIFF ultimately wasn't able to resume operation after countless films, files and other materials, collected over a decade by BIFF sponsor Li Xianting Film Fund, were confiscated by police.[70]

Grassroots film festivals in China weather periodic repression, but many critics say the 2012 indie crackdowns were unusually harsh. Zhang Xianmin, who served as a promoter and consultant for CIFF, termed it the "year of demolition" in describing the government's tough posture that year. The real cause for the sudden shift in political climate "had something to do with the changing of the guards at the top (e.g., Chinese President Xi Jinping's ascension as party secretary in late 2012), and an incentive to 'clean things up' before the new leaders arrived." Zhang said.[71]

However, during a 2015 panel discussion about China's censorship held in Taiwan, exiled indie film-maker Ying Liang said growing crackdowns and tightening state control were also driven by outside factors. One such influence was the Arab Spring, some say, which started in Tunisia in 2010 and went on to inspire pro-democracy protests in China in 2011.[72] Beijing has a long-held fear of social disorder and has a strong distaste for large crowds congregating without its permission.

After 2012, Chinese-language festivals that are "more official" in nature have emerged as important launching pads for some novice indie filmmakers. These include Xining's FIRST International Film Festival in the northwestern frontier of Qinghai; the historic Golden Horse Award in Taiwan; and most recently, Jia Zhangke's Pingyao Film Festival, launched in 2017 in Shanxi's Pingyao old town and touted as the "Boutique Festival for the People."

The FIRST Int'l Film Fest, sometimes referred to as China's Sundance Film Festival, is a unique entity that got its start in 2006 in Beijing as a student DV festival, before reinventing itself and relocating to Xining in 2011. Partially funded by the Xining Municipal Government and China Film Critics Society, the organizers work with celebrities and film experts, focusing on the "discovery and promotion of emerging filmmakers and their early works." [73] Before long, FIRST had established itself as the go-to platform for newcomers whose features might veer away from the social and political party line. This festival boasts a stellar record of propelling films onto bigger stages.[74]

Hao Jie was one such director who benefited hugely from FIRST's dedication to helping newcomers. Hao's debut film *Single Man* won best director prize at FIRST in 2012. In 2013, he seized the opportunity again at FIRST with his second feature *The Love Songs of Tiedan*, which won the film festival's best film and best director prizes that year. He went on to win the Network for Promotion of Asian Cinema (NETPAC) award for best Asian film at Taiwan's Golden Horse Film Festival.

Similarly, first-time director Xin Yukun won best film and best director awards with *The Coffin in the Mountain* in 2014 at FIRST, which provided momentum for his subsequent win of the Grand Prix award at the 30th Warsaw International Film festival in Poland that same year. And in 2017, Huang Ji's second feature *The Foolish Bird* won the festival's Best Artistic Originality award, which led to her subsequent win of the Best Fiction Film award at the South Taiwan Film Festival.[75]

For much of the Golden Horse Film Festival's 50-year history, the high-profile Taiwan-based event showcased Taiwanese and Hong Kong films. After 2010, however, it started focusing on first-time directors from the Mainland following the initiation of a new director's award that year. In 2015, after awarding Bi Gan its best new director prize for *Kaili Blues*—a mystery drama based in southern China's Guizhou—the Golden Horse went on to award several new auteur directors discovered at FIRST. They include Zhang Dalei (*The Summer is Gone*, 2016) and Hu Bo (*An Elephant Sitting Still*, 2018), with both winning not just the best new director award, but also the top prize for best film award. These prizes provided the young indie directors (Hu Bo passed away in 2017, and his film was awarded the prizes posthumously) with the most rewarding affirmation they could hope for, propelling them to stardom and commercial releases.[76]

Some indies are also supported by Jia's government-backed Pingyao International Film Festival (PYIFF), which is emerging as one of China's newest and most influential events to scout fresh talent. In 2018, for example, it helped launch Bai Xue's career. Bai won both the Fei Mu Award and the best actress award for her debut film *The Crossing*, while Zhang Dalei won the Work-in-Progress Lab Award for his second film, *In Winter*.[77]

▷ The Independent "Roots-seeking" Generation (2010 to 2019)

Although the commercialization of cinema by the younger auteur filmmakers did not come about overnight, Li Yang, film professor at School of Arts of Peking University, maintains that the market began to see a clear rush around 2010 to a new type of art-house *duli pian* (independent films) that are not only non-government-backed and smaller in budget, but also come with a "dragon logo" stamp of approval from film authorities.

"Independent" as a Deliberate Choice

Li believes this new kind of cinema is created by indie moviemakers who chose full ownership rather than become victims of circumstances like their predecessors. More savvy and creative than their older peers in raising funds, these directors are becoming a new and powerful force in China's art film market. In addition to selling their houses or borrowing money, more of them also use crowd funding or money received from foundations or non-profit studios, debunking the myth that you cannot make good movies on a limited budget.[78]

More importantly, Li notes that these younger filmmakers, mostly the *balinghou*, have learned to balance the system and the market—neither directly criticizing state ideology nor overtly courting commercial appeal. Compared with earlier independent filmmakers, they have intensified their search for emotional and social depth through personal narratives while remaining critical of society. "In the new independent cinema, the periphery and the center are no longer static players trapped in a binary stalemate," Li said. Instead, their films challenge the notion that gloom, marginalization and tension are necessary themes in chronicling Chinese life. Some of the examples Li gives in this category include Bi Gan's *Kaili Blues*, Xin Yukun's *The Coffin in the Mountain* (see chapter 5) and Zhang Dalei's *Summer Is Gone*.[79]

Li says, in some ways, the emergence of this new type of indie cinema is inevitable, as 21st century social, cultural and film-industry changes affected how a new generation interacts with the market and the authorities while still struggling to preserve its integrity. Because this new cinema is less dependent on financial support that restricts or interferes with the creation process, the director has greater control over shooting and editing. This sets it apart from mainstream commercial movies and government-sponsored melody films (a reference to films that embody official ideologies that are promoted by the state).[80]

A Clear Shift to the Rural and the Native

What Li Yang fails to mention is that the three representative *balinghou* filmmakers he has highlighted all share rural roots and sensibilities. *Kaili Blues* and *Summer Is Gone*, for example, both focus on personal stories that occurred in Guizhou and Inner Mongolia respectively, while *The Coffin in the Mountain* is a crime story that takes place in a remote village in central Henan province.

Observers add that this rural orientation extends beyond the three newcomers to others in the generation who are also from China's countryside. This leads them to focus on people from similar backgrounds. In an interview, BFA professor Zhang Xianmin used the term "native land" to describe these emerging filmmakers because they use their own hometowns set in the frontier regions of Tibet, Gansu, Guizhou and Inner Mongolia as backdrops for narratives.[81] He believes this is the result of a rising regional awareness on the part of ethnic minorities.

British film scholar Yu Qiong concurs, although she terms this approach "roots-seeking" cinema. Yu believes this rural focus is heavily influenced by Jia Zhangke's "small-town aesthetics" and his now-famous hometown trilogy of *Xiao Wu* (aka *Artisan Pickpocket*), *Platform* and *Unknown Pleasures*—based on his upbringing in Shanxi's Fenyang.[82] She noted that many young filmmakers have now completed their own versions of hometown trilogies, what she terms the "roots-seeking waves."

A Penchant for Personal Narratives

Although 5th and some 6th generation filmmakers also focused on provincial China (though many of their films were set during the Republican era), critics note that the new cinema pointedly lacks historical references or an allegorical framework. Instead, said film scholar Yang Junlei, many new indie directors avoid challenging the authorities by focusing on personal narratives, steering clear of the correlation between history and the fates of individual characters. One example she gives is Hao Jie's debut film *Single Man* (also see chapter 3) about four elderly rural bachelors. Although Hao has anchored it with four historical points: 1942, 1945, 1966 and 1975, he does not explicitly say how historical events affected the individuals in his narrative.[83]

To Yang, the historical points in *Single Man* are little more than snapshots in a single character's life rather than monumental events with a lasting effect on the entire population.[84] This a far cry from the treatment of early movies by 6th Generation filmmakers, Yang says. In Wang Xiaoshuai's *Shanghai Dreams*, Jia Zhangke's *Platform* and Jiang Wen's *In the Heat of the Sun*, for example, even the most insignificant characters are aware of how their fates are shaped by the arc of history.[85]

While these filmmakers focus on the bottom of society and the marginalized—an echo of early 1990s independent films—film scholar Yin Hong sees a conspicuous lack of a "theme" in newer productions. What's presented to the audience is more like a "state" of life. This "state" is often not dramatic given the lack of conflict or contradiction in the storytelling. The values conveyed in these images are more about contemporary living conditions and a recognition of the tenacity of humanity despite great adversity.[86]

A remarkable rush of new female directors

Critics also remark at the sharp increase in female directors since 2000, complete with their fresh, alternative perspective. According to a 2017 survey on Chinese filmmakers born between 1975 and 1994, some 17 percent of the 60 surveyed are women.[87] A 2020 survey of 187 directors from similar age brackets found that the percentage of women has increased to 28 percent. While the proportions remain relatively low, the percentage has increased significantly.[88]

Among China's better-known young female directors include Huang Ji (*Egg and Stone*, see chapter 2), Liu Jiayin (*Oxhide*), Li Yu (*Lost in Beijing*) Yang Lina (*Longing for the Rain*), Vivian Qu (*Angels Wear White*), Song Fang (*Memories Look at Me*), Emily Tang (*All Apologies*) and Yang Mingming (*Girls Always Happy*). Many have tackled taboo subjects ranging from sexual abuse of left-behind children and women's unfulfilled sexual desires, to the tragedies of China's one-child policy and sexual misconduct by government officials. Taking full advantage of the digital revolution, these young women have ventured into once off-limit topics, making new contributions to China's indie cinema.[89]

Jia Zhangke's film practices and small-town aesthetic, including his use of "raw reality" techniques, low-budget narratives, amateur actors, "on the spot" improvisational filming and use of local dialects, is credited with inspiring many younger followers. Mei Yang, a film scholar at the University of San Diego, points to exiled independent director Ying Liang as one who has benefited hugely from Jia's influence. Ying, originally from Shanghai, made *The Other Half* (2006) and several other films about Zigong—a small city in Sichuan where he once lived—that shed light on the local psyche. Yang said Ying's multi-tasking approach working as director, screenwriter, photographer and editor, in turn, inspired more filmmakers than is sometimes acknowledged within the academia.[90]

Several regional filmmakers featured in this book acknowledge that Jia's rural orientation directly or indirectly influenced them, including Li Ruijun, Hao Jie and Yang Jin. Hao singled out *Xiao Wu* in particular, given its intimate and moving story about an individual's life. Hao said he used to be very embarrassed by his provincial background, but Jia's films helped him realize that "in front of the silver screen we are all equal and that we all have the right to express ourselves."

Similarly, Zhai Yixiang, the youngest artist in this book, said Jia's *Still Life* provided encouragement because Jia's style was simple and within reach, "basically about the chronicling of a place." Zhai also credits the single-handed approach conveyed by Ying Liang during his training at the Li Xianting Film School.

Even Xin Yukun, who works exclusively on crime films and was more a fan of Korean than Chinese auteur films, said Jia's experience as a non-matriculated student at BFA emboldened him to apply repeatedly at the prestigious film academy with its demanding entrance exams. Xin wasn't accepted as a regular student there either, but managed to enroll years later in a shorter certificate course in cinematography.

The first four "hometown" filmmakers in this book made their name using non-professional actors usually hired on location. This approach not only helps them save money, but also supports the use of regional dialects as the main language for their narratives—a practice advocated by Jia Zhangke. Although Xin Yukun and Zhai Yixiang, each with two films to their credit, don't plan extended narratives centered on their hometowns, both used their villages as backdrops and tell contemporary, rural-based stories about people left behind by modernization. These six *balinghou* artists, from as far west as Gansu and as far north as Inner Mongolia, to inland China's Shanxi, Hunan and Zhangjiakou, and to Jiangsu of the Southeast, have greatly enriched the repertoire of China's regional indie cinema.

Jia's early films, such as *Platform* and *Unknown Pleasures*, chronicle the struggles and confusion of lost youth trapped in a remote small town as the pace of modernization inexorably rolls forward. In contrast, the younger generation's "roots-seeking" pictures are "follow-up" portrayals of rural life, reflecting a momentous urbanization program implemented soon after 2000.[91] Zhou Zhongmou, for one, argues that Li Ruijun's hometown narratives (chapter 1), set in northwestern Gansu province, are no longer about the frustrations of lost village youth, but have advanced to illustrate the "emotional dilemma" and complex nostalgia of villagers as their hometowns disappear.[92]

While many of Jia's main characters feel powerless and anxious about being left behind, they still have their local community for support, Zhou said. In contrast, "hometown" is no longer a constant in Li's films as the relentless bulldozers eventually destroy it before their eyes. In this case, hometown remains a physical location, but its structure, traditions and cultural connotation are erased, no longer able to provide emotional stability. As such, Li's hometown narratives are about being a "stranger" in one's home, and the nostalgia associated with that loss, Zhou argues.[93]

Although some may dismiss the *balinghou* regional filmmakers' body of work as merely a sort of postcard of their hometowns, both Yu Qiong and Mei Yang believe many of these tales are a microcosm of contemporary China. They chronicle the transformation of hometowns and the resulting losses and anxiety during a period of unprecedented social and economic change. Yu, in particular, believes these films have helped establish a new regional aesthetic of "hometown realism."[94]

Among new indie filmmakers, Hao Jie and Bi Gan both benefited greatly from changing market conditions and new government policies. However, Hao's *My Original Dream* and Bi's *Long Day's Journey into Night* may not have attracted significant investment without a golden decade between 2006 and 2015. During that period, China's annual box office growth rate exceeded 25 percent, making it possible for many in the industry to reap a windfall and build up capital.[95] Success breeds success as investors and speculators from non-traditional film funding sources flooded the market, fueling a growing hunger for new talent, even as audience tastes grew more selective.

For years, hoping to rival Hollywood's global soft power, the Chinese government tried to prop up homegrown moviemakers using cheap real estate for studios, theater subsidies and various other forms of support. As these programs intensified, real estate tycoons, former coal barons, and advertising firms and other carpetbaggers elbowed their way in. According to Bloomberg News, between 2005 and 2015, the number of film-focused private-equity funds in China increased to 160 from five. Even tech companies such as Alibaba Group Holding Ltd. leaped in, investing in everything from studios to ticketing companies.[96]

Despite this massive buildup in movie theaters and commercial productions, studios and investors paid little notice as moviegoers got younger, their tastes more diverse. A report released by Maoyan Entertainment—an online ticketing service—found nearly 80 percent of film viewers are from the "post-1985" bracket, with younger viewers growing steadily.[97] Today's Chinese moviegoers are becoming more discerning, with fancy visual effects and token Chinese actors no longer a guarantee of box office success. In contrast, a few low-budget domestic films by young directors on everyday themes have proved as popular as big-budget Hollywood productions.

According to Yang Lei, the vice president of Alibaba Pictures Group, while Chinese audiences are among the world's youngest, the country's directors are among the oldest. "So, you end up with a bunch of post-1960s and post-1970s directors serving a mainstream audience born in the 1980s and 1990s, which is disproportionate," Yang said.[98] Sa Dan, a researcher at China Film Archive, also laments that after so many years, "we're still counting on old guards such as Zhang Yimou and Feng Xiaogang (both born in the 1950s) to try to draw the crowds to the theater." It's clear that there's a dearth of young talent and good scripts with interesting plot lines. [99]

Yet many studios have balked at investing in unknown and untested filmmakers. They became somewhat inclined to do so after *Black Coal, Thin Ice*, a thriller with visually arresting scenes by art-house director Diao Yinan, emerged as a surprise hit in 2014. The detective tale, which won the Golden Bear for best film at the Berlin International Film Festival that year, raked in US $12.8 million in its first two weeks. [100] The film's producer Hong Tao says Diao's success was not entirely surprising given that many young moviegoers were tired of formulaic films and hungered for a change, making them more willing to give thought-provoking art-house and indie films a chance. [101]

Another reason for his success, Diao said, was that *Black Coal, Thin Ice* carefully skated the line between art, acceptable political views and audience taste. He adds that he consciously made an "art-house for the mainstream" film by injecting commercial elements into a gritty script. "If you tell a good story, you can also honestly express your views and attitudes towards society, life and humanity," Dian said in a CNN interview. [102]

Diao's box office success, coupled with the industry's maturation, led to the idea that indie cine-ma could be a pipeline for talent. This prompted more investors to court directors with projects that are not only fresh, but are also politically acceptable. This gave them a better chance of passing the censors and gaining commercial releases. It is all the better if these films won prizes at international festivals, boosting their directors' name recognition. As Yang Cheng, a post-80s producer and founder of Nezha Brothers Pictures, said in an interview, "China's market is swimming in money, but there's a real shortage of new talent." If local companies want to discover fresh blood, he added, it wouldn't take them long to discover it in indie cinema. [103]

In that sense, Hao Jie and Bi Gan both timed their careers well, using the market bubble to break into the mainstream. Li Ruijun, (chapter 1) who won several prizes at foreign festivals and was short-listed by Cannes, Venice and Berlin, meanwhile, attracted some 10 million RMB (US$ 1.4 million) from four investors, allowing him to produce his fourth feature film, *Walking Past the Future* (2017). Among these, the most famous partner was Anle Pictures—a top firm and the main distributor for films by Ang Lee and Zhang Yimou.[104]

Xin Yukun (chapter 5), a crime and suspense film addict and a Coen Brothers' fan, managed to break into the commercial market by focusing on a crime and detective story with a cleverly conceived plot, following in Diao Yinan's footsteps. In 2015, Xin's directorial debut, *The Coffin in the Mountain*, a suspense crime story set in a deserted Chinese village, emerged as a surprise indie hit, grossing $1.5 million at the box office despite its modest production budget of 1.7 million RMB (roughly $ 243,000).[105]

Two years later, Xin was able to cash in on his early success to make his second crime feature, *Wrath of Silence*—another auteur-commercial hybrid that reveals the darker side of society. Production help came from the Bingchi Lab initiated by Xining's FIRST International Film Festival. This film attracted 20 million RMB ($US 2.8 million) in investments, over ten times the budget for his first film. In fact, Xin turned down several more lucrative offers from major studios to make his second film, but opted to go with Bingchi Lab in order to maintain more autonomy.[106]

▷ The End of An Era?

The golden period of Chinese cinema didn't last as long as many hoped, however, particularly for novice filmmakers. The first sign of trouble came in the summer of 2019 during the Golden Horse Award ceremony, when a controversy involving a Taiwanese director's speech in favor of Taiwan's independence broke out. Chinese film authorities retaliated immediately by blocking all Chinese filmmakers and industry professionals from participating in future Golden Horse events. This essentially ended many young filmmakers' access to one of their most supportive and viable channels.[107]

A few months later, in January 2020, CIFF organizers formally announced that the festival had "halted indefinitely" any future events because it had become "impossible" to hold them in China's current political climate.[108] The statement essentially marked the end of an era given that the 17-year-old CIFF was the last of the three largest grassroots festivals to close shop. Originally started in Nanjing and priding itself on its independent spirit and creative expression, CIFF had shown some 1,000 films at various locations. Many of those titles touched on politically or socially sensitive topics, with a few effectively genuine underground titles that lacked the official "dragon logo" required for public screening.[109]

CIFF's announcement was hardly a surprise given the gradual, sometimes intermittent tightening seen since the late 2000s. After 2012, the festival was all but driven underground. Zhang Xianmin, CIFF's festival consultant, said that for over a decade, he and his colleagues had been 'closely observed,' though the government's attitude was far from unified. Some local officials in Nanjing and Jiangsu were 'very resentful' of the festival and its organizers while others expressed "cautious friendliness" towards individual filmmakers. "I do get invited in from time to time to 'have coffee' with officials for different reasons. But I also understand that many from the censorship department needed to justify their existence," Zhang said during a 2017 interview.[110]

For a while, CIFF tried to avoid scrutiny by operating quietly with a limited, close circle of insiders. Although festival organizers focused on experimental films to circumvent run ins with the authorities, the schools, work units, theaters and restaurants that worked with CIFF faced constant pressure from authorities, a second-derivative pressure that ultimately made it impossible to continue.[111]

Worse, the 2016 new film law, implemented in March of 2017, (for a more detailed discussion, see chapter 7, an interview with Wang Fei) made explicit what was previously a gray area. In article 24 under "Film Distribution and Screening," it clearly states that enterprises and individuals, households, industrial and commercial entities able to screen films "may only do so in fixed screening venues with the approval of the film department of the local county people's government." The law also makes plain that any filmmaker expecting to take part in a film festival must receive a screening license from related authorities.[112]

After finishing its 2018 exhibitions (their 14th edition), CIFF skipped the 2019 season before formally ending the festival in 2020. Other art-house festivals with more "official" status such as Xining's FIRST have expanded to fill the gap, though they require that all films be approved by the state before being considered.

What does this mean for emerging players? For Zhai Yixiang (chapter 6), the shutting down of these grassroots festivals means novice filmmakers are losing the opportunity to meet with like-minded artists, brainstorm, gain feedback and garner much-needed encouragement and support. Zhai also credited CIFF for allowing him and Bi Gan to showcase their first films. (Zhai's directorial feature *This Worldly Life* was selected by CIFF in 2014, while Bi Gan's *Kaili Blues* won CIFF's Special Jury Prize in 2015). Without these venues, Zhai fears that many ambitious young filmmakers won't get their shot.

Zhai said in a 2019 interview that he feels his second feature, *Mosaic Portrait*, which touches on the sexual abuse of a young girl, was directly affected by the stricter, new censorship rules. That follows because such topics are increasingly out of bounds, even though films with similar topics, including Vivian Qu's 2017 feature *Angles Wear White*—about two young teens sexually assaulted by a government official—had little trouble securing a screening license shortly before the implementation of the new film law. Bad timing robbed him of the opportunity to secure a hard-to-come-by screening permit, he recognized. Zhai said he has been negotiating with censors about a screening permit for *Mosaic Portrait* since 2018, so far without success, and the film may never see the light of the day.

In this new political environment, Zhai believes even not-for-profit companies such as Blackfin Productions and Heaven Pictures will now insist that films they support pass censorship hurdles. Zhai's debut *This Worldly Life* never passed censorship, but was still green-lighted by CIFF in its 2014 competition.

Zhu Xin, a first-time director born in 1996 (*Vanishing Days*, 2018), points out that more official events (with licenses to hold events) at Xining's FIRST and Pingyao film festivals have a markedly different character than grassroots film festivals such as CIFF—there are stricter requirements on quality and subject matter. This stems in part from the stipulation that all showings be held in proper theaters, not in more casual venues. Related to this is that grassroots film festival screenings also tended to be much more intimate and spontaneous, involving more spirited discussions with filmmakers, compared to the formal, scripted feel of official events.[113]

Indie films without a "dragon logo" also used to be able to attract mainland distributors by first entering foreign festivals, effectively a workaround. According to Wang Yishu, head of screening affairs for Xining's FIRST Film Festival, the film bureau now requires that all films pass the censors before screening anywhere in the world if they want to return home for theatrical runs. This closes a common financing door in the past used by the likes of Jia Zhangke (*Xiao Wu*, 1997), Lou Ye (*Summer Palace*, 2006) and Li Yang (*Blind Mountain*, 2007). [114]

But some say stricter censorship isn't the only culprit. They also blame the "illusion of fast fortune" spurred by the rapid growth of commercial cinema as another main deterrent that has diverted talent and new blood from China's indie sector. Zhang Xianmin, for one, believes "with too much money in the film market chasing too few projects," young directors today are spoiled for choice. They get snapped up for big projects soon after graduation or after completing their first few shorts, affording them little time to mature.[115]

Indeed, in a 2019 interview with this author, CIFF co-curator Wang Fei echoed this view, adding that they have witnessed fewer and fewer quality independent submissions in recent years, which all but defeats the purpose of having the festival. At one point, CIFF resorted to accepting films with a "dragon logo" as a way to cope with a shortage in quality submissions, Wang added. During their 2011 edition, at the suggestion of then curator Wang Xiaolu, CIFF created a special category for "films with a 'dragon logo'."[116] But this decision, according to Wang Fei, was sharply criticized by some indie filmmakers who insisted that CIFF maintain its relative independence from authorities.

This "fast fortune" period proved more short-lived than many had expected, however. As tax policies tightened after 2019 following mega star Fan Bingbing's infamous tax evasion scandal in 2018, a chill has swept through China's entertainment industry.[117] In the face of the crackdown, the market value of several leading film companies cratered by 70 percent. Growing investor nervousness has prompted studios to further reduce output.[118]

Sadly, this desperate situation was made worse by the unprecedented revenue decline as thousands of movie theaters shuttered because of the Covid-19 outbreak starting in 2020. Due to the pandemic, China's box office was expected to fall to US$4.2 billion in 2020, less than half of 2019's US$9.2 billion, according to *Content Commerce Insider*,[119] and some believe a full recovery could take years.

What is certain is that the money that has sloshed around China's film market in the last decade has now largely disappeared, at least for the foreseeable future. As more and more investors leave the market, opportunities for the likes of Bi Gan who managed to break into the mainstream with a single feature film credit may well be a thing of the past.

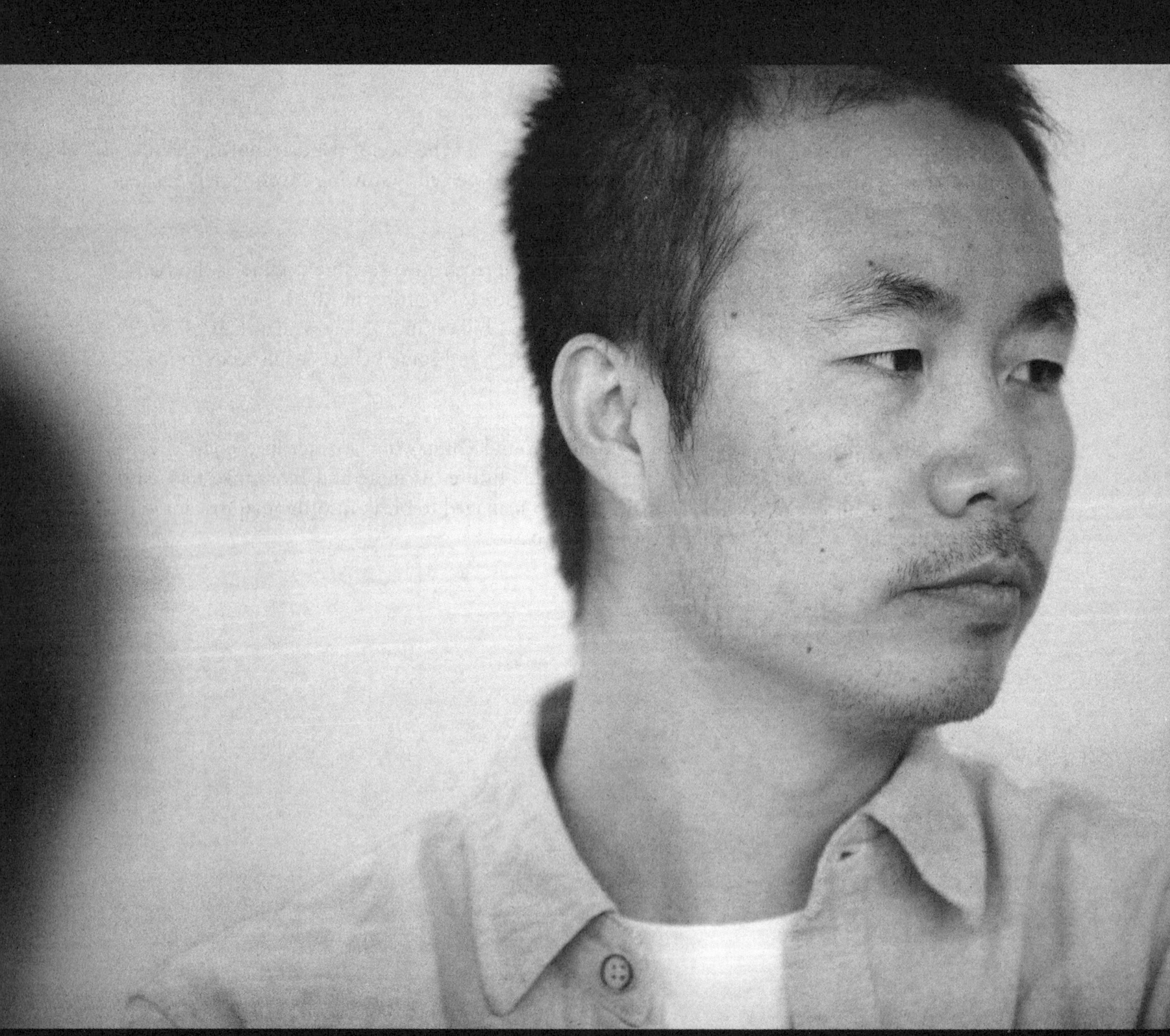

Director Li Ruijun

CHAPTER 1

LI RUIJUN
Transformation and the Transformed

A Short Introduction

Li RUIJUN is a rising star in China's independent cinema. Among his generation, he is best known for his consistent and thorough exploration of the meaning of hometown and his treatment of the dramatic transformation of rural China in recent years. Li was born in Gansu Province in Western China in 1983 and has a background in music and painting. In 2003, after graduating from the Communication University of Shanxi, he moved to Beijing and started his career with a short feature, *The Summer Solstice* (2007). He went on to write and direct four more films about his hometown Gaotai, including *The Old Donkey* (2010), *Fly With The Crane* (2012), *River Road* (2015) and *Walking Past the Future* (2017), all of which were either showcased at European film festivals (Venice, Berlin and Cannes) or won awards elsewhere (Hong Kong Film Festival, Australia's Golden Koala Chinese Film Festival and the Brasilia International Film Festival.)

Seen as a social realist, Li's movies focus on the tie between people and the land, especially the rural attitude towards family, home, life and death of the Chinese countryside in transition. Although Li's hometown narratives are compared with those of Jia Zhangke, scholars note that Li's films are no longer about the frustrations of young people left behind in backwater villages. Rather, they go deeper to reveal the "emotional trauma" and complex nostalgic feelings of local farmers who have witnessed the deterioration of their ecological environment in the government's headlong rush to reform and modernize the countryside. Desertification of the arid grassland and abandoned villages portrayed in *The Old Donkey* and *River Road* both illustrate such devastation.

The Old Donkey and its sequel, *Fly With The Crane,* both deal with elderly farmers and their relationship to the land. They are juxtaposed against a society that pushes reforms and new policies relentlessly. *Fly With The Crane*, based on a short novella written by renowned author Su Tong, takes a hard look at an old farmer's contemplation of death. *Walking Past the Future* is based on an original script about two generations of a rural family working as migrants in the bustling southern metropolis of Shenzhen. When the parents reach retirement age, they return to their hometown in Gansu, only to find their ancestral home repossessed under a rural-reform policy. *Walking Past the Future* had a higher budget than any of Li's previous features at roughly 10 million RMB ($1.5 million). The film was chosen in the *Un Certain Regard* category at the Cannes Festival 2017, the only Chinese entry that year.

Changing family structure and instability is another constant theme in Li's films. In *Fly With The Crane*, Old Ma's three sons have left town to make money in the city, and Old Ma's wife is long dead. The absence of the "mother" figure is perhaps the most poignant allusion to a lopsided family power balance in rural society. In *The Old Donkey*, the mother figure is also conspicuously absent, and the daughter character must take care of the elderly father while tending the fields. In Chinese literary works, "mother" often symbolizes the earth. The absence of "mother" is a metaphor for the painful disappearance of hometown.

Few of the actors and actresses appearing in Li's films are professionals, with most hired from among his friends and relatives in Gaotai (with the exception of the cast in *Walking Past the Future*). Through these films, Li opens our eyes to this uniquely rustic region of Northwestern China, showcasing its haunting beauty and the wild abandon few people have seen outside of China.

Hometown narratives are a popular genre with millennial indie filmmakers. But one thing that distinguishes Li is how devoted and persistent he is in showing the impact that reforms and policies have had on villagers and their families—a theme many from the *balinghou* generation shy away from. In order to remain independent-minded, Li refused repeatedly to take money from wealthy investors for commercial films. He also chose to live for many years far from central Beijing in a dingy row house in order to save enough money for his film projects, which may have kept him grounded. He is committed to telling stories about China's underclass blindsided by the wrenching speed of social and economic changes.

Filmography

The Summer Solstice 夏至 (short film, 2007) - director, screenwriter, actor, editor, production manager

The Old Donkey 老驴头 (feature film, 2010) - director, screenwriter, composer, editor

Fly With The Crane 告诉他们，我乘仙鹤去了 (feature film, 2012) - director, screenwriter

Present 礼物 (short film, 2014) - director, screenwriter

River Road 家在水草丰茂的地方 (feature film, 2015) - director, screenwriter, editor

Walking Past the Future 路过未来 (feature film, 2017) - director, screenwriter

Interview

I first met Li Ruijun at a screening at Beijing's Italian Culture Center in the spring of 2016. Li, a rather small-framed man with a mustache, wasn't very assuming. But his film has left a very strong impression on me. The film screened that evening was *Fly With The Crane*, and its unvarnished look at old age and death touched me in a way I hadn't expected. The stark beauty of Gansu featured in the film was also impressive. The following month, I interviewed Li for a magazine article I was working on at the time that eventually led to this book. In June 2017, after Li finished screening *Walking Past the Future* at Cannes, we sat down again at a café near Beijing's Third Ring Road, at which point Li updated me on his thinking and motivation behind making the third film in his Hometown Trilogy, *Walking Past the Future*. (The other two are *The Old Donkey* and *Fly With The Crane*.)

How did you decide to become a filmmaker? And was it difficult for you to make your first films?

I was good at arts and crafts but not at math or science, so my father sent me to a special high school to study painting and drawing. When I graduated, my teacher suggested that I learn how to do commercials at the Communication University of Shanxi. It was while I took some of those courses, which included watching a lot of movies to learn how to tell stories, that I discovered my love of film.

It was a rough start. In 2006 while filming *Summer Solstice*, I had an investor pull out at the last minute. I was in trouble because I'd already set up a film crew and needed 300,000 RMB (roughly $50,000). At that time, I was using film, so it was very expensive. My dad had a chunk of savings put aside to buy a house. He ended up lending me that money. I cobbled together the rest from relatives and friends and finished shooting the film. It was really rough there for a while because people thought I was a hoodlum since I didn't have a steady job and wasn't making money like other people. I got a lot of support from my director friend Yang Jin, who worked for free as the cinematographer and recording artist for *The Old Donkey*. It was only after I won 10,000 euros at a film festival (in 2010) for a screenwriting award for *The Old Donkey* that my parents heaved a sigh of relief. Luckily, I got another 20,000 euros at Rotterdam as a post-production award for the same film, which allowed me to pay back some of the money I owed my parents and friends. I also worked temporarily as a TV director to finish paying off my debts.

What motivates you to make independent art films? Is winning prizes at international festivals important to you?
I don't set out to win prizes at festivals when I'm making films. You just can't predict which films or themes will be picked for each festival. Besides, judges are different each year, and who will be a judge for your film and what gets chosen is entirely based on luck. So I don't get a swelled head just because I happen to win a prize or two.

I make films entirely based on one question—whether it is worth doing, and whether it will move people. Movies are not just entertainment to me, but also a space for us to reflect and chronicle society. As a human being, I simply cannot let go of the social issues around me and pretend that I don't see them. For me, filmmaking is a window to understand the world. It's also a way to communicate with the world; a way for me to record the transformation of China, the lives of the people and their

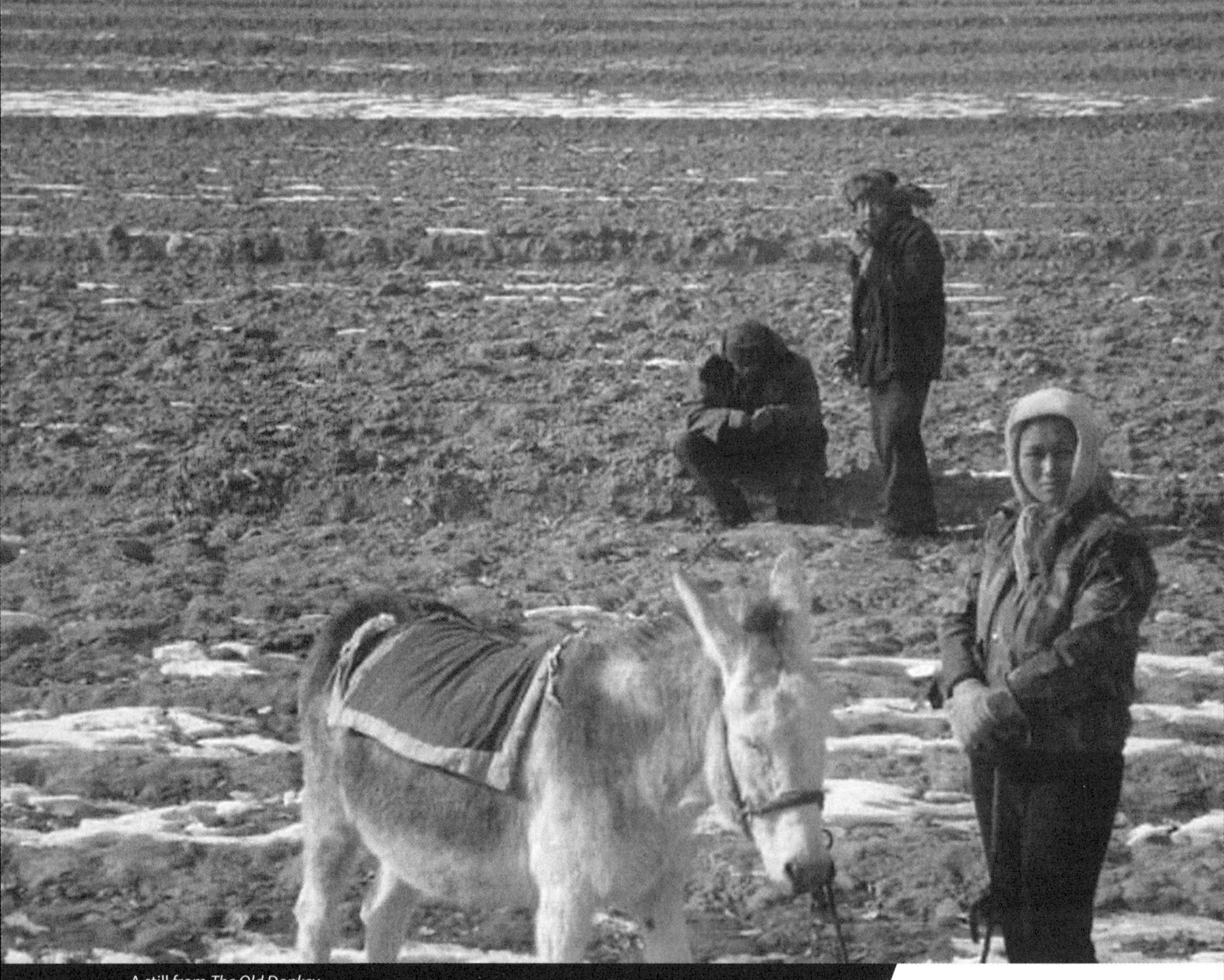

A still from *The Old Donkey*

struggle in the face of transformation. And yes, there is a bit of focus on the meaning of life as well. I hope through my films I can help change the world by evoking some kind of reflection among audiences about what's happening around us, and make them pay more attention to the less fortunate.

You made several movies about the elderly living in rural Chinese villages, including *The Old Donkey* and *Fly With The Crane*. Why are you so interested in issues related to this particular group of people?
I go back to my village all the time in Gaotai, Gansu Province, and I'm familiar with many issues that concern these older people. Society pays little attention to old people left behind in rural China, or their worries about life and death. Yet there are close to 200 million elderly in China, (according to news reports, roughly 10 percent of China's population is now over the age of 65) and how can a group that size be ignored? Right now, we only seem to be interested in the future, not the past. But the future and past are connected, and we'll all get old one day. We should care more about older people's concerns.

Growing up I also had a lot of questions about life and death. What's the purpose of life? Why is it that many peasants prefer to have boys rather than girls, etc. While filming *The Old Donkey*, for example, I found many answers. I found out why Chinese peasants are so insistent on having sons—because as farmers, they don't enjoy any social welfare benefits. I know this because my mother was a farmer. And since daughters will leave sooner or later after getting married, having sons is about the only way farmers can ensure that someone will look after them when they get old.

In *The Old Donkey*, we see how the elderly fight to the bitter end against the county's decision to redistribute their land to those who agree to use agricultural machinery. Land grabs are a serious issue in rural China. How much of the story is based on events in your hometown?
Land reform started in 2009 across China, not just in Gansu. This caused a lot of conflict. Although the central government said land reforms should not be implemented by force, regional governments often went ahead, ratcheting up tensions. These problems were especially common a few years ago. Unfortunately, many policies are made without taking into account the situation on the ground.

In *The Old Donkey*, you focus on how family relationships are being transformed in fast-changing China, especially for the elderly left behind without anyone to care for them. For example, none of the three sons in *The Old Donkey* is there for the old man when he's sick. Ironically, it's the daughter who ends up taking him to the hospital. Is this arrangement intentional? Why?

You could say that I intentionally depicted all three sons absent from the village but it is also based on reality. In rural China, almost all young men head to the city as migrant workers. Women are generally left behind to take care of older parents and tend the fields. In many ways, the wives of migrant workers are forced to pick up the slack, their load doubled as they juggle farming and domestic chores.

In the original version, there was a reference to the Great Famine in 1960 that did not survive the cut. In that unused scene, several old men gather around a table and talk about how they saved their limited food rations for their sons during the famine years and let their daughters starve to death. The characters thought they had no other choices because they needed the boys to care for them later. As an old saying suggests, "Raise boys for your old age." They believed their daughters would marry and leave town and cannot, therefore, help them secure their old age.

So, in the end, none of the grandfather's three sons stay in the village to take care of him when he's old and sick. It is his youngest daughter who stays and helps him tend the field, bringing him lunch and going to great lengths to get him to the hospital when he falls ill. Other old people in the village are jealous of Old Donkey's daughter because they don't have anyone left to care for them. I guess what I'm trying to say is that the Chinese tradition of raising boys for your old age has not survived the changing times. The fact is that as young males leave the village for better opportunities, they leave their aging parents behind unattended. There's a real gap between tradition and reality in Chinese society right now. What happens to these older people? How will they cope with their lives and old age? These are urgent questions I wanted to raise in the movie.

In your movie _Fly With The Crane_, we see the grandfather character so opposed to the idea of being cremated that he asks his grandchildren to secretly bury him "alive." Why is it that older people in rural China are so against cremation, to the point that some would rather die prematurely to ensure their traditional burial?

I think it has a lot to do with the fact that they work on the land all their lives. When you work day in and day out with the earth, your livelihood relies on harvesting from nature and you come to see the power of the earth and how it perpetuates the life cycle. Harvest is life itself, and the earth is what bestows life. Life begins and ends with the earth. So, to them, it's a very natural thing to want to bury their bones in the earth, return them back to the soil and make this final contribution to the land. They see being cremated as breaking that cycle. That's why in the film, the old man thinks seriously about dying early to ensure a traditional burial, rather than waiting to die later and be cremated. This attitude is very common and very real.

Take An'qing, a city in Anhui Province, as an example. Several elderly people there saved money for years, perhaps even decades, for a coffin. They committed suicide in April and May of 2014 ahead of a June reform deadline that made traditional burials illegal. After the deadline, cremation was the only way villagers could dispose a body. Many policies in China are made without taking into account the practical situations. It may be reasonable to implement a cremation policy in cities, given its environmental benefits and limited land resources, but less crowded areas such as northwestern China should not be subject to the same policy.

I also want to add that for my relatives and many older folks in my village, death is part of life, they're not afraid of it or particularly superstitious. In fact, my great uncle—who won a prize at the Australia-based Golden Koala Chinese Film Festival for playing the lead role in _Fly With The Crane_—is no different. When we heard he'd won the best actor prize, we scrambled to find him something presentable for him to wear. We were in such a rush we forgot to bring any formal clothes, and in Australia, we couldn't find anything that he felt comfortable wearing. Eventually we stumbled on some funeral homes in Chinatown selling special clothes meant for the dead. My great uncle was very pleased with what we bought and didn't feel strange or unlucky at all by their association with death. He wore his "long-life" outfit at the ceremony to accept his award.

In *Fly With The Crane*, you used a lot of long takes, and the pace of the film is extremely slow. What was your thought in using this approach?
I did this deliberately because I wanted the audience to get a sense of what the passage of time is like from the old man's perspective. "Should I choose this moment to die or not?" is a very important decision for the grandfather, and he needs a lot of time to think about it. The passage of time is really life itself. I believe the psychological rhythms of an old man come in waves, and I wanted to express this in the movie. In the film you will notice it's the children and old people who end up spending a lot of time together because they are the ones with a lot of time on their hands to ponder the meaning of life and death. The adults, on the other hand, are too busy or too worried about making money.

I also feel as human beings, we come into this world without any choice over when and where we're born. But we *should* at least have the right to choose *when*, *where* and *how* we die. In the movie, the grandfather's friend's last wish that he has a traditional burial is ignored and he is ultimately cremated. That gives the grandfather a lot to think about when he considers whether to take things into his own hands while he still has time.

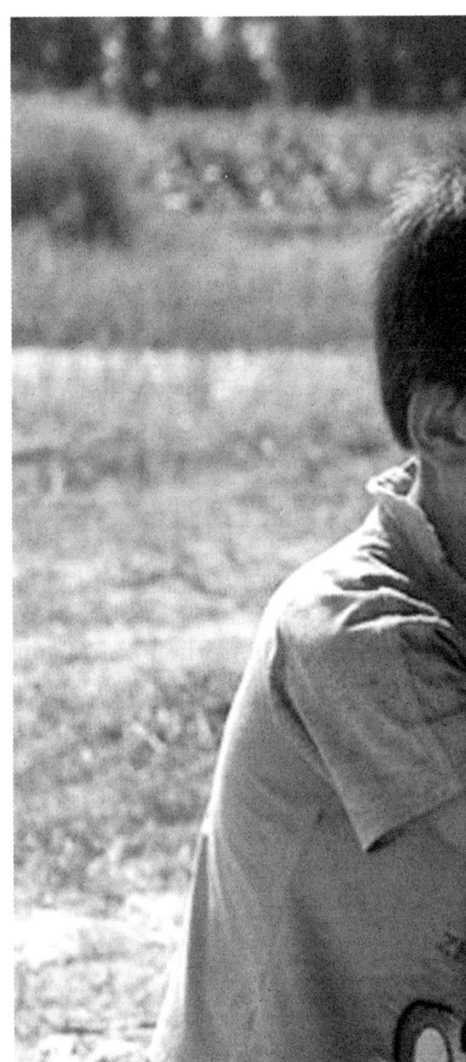

Fly With The Crane asks the tough question: should we have a choice in how we die?

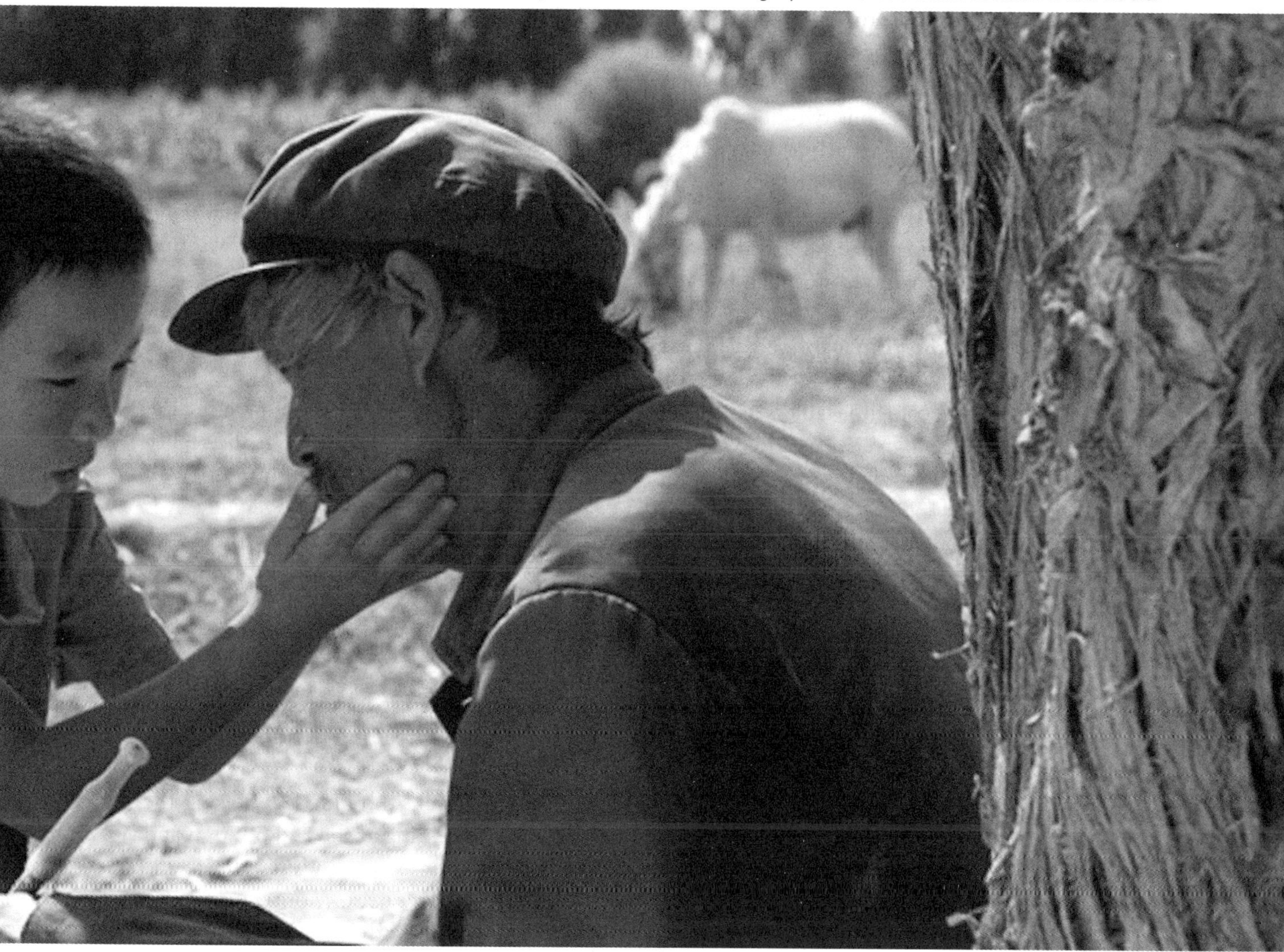

River Road, your third feature, is about two young boys crossing the remote Northwestern desert on a camel's back as they search for their missing father. Can you tell us more about this film?

The film is a road movie about two boys from the Yugur ethnic minority left behind in a remote village with their grandfather while their father works in the city. When grandpa dies, the two estranged boys are forced to cross the desert together to look for their father and their home. On the road, they witness the devastating ecological destruction and desertification of their ancestral land, which is dying due to natural and man-made climate change. Along the way, the two warring brothers must find a way to reconnect and work together to survive the dangerous journey.

And at the end of the film, you see a factory in the middle of the desert, which is quite shocking….

The film is really an ecological fable. The speed of China's industrialization is extremely fast. The two boys hope to find a greener pasture when they start the search for their father. But the reality is very disappointing, and that is something a lot of younger people must face in the future. We all want to improve our society, but when the pace is so fast that it interferes with our everyday lives and the environment, then creation becomes rather meaningless. China used to be a nation very mindful of living harmoniously with the environment. But economic development has taken priority over ecology, so the losses really outweigh the gains. Unfortunately, when the entire Chinese population is focused only on making money, few are interested in the wellbeing of our souls.

For *River Road*, I understand you had to apply for a screening permit required to screen in China and at international film festivals. How did you handle the screening permit for *Walking Past the Future*?

It's slightly complicated in the case of *Walking Past the Future*. We were thinking of entering the film at Cannes Festival 2017 but were behind schedule. We finished filming at the end of 2016 and had a 150-minute long, half-finished rough cut. We were half thinking of sending the film to the censorship bureau in May. You don't want to seek their approval too early because once a permit is given, you can't make further changes to the film. Although we didn't think the 150-minute edition

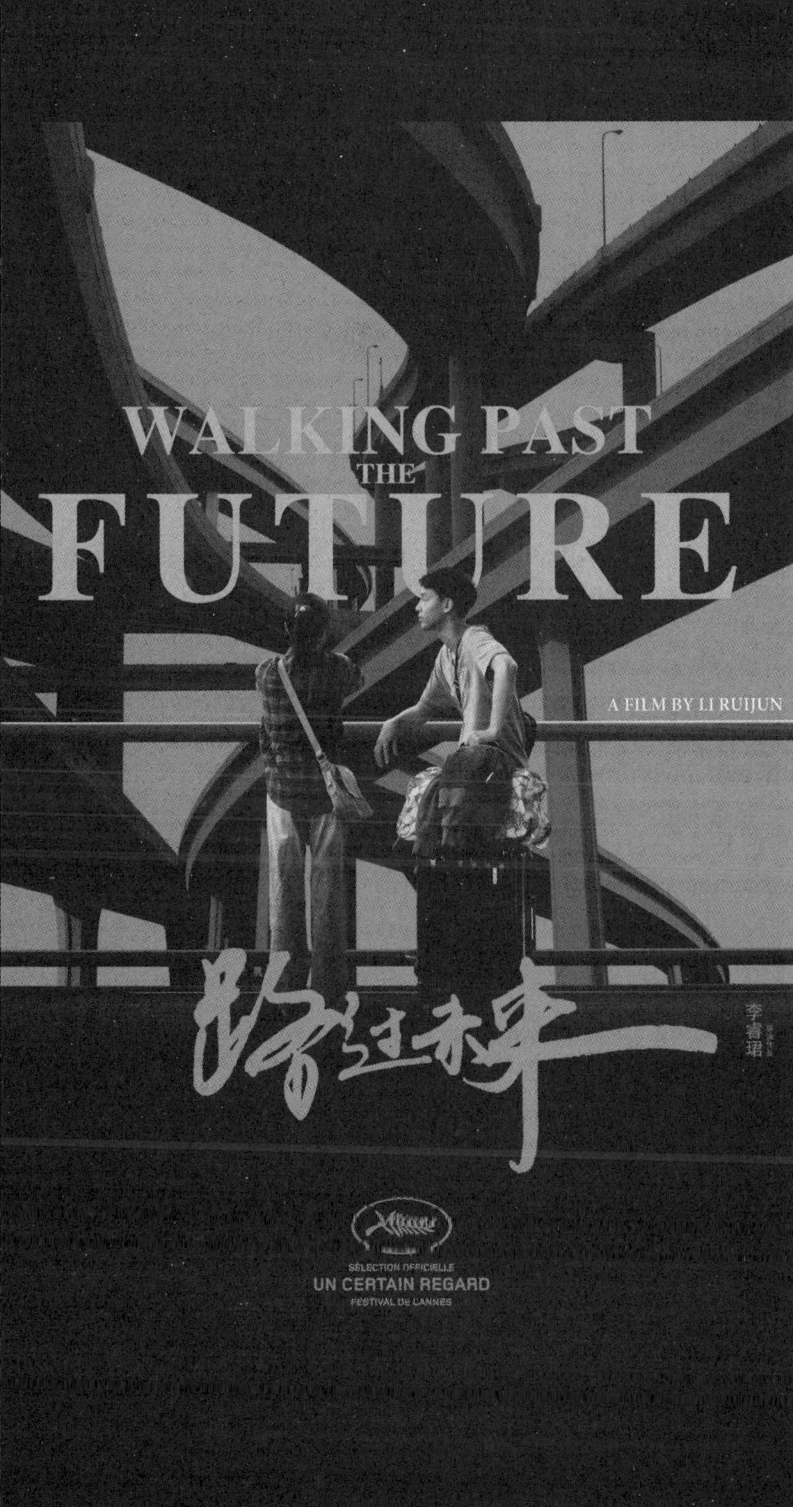

was ready for screening at festivals, some of my team members suggested that we send it to Cannes anyways for feedback, and we did this in February of 2017. We heard back from Cannes about a month later, and were encouraged when they suggested that we send an updated version. We followed up by sending in a 120-minute edition. Then another month went by and we heard nothing. We took it to mean we hadn't made the cut, and thought we'd try again in 2018. But then in mid-April, we received word that *Walking Past the Future* made it onto the very final list. We were overjoyed, and immediately sent the film to the film bureau for approval. It only took the authorities two days to give the

Walking Past the Future is a take about migrant workers working in urban China.

okay, and they suggested very light changes. This in part, I think, had to do with the fact that in 2016, not a single Chinese film had made it onto the final list in any category at Cannes. In 2017, my film (as well as a Chinese short film by Qiu Yang) were the only Chinese features that made it to Cannes.

Walking Past the Future is very different from your previous films in part because it's a much bigger production, both in terms of budget and production time. What did you find most challenging about making this film?

When I made _The Old Donkey_ and _Flying With The Crane_, I made them in a village I'm very familiar with because I grew up there. I also had absolute control over how many days to do the shooting. And the villagers knew me well and were very cooperative, keeping quiet whenever I asked them to. With _Walking Past the Future,_ it was entirely different. Most of the shooting was done in Shenzhen, a very busy city. This meant we had to juggle with complicated traffic rules. At certain hours, for example, we couldn't drive into a narrow street with a big truck and had to make do with a smaller car. We also had to apply to many different government departments, including a hospital where we did a significant part of our filming. We had several scenes that required shooting on a very busy street, and it was extremely difficult to keep everyday pedestrians from walking in front of the camera. We had to dispatch many crew members onto the street to explain and ask for their cooperation. Logistically, it was very challenging and a bit of a nightmare, not to mention our having to constantly shift our film crews between locations.

You also added a few professionals, like Yang Zishang and Yin Fang, as the lead actor and actress in your otherwise all non-professional cast. How did that work out?

I found working with a professional cast easier than with non-professionals because their performances are much more effective. When I worked with non-professional actors, I often had to spend one or two months teaching them how to read the screenplay, how to memorize their lines and how to act, and we took a lot of time rehearsing. However, when working with professionals, you have tighter time constraints because they have very busy shooting schedules. In this case, they would only give me 15 to 18 days of their time, so I had to work around their schedules by first completing all the scenes involving them. This often meant setting up and dismantling different sets over and over again because the scenes are shot out of sequence. It ended up taking a lot of time. When working with non-professionals I didn't have to worry too much about time schedules. I usually shoot the scenes chronologically, which allows me to better concentrate on the story. This film also involves a much bigger cast because it's a story about the destinies of several characters, and this also adds to the challenge.

Some Chinese reviewers have criticized *Walking Past the Future* for trying to tackle too many issues, including skyrocketing real estate prices, bankruptcies and paid drug trials. What is your response?

Actually, some of the Chinese critics say they didn't understand the film, which is very ironic, especially coming from China. Some also say the film lacks "positive energy," and that I'm selling "bitterness" to the audience. What I am expressing in the film, in fact, are issues and problems that I see happening everyday around me. If these critics don't understand, then either it is because we don't live in the same world, or that they simply haven't paid full attention when watching the film. I actually suspect that some of them didn't even see the movie, yet they felt justified in joining the clamor, even demanding that my film exude positive energy. They're merely regurgitating the established official view. There is very little original thinking coming from these critics. This isn't the type of audience I'm aiming for. A Mexican viewer in the audience had a very different response. He said he felt very close and familiar with the characters' fates and felt the movie could have been a Mexican film. A German moviegoer had a similar reaction. So, I felt the destinies of many Chinese are becoming more and more similar to those who live in other countries, including those of refugees.

You have gone from making films about Gansu to now making a movie about a big city. Will you be focusing more on big cities and urban residents in the future?

As a rule, I don't have an interest in big city settings. But Shenzhen is different. It's not just another big city—it's China's fastest growing metropolis. Since *Walking Past the Future* is about China's social transformation in recent years, I find Shenzhen the one place that best exemplifies the metamorphosis that China has endured since 1949. Shenzhen used to be a sleepy fishing village at the dawn of the 1950s. The houses you found there were all one-story houses. China used to be an agrarian society. The image of China from those days was rather like a humble, one-story brick house. But because of policy changes, it suddenly shifts gears and rapidly develops itself, building rows and rows of shiny skyscrapers. The process is very much like what has happened to Shenzhen—a model city so radically transformed that it completely reinvents itself within a couple of decades. The metropolis has been crowned China's first Special Economic Zone, a showcase of the country's economic success. Because of its miraculous transformation, the government has decreed that any new experimental tests begin in Shenzhen. This is why Shenzhen is the only city that can represent all the changes that China has gone through.

If you could sum up the one theme that connects all your films, what might that be?
I've never really considered the themes of my movies, but if there were one common thread, I'd say it's the relationship between *transformation* and *those who are forced to transform*. In China, policies are very top-down, very subjective and not at all well planned. And despite the government's best intention to improve lives, many policies have in fact backfired. And in the process, a lot of resources are wasted.

What would you be working on next? And would it be related to Gansu again?
I don't know yet. I don't like to plan my projects too far in advance. I will consider topical issues that catch my eye. It may be related to Gansu, but themes may vary—it all depends, and I don't want to limit myself. But it will definitely have something to do with ordinary people.

Now, the Chinese film industry is abuzz with talks about making commercial films and turning them into lucrative mega hits. How do you stay true to yourself as an auteur filmmaker without giving in to temptation?
I've been making indie films for a decade now. It has been a tough journey staying in this field doing what I love. There are many people out there who dream of becoming a filmmaker but never succeed. I'm among the few very lucky ones living this dream. Not only can I realize my vision making the kind of films I want to make. I also haven't been interrupted and my work has been

very steady. This in itself is very satisfying. I think perhaps it's because I put everything into film-making. That's my only priority in life and I don't really care about having other comforts so long as I have enough to eat. Life is full of temptations and you can't possibly fulfill all your desires. There's a saying in Chinese that says until you know what to give up, you can't get what you really want. If you want too many things, you will end up with nothing, it's that simple.

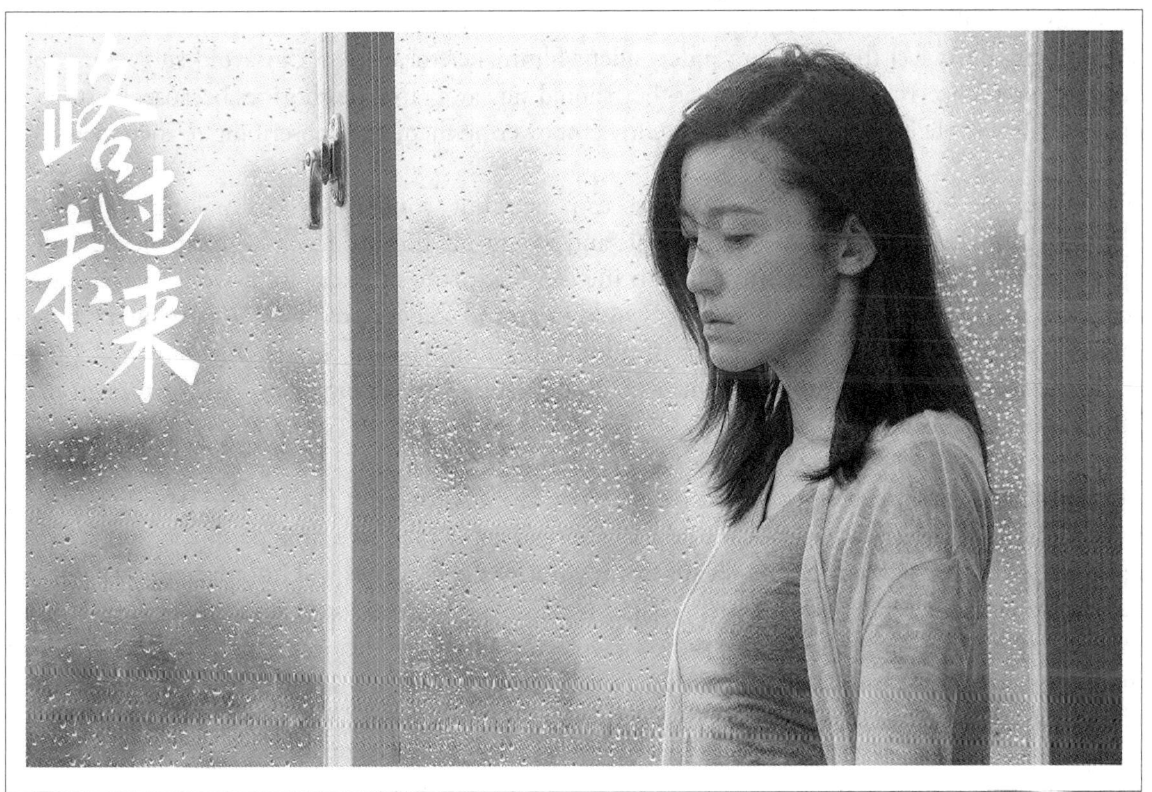

A still from *Walking Past the Future*

I'm not saying I absolutely won't touch a commercial film in the future. If an investor approached me and told me we ought to make a certain type of film because it's popular and lucrative, then I'd definitely say "no thank you." But if there's a story that I really like that's also got a commercial element to it, then I wouldn't refuse.

Chinese authorities recently amended the film law effective April 2017. You're already an established filmmaker. Will the change affect your filmmaking?
Of course, it will affect me. I imagine I will become less free. I'm actually very conflicted about it. Some of my peers feel that being an independent filmmaker means you can avoid subjecting your films to censorship. They feel strongly that they should stay away from authorities because, by subjecting your films to their rules, you're inadvertently empowering them and subscribing to their views.

While I see the logic in this argument, I also can't help but wonder why I'm making films in the first place. I make films about ordinary people and I want my films to reach as many ordinary people as possible. If I did not send my films to the censors, many ordinary folks would never have a chance to see my films (because these films would not stand a chance of being released in a Chinese theater.) So, in the end, what's the point of my making films? I have to ask. Without the Chinese audience, would I not end up a filmmaker bent on "selling China's bitterness" to the foreign market, as some critics charge?

My films are set in China, and I want those living in the environment I portray to be able to watch these films. So, I feel I have to work with the system and apply for a screening permit so my films can reach more Chinese viewers. My hopes are that eventually the film laws will improve, especially if the censorship bureau adopts a rating system. Right now, we are under a lot of pressure, and we end up thinking a lot before we even start our projects, worrying about whether our approach will ultimately make the cut or cause trouble for our production companies. The new law has made it a punishable offense for any producer to screen films in public without having a proper screening license.

Before the law was enacted we were able to participate in film festivals without applying for a *long-*

biao. We could always apply for it afterwards if needed. Now, this isn't possible. Getting a permit is mandatory if you want to participate in any film festival, domestic or international. Any violation, when discovered, will not only mean hefty fines for the filmmaker and producer alike, it also subjects them to very tough punishment, including being barred from touching any film for a long time. So we really want to avoid causing trouble for our producers by not following the rules. The only way I see getting around this bind is to invest my own money in a film that might be too sensitive. That way, if there's a problem with the film, I'll be the only one responsible.

What about up-and-coming indie filmmakers? What sort of impact will this law have on those who have not yet made their first film?
New filmmakers, given their lack of experience, won't know what the censors allow and what they don't. This is a huge disadvantage. Another worry is that many of their imaginative ideas will be killed out of fear they will offend the authorities, that self-censorship will destroy their creativity before they even begin. Afterall, the rules outlined by authorities are not very clear. Even movies streamed on the Internet face more scrutiny, and the government can remove content anytime. These days, Internet providers are also less willing to air films that don't have a screening license.

What do you see happening to Chinese independent film?
I'm not very optimistic at this stage. There are also a lot more opportunities for young filmmakers to make commercial films. This means a lot more temptation and distraction for those interested in making independent films. This is why I feel we're at a stage where things are rather gloomy.

Case Study: *Fly With The Crane*

The second work of Li's "Hometown Trilogy", *Fly With The Crane,* tells the story of an elderly farmer from a small village in Northwestern China who must decide whether to take control of his own death. This comes after he finds out that the preferred, traditional burial option in his area will soon be disallowed. It is an intimate, thought-provoking film that takes an unflinching look at

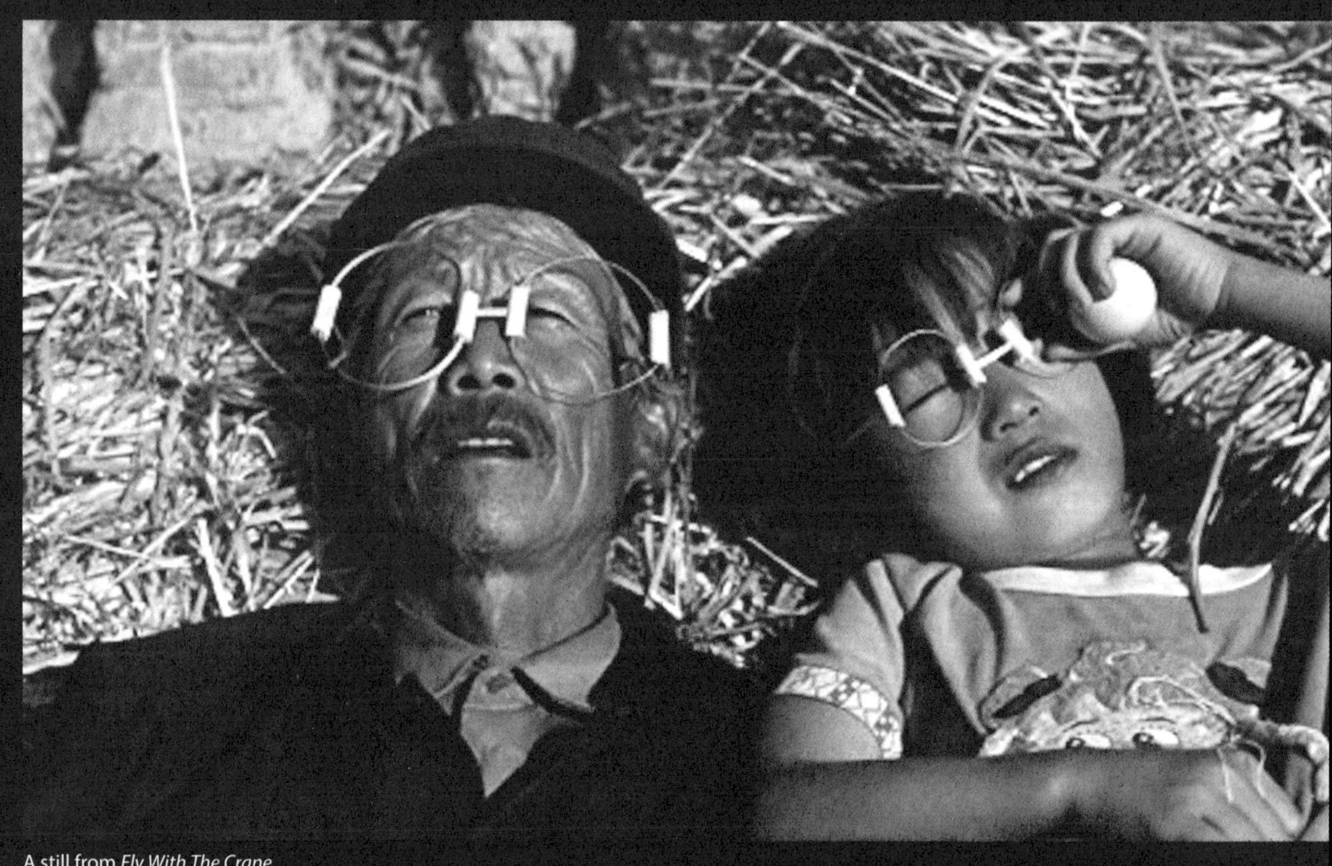

A still from *Fly With The Crane*

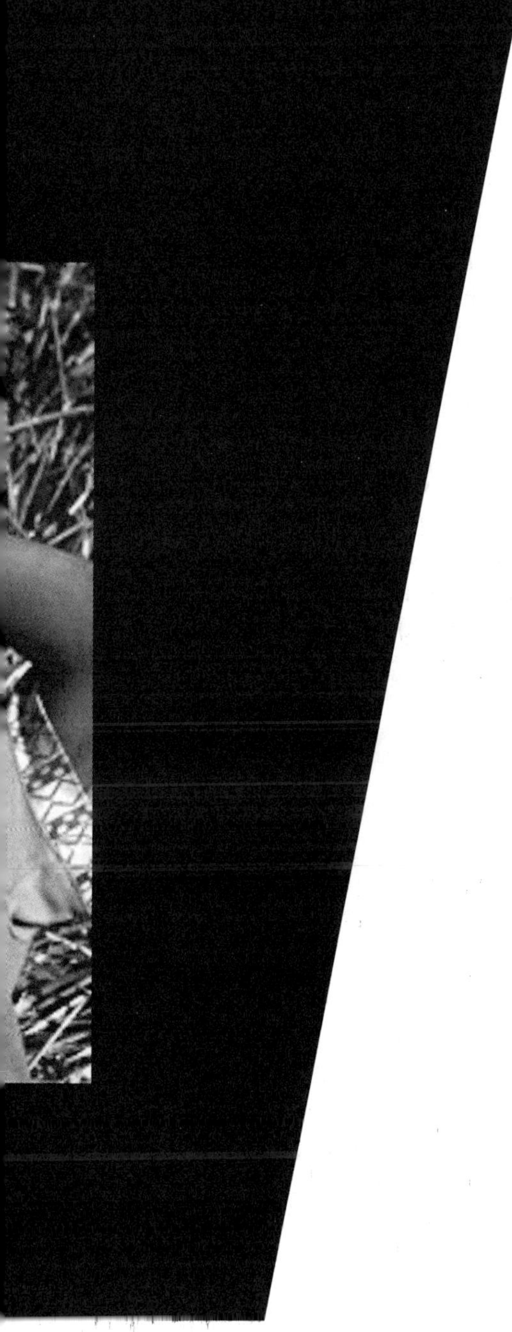

aging, life and death in rural China—a rare look at a group that's easily overlooked.

Similar to *The Old Donkey*, Li's debut feature, *Fly With The Crane* is about the changing human relationship with the land. Unlike the first film, however, *Fly With The Crane* is less a denouncement of unfair local land policies than an old man's simple love for the earth, life and his touching relationship with his grandchildren.

The film is slow-paced without being tedious or sentimental, and maintains tension throughout by contrasting the lively games of the grandchildren against the slow, contemplative stillness of Old Ma. The old man's inner struggle over his preferred death is also skillfully set off by the brilliant colors and idyllic exterior of the countryside.

Ostensibly based on renowned Chinese novelist Su Tong's short story with the same title, in fact only its final 20 minutes is taken directly from that story. The script's first 80 minutes are written by Li based on his experience living with the elderly in Gaotai, his hometown. The film cost 1 million RMB (roughly $154,500) to make, and the decision to shoot it using an amateur cast was partially motivated by cost, although a more important consideration was to make it almost entirely in the local Gansu dialect—a language most professional actors wouldn't be able to handle.

The film is partially funded by Heaven Pictures, a non-profit media firm devoted to promoting art-house films. When Beijing authorities heard that the 69th Venice International Film Festival had allowed *Fly With The Crane* to compete in 2012, they approached Li and asked him to make changes and cuts before the premiere. Li declined, and the picture was screened in its entirety at the festival. Perhaps in 2012, the censorship rules were still relatively lax, Li said he did not face any consequences for that decision.

The Director's Take

What's an independent film?
An independent film relies on independent thought and spirit, one that is not influenced by opinions other than the director's own. An auteur will not consider the marketability of the film, nor rely on other people's financial help to complete it. S/he will make the film as a way to express a thought or idea.

Do independent films need to have a social function?
Yes, independent films should have a social function, and they need to be experimental, reflective and critical of society.

Why do you make films? And who is your audience?
Making films is more like an instinct for me because I have thoughts and ideas to express and film is the best vehicle for me to communicate those with the world. When I make films, I don't think about my audience, I simply do it according to my own vision.

What's the first film you ever saw and what were your initial reaction?
It was an anti-Japanese war film made by the government, though I can't remember which one it was now. At the time I thought movies were very entertaining.

Which single movie made you realize that film is an art form?
Vittorio De Sica's *The Bicycle Thief,* which I watched in 2001 in college.

What is your favorite film of all time?
Fei Mu's *Spring Time in a Small Town* because it's timeless, and the film was way ahead of its time.

Who's your favorite director of all time and why?
Theo Angelopoulos. His films are very philosophical, and the stories seem very simple but are actually very thoughtful and complex.

What in your opinion are some of the qualities that the best films share?
Sincerity and a high level of completion, and the length of time it remains in people's memories.

What's your best quality as an independent director?
This is not something for me to decide. I will leave that to the critics.

Name one Chinese film you've seen lately that you consider great and why?
Vivian Qu's *Angels Wear White (2017).* It is a courageous film that touches upon a social issue not tackled before, namely sexual violence against underage girls in Chinese society.

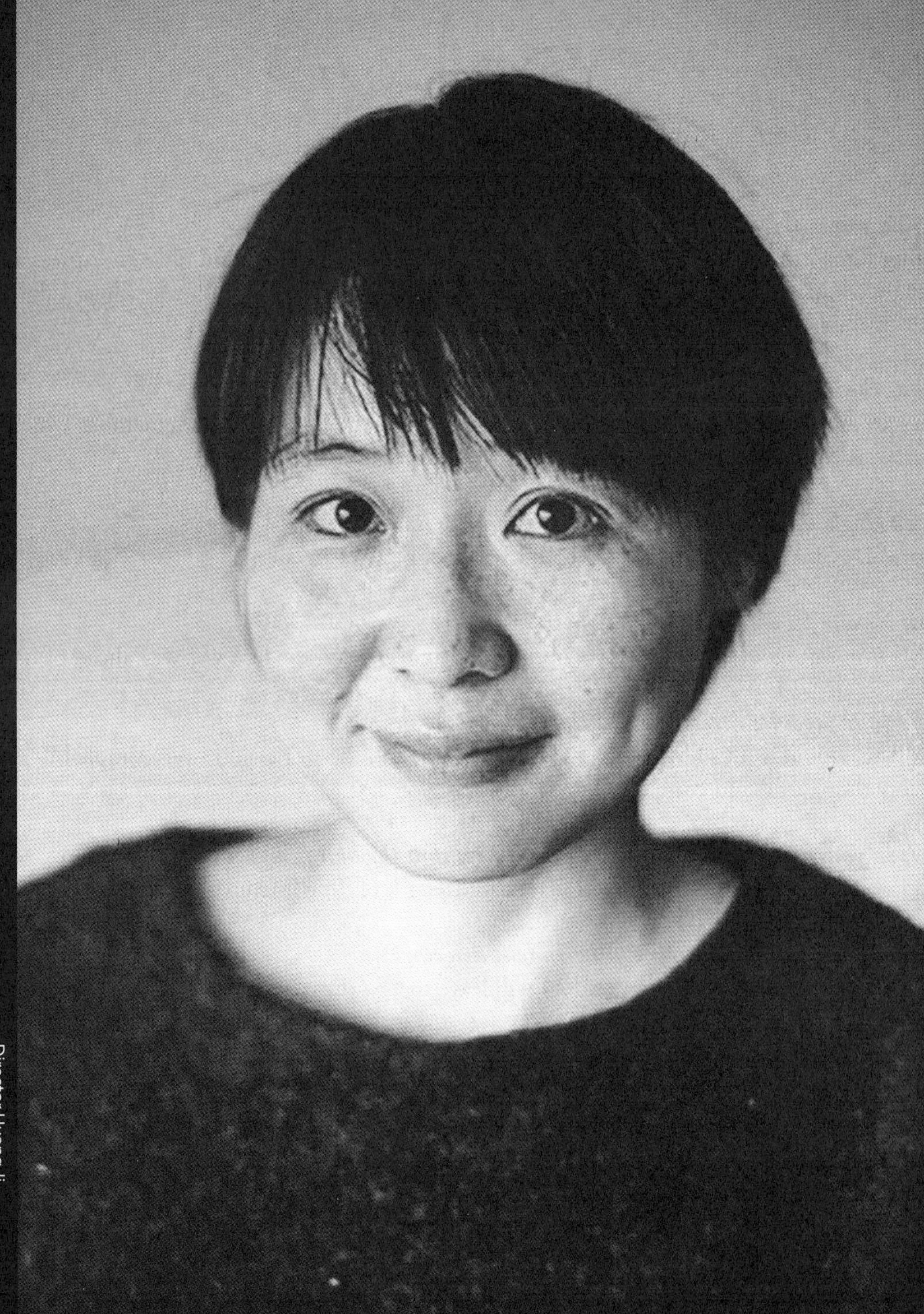

Director Huang Ji

CHAPTER 2

HUANG JI
Portrait of A "Left Behind" Daughter

A Short Introduction

HUANG JI is a Beijing-based independent director noted for her "feminine perspective" and credited as the first feature filmmaker to put a spotlight on China's so-called "left-behind children". These are disenfranchised children and young teens left behind mostly unattended in rural villages while their parents migrate wholesale to developed coastal cities for better jobs and moneymaking opportunities. (The "China Child Welfare and Protection" Report 2019 estimated that in 2018, there were some 6.9 million left-behind children in rural areas across China.) Her daring portrayals of sexual exploitation of young girls left behind in small-town China shattered a longstanding taboo on discussing this issue.

Born in 1984 in Yiyang in the Southern Central Chinese province of Hunan, Huang graduated from the screenwriting department of the prestigious Beijing Film Academy (BFA) in 2007. In her semi-autobiographical directorial debut *Egg and Stone* (2012), Huang zooms in on a young girl left behind in a rural village for close to a decade by her neglectful parents, and how she is forced to fend for herself in the face of many unfortunate events. Filmed with a non-professional cast in her hometown and help from her cinematographer husband Ryuji Otsuka, the feature shocked China and grabbed headlines at international film festivals. It eventually won Huang the top Hivos Tiger Award for Best Feature Film at the Rotterdam International Film Festival in 2012 and the Grand Prix at the Tarkovsky International Film Festival-Zerkalo in 2013.

Huang's second feature, *The Foolish Bird* (2017), is a sequel. Shot with the same non-professional cast, the film is a painful, coming-of-age story about a forgotten 16-year-old girl who, after being left and ignored for years in a small town by her parents, grapples alone with corruption, sexual violence and omnipresent social media. The movie won the 67th Berlin International Film Festival Special Mention of Generation 14 plus International Jury prize.

Both of Huang's films were produced by Yellow-Green Pi—a Beijing-based film production company founded in 2009 by Huang and her husband. Otsuka worked as producer, director and cinematographer, Huang as screenwriter and director. Huang and Otsuka's teamwork gives them an edge, allowing them to collaborate with Japanese TV stations on documentary productions. This comes as the two continue to express themselves through small-budget, independent features, which they take to international film festivals for potential collaborations. Since our interviews, Huang has started on her third film, *Stonewalling,* the last of her "Hometown Trilogy."

Filmography

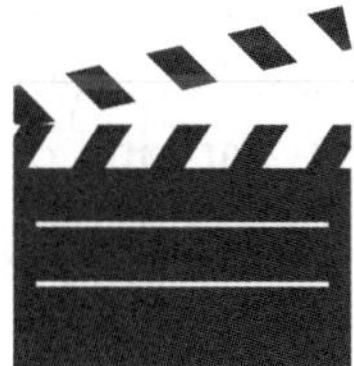

Underground Mark Six 地下 (documentary, 2004) – director
Lingling's Garden 玲玲的花园 (short film, 2007) – screenwriter
The Warmth of Orange Peel 橘子皮的温度 (short film, 2010) – director, screenwriter
Egg and Stone 鸡蛋和石头 (feature film, 2012) – director, screenwriter
Trace 痕迹 (documentary, 2013) - director
The Foolish Bird 笨鸟 (feature film, 2017) – co-director, co-screenwriter (with Ryuji Otsuka)

Interview

I met Huang Ji through a friend. Due to her hectic travel schedule and demands as a working mother with a young child, it took us quite a while to sit down and talk. We first met at a café near her house in Tongzhou—an eastern gateway to Beijing roughly 40 minutes away by train—and our interview was initially meant for an article about *Egg and Stone*. In the summer of 2017, I was invited to Huang's opening for *The Foolish Bird* at Beijing's Ullens Center for Contemporary Art (UCCA), where she had an extended Q & A session with the audience after the screening. This chapter essentially is based on these two events, with additional material added later through follow up email and Wechat exchanges. Huang, a left-behind daughter herself, has vowed not to leave her own daughter behind even for short periods while working, and tends to take her everywhere, including to film festivals and screenings. During the Q & A session at UCCA, Huang juggled between answering questions and keeping her young daughter occupied. She was unapologetic about this and said it is extremely important that she doesn't repeat the mistakes her parents made by favoring moneymaking over family relationships.

You've gone to BFA and made several films. What motivated you to become a filmmaker?
As a young child growing up in Hunan, I really loved funeral portraits. In the old days, many folks in the village took their portraits only once in their lifetime—when they knew their end was near. These portraits were meant for family members for safekeeping because, without them, their loved ones may soon forget what they really looked like. And every time I heard firecrackers on the street, I knew someone had died. The funny thing is, people didn't seem very sad at funerals. So, it got me thinking about many things: "What is life all about?" "Why do we exist?" and "What kind of trace will we leave behind when we're gone?" That's how I became very interested in film and photographs, which eventually led me to filmmaking.

You have made three films about young women related to the theme of sexuality, including *Egg and Stone*, a short film called *The Warmth of Orange Peel*, and now *The Foolish Bird*. Would you say you're the first Chinese director to tackle this theme in a feature film?
Actually, I'm not the first because Hao Jie, another filmmaker from my generation, made a trilogy looking at sex in the village (see chapter 3). His *Single Man* and *The Love Songs of Tiedan* are both about single village men and their sexual frustration. But I'm the first to tackle the theme from a female perspective, especially about how young, left-behind girls in rural China are forced to cope with sexual exploitation all on their own.

Egg and Stone garnered a lot of attention at international film festivals, winning many awards. Do you think this is due to its unusual theme, or more because of your treatment of the subject?
Objectively speaking, the film is a very honest and believable portrayal of the everyday life and feelings of a young girl left behind in the village by her parents. And even though it's not an easy life because the young girl is sexually exploited, she is not portrayed as a victim because the film is not about denouncing her abuser per se. In other words—and this is a very important point—the film is not out to make a deliberate point about justice. Rather, it's a film about the protagonist's mood changes, which are tied to nature and her surrounding environment in the village.

Another unique feature about the film is that the narrative is organized in a non-traditional and non-linear way. If film is an art form involving space and time, then in *Egg and Stone* you'll notice that the narration is seen through a woman's menstrual cycle instead of the conventional linear calendar, and this helps make the film stand out. There's a very strong feminine touch in the way time is handled here. This starts from the beginning, when the protagonist realizes in anguish that she has missed her period, to the end when she rejoices at the knowledge that she's menstruating again. Of course, I think Otsuka's cinematography is also crucial because the film comes across as very beautiful and poetic. As some of the judges (at Rotterdam) said, "He was able to weave his film language into the story line." Otsuka's beautiful shots help make audiences feel more empathy for the main character, making them want to protect her.

Speaking of Otsuka, can you talk about the cooperation between the two of you? In what way do you think this collaboration has helped your work or the way you express yourself?
I met Otsuka at BFA and we started collaborating officially with *Egg and Stone*, even though we already had a working relationship when I was shooting *The Warmth of Orange Peel*. That was the first time Otsuka visited rural Hunan, and the first time he tried to capture the villagers with his camera. *The Warmth of Orange Peel* is about the sexual awakening of a ten-year-old girl living in a small village. It's a very personal story based on my own experience, and it was Otsuka who helped me identify what's distinctive about my work as a filmmaker. He really pushes me to confront my own emotions.

One thing that separates me from other directors is my deep interest in the individual. While quite a few male directors tend to approach social issues from the larger worldview, or that they prefer to pay more attention to how power structure works, I am much more into how individuals, particularly women, see and feel their world. In *Egg and Stone*, for example, rather than treating the protagonist as a victim, or focusing on the social impact, I zoom in on the young girl herself. In other words, I've totally reversed the conventional approach of first seeing things from the bigger picture before getting down to the small and the concrete. This approach to my filmmaking is further amplified by Otsuka's help through his unique film language.

In *Egg and Stone,* Yao Honggui plays a "left-behind" daughter in the countryside

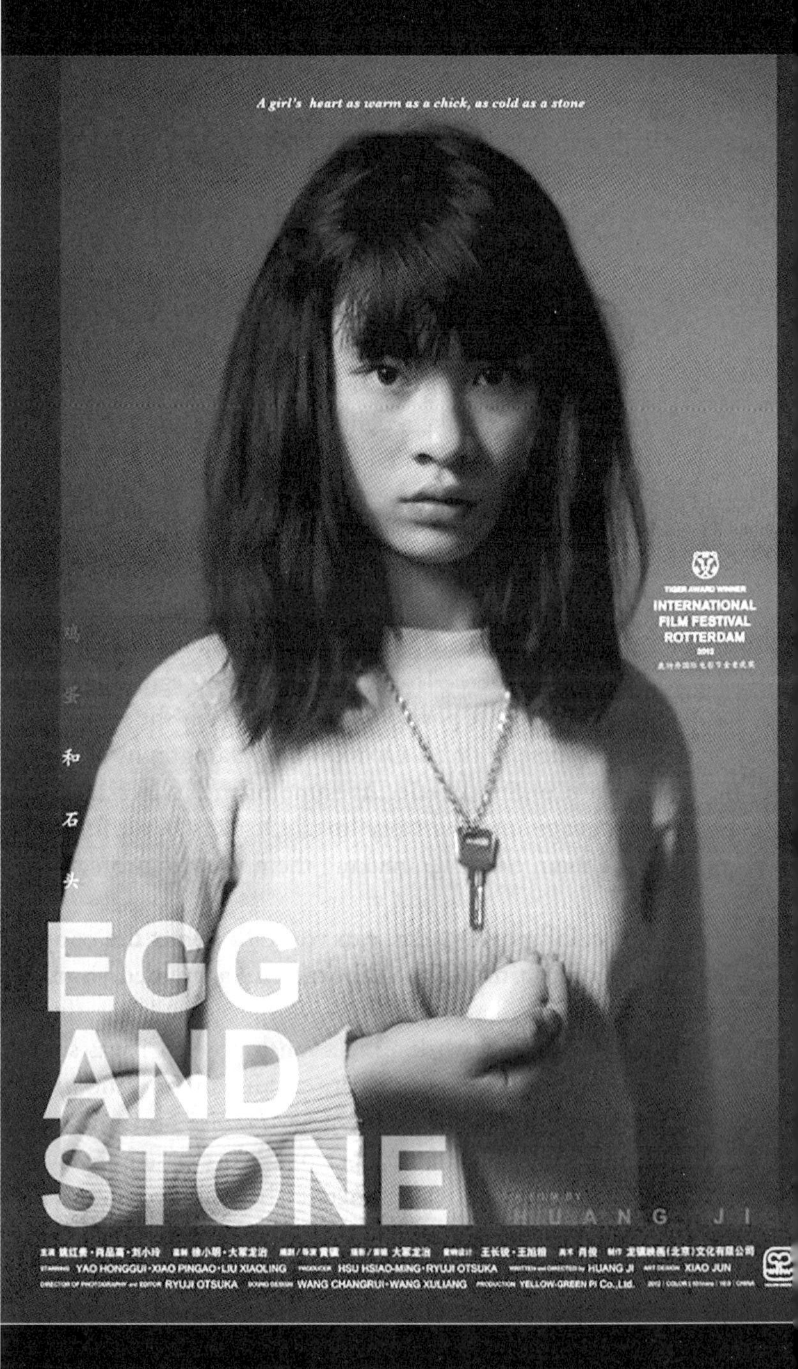

Unlike many cinematographers who tend to be rather heavy-handed with serious topics, Otsuka has a very different take. He would ask the question: "Which one is sadder when broken, a beautiful thing or something that's not so beautiful?" With that in mind, he would make the village and the young girl appear as aesthetically pleasing as possible on camera. His cinematography transcends national boundaries, and my very local sensibility is equally borderless. And this is how we came together as a team.

"Left-behind children" is a topic not talked about much in Chinese feature films, especially when they're involved in sexual abuse. What is it that you most want to convey through _Egg and Stone_?
I think relationships between left-behind children and their adult relatives are complex, especially when it comes to feelings. There's a mutual emotional dependency between the children and their relatives. However, sometimes things happen unexpectedly. It could have been a cold night, or perhaps because there is nobody else around, and in a matter of seconds, things can get out of hand. My intention, however, is not to blame anybody, but more to show how sometimes instincts and loneliness in a very isolated place can be a factor that leads people to do things they don't intend to do in the first place.

You may wonder why people in the countryside have become so _lonely_. I think it has something to do with people losing touch with their spirituality and the fact that we've lost what was once a very vibrant rural popular culture. In the old days, we used to have a theatrical culture involving cross talk. Not anymore. All we see today is people indulging in playing mahjong all night, as we see the Auntie character do in _Egg and Stone_. And the uncle may have felt left out because his wife is never around. To me, the most interesting themes I want to tackle are not about nations or politics, but about human nature, and how humans relate and react to their environments. City folks and country people, for instance, react to their respective environments very differently. And this is the same anywhere you go.

Your short film _The Warmth of Orange Peel_ is also related to the subject of sex, but from a very different perspective. What is it that you're trying to convey in this film?
The Warmth of Orange Peel is about the sexual awakening of a ten-year-old "left-behind" daughter living in a small village during a very cold winter. Lacking proper guidance about sex at school,

the girl becomes curious about her father when he returns for a visit, and the girl begins to see him more as a man than as a parent. It was based on my own experience. My parents briefly returned to live in the village when I was 12 and left again when I was 14. It was during this period when I started middle school that I became very curious about sex. I think I was missing the feeling of warmth both physically and emotionally.

In *The Foolish Bird*, you put your focus on teen sex. Why is this theme important to you?
In this film, I come back to address the issue of sex because I feel that for many young girls who grow up in rural China, sex is the one thing that remains a huge headache for them. And yet most will find it difficult to verbalize their sexual urges and related troubles. Other problems are relatively easy to solve, but not sex. Many social problems in rural China I feel are related to women and sex because the village women are the least able to verbalize such things. The film is about a 16-year-old high school girl's troubling experiences with love, sex and money in a small village. She's so starved for attention and human contact that she randomly calls strange men up, foolishly allowing them to take advantage of her. The film is not necessarily a sequel to *Egg and Stone* per se, though Otsuka and I took to filming it again in my hometown using the same non-professional cast we'd worked with before.

The lead in both *Egg and Stone* and *The Foolish Bird* is a non-professional teenage actress named Yao Honggui. I understand you plan on using her again in a third feature-length film. Is there a particular reason you keep working with her?
Actually, I thought of using Honggui for my second and third films as soon as I finished shooting *Egg and Stone*. The shooting of my first film gave me the idea of completing a trilogy built around the different stages of a young woman's coming of age in the village, which in many ways mirrors my own experiences growing up in Yiyang during the 1990s. So, the first one is set when the young girl is 14, the second when she is about 16 and the third will be when she is around 22 or 23.

Another factor is that I really like that Honggui is much less affected by popular culture than her peers. Although she's also a left-behind daughter, she doesn't go shopping much, doesn't wear makeup and seldom listens to popular music or watches television. In other words, she's still quite pure and remains mostly in her own world without being influenced by the language perpetuated by popular TV culture.

More importantly, I've built a very good and trusting relationship over the years with Honggui. We have a good understanding of each other's needs, so it makes it much easier to continue working together.

The Foolish Bird is about juvenile delinquency in rural China based on your own experience. But today's social environment is quite different from the 90s when you grew up. How did you handle this change in social environments in the film?
Of course, the environment where the protagonist Lynn grows up is quite different from mine. In the 90s I grew up an attention-starved, neglected young girl, and I used to call men who were total strangers for a bit of attention. In those days, we didn't have cellphones or social media. So, I used landlines to do my calling.

When I first did my research for _The Foolish Bird_, I was worried that the gap in social environments between then and now might be too great. But then I realized young women today in the village suffer from the same kind of loneliness I felt back in the 90s. I also felt that it's more relevant and meaningful to make a film about the reality of young village women today than do a film looking back at the 90s. That's why I decided to observe Honggui's as well as her friends' lives and focused on the theme of loneliness in the village. In _The Foolish Bird_, you see that cellphones play a big role and are used as a vehicle in various ways to fill the huge vacuum left in the heart of the young protagonist. For example, Lynn would steal cellphones before giving them away as gifts to her best friend and a boy she has met randomly, in exchange for friendship and sexual attention. Or she would sell them to strangers for materialistic comfort.

Related to the theme of loneliness is also the huge communication gap between adults and their teenage children, with adults often taking very little interest in what's happening with the young-sters. In the film, for example, Lynn's mother rushes back home unexpectedly because she needs to take care of some financial matters. When mother and daughter come together, they can't talk to each other because so much time has lapsed since they last saw each other. And even if Lynn wants to talk to her mother, she doesn't know where to begin.

The two occupy the same intimate space. But emotionally, they are very far apart, each lost in her own thoughts about various problems. So, the two just sit there in silence until the mother has to rush off again to the city. There is no hugging between the two, just Lynn looking up briefly from her cellphone and sending her mother off with her eyes. This scene is based on my own experience. So, although the social environment may have changed, the feelings have not.

A poster for *The Foolish Bird*

I noticed that in *The Foolish Bird*, you didn't take many frontal shots. Instead, the camera angle tends to be mostly from behind the protagonist, making it as though we're following the heroine everywhere. Can you explain the significance of this approach?

In *Egg and Stone*, the protagonist is still a young teen, and she's mostly a passive character perplexed by her predicament, including having to deal with a relative who's also a sexual predator. The story is really about the changes in her inner world, which is why the film is mostly shot in her room.

In *The Foolish Bird*, the young woman has grown up a bit more, and no longer wants to be trapped in her room. She wants to take the initiative to meet people and engage in different relationships, but she doesn't know how to make decisions for herself because she has received no guidance from her absentee parents. Under the circumstances, she relies on the advice of her best friend May, who instructs her to steal cellphones. When May eventually refuses to take her calls, Lynn starts to pin her hopes on a new boyfriend, thereby exposing herself to sexual exploitations.

Lynn is very confused, so everything she does takes on a very uncertain, tentative quality. Her body may be moving, but she has no idea where she's going. Otsuka and I decided to take shots from behind her so we can better observe her anxiety and indecision, and magnify her confusion. If we took frontal shots, we'd be suggesting that she has a plan and knows where she's going, which of course is far from the truth.

In *The Foolish Bird*, you also have a minor salesman character pushing air purifiers on elderly men and women. Can you tell us why you added this subplot?

This subplot is an extension of the loneliness theme I wanted to express about small town villagers, including the older people. The elderly villagers are particularly venerable to sales scams because their sons and daughters are not around and they desperately crave some kind of attention. So when a friendly sales person comes to them pushing his wares, they become easy prey. This is fact, not fiction. I know in my village of Yiyang, there are quite a few elderly people who spend lots of money on electronic products they don't need but buy them as a way to fill the gaping holes in their hearts. In their desperation, they don't see these as sales scams. In fact, they want to believe that the young salespeople are genuinely kind and care about their wellbeing. Like the lead in the film, lonely people all use modern gadgets to temporarily relieve the emptiness they feel inside.

This is the third film you've set in your village of Yiyang. (The first film is *The Warmth of Orange Peel*, followed by *Egg and Stone*.) Is this more out of budget considerations? Or is there something particular about Yiyang that draws you back repeatedly?
One reason is that in 2003, when I was a student at BFA, I felt very insignificant as an outsider because Beijing was the first major city I'd ever lived in after leaving Hunan. Not knowing the city well, I didn't have any sense of attachment to the place, much less the confidence to engage in social discourse. Hunan, however, feels different to me because it's my home. In a way, perhaps it's more appropriate to say that, for many filmmakers raised outside of big cities, we don't feel we have the *right* to talk about urban China, even though since 2000, rural youngsters like me started to have more opportunity to be educated in big cities. So, for us, coming to the cities to make films doesn't make sense. In that sense, it's much more accurate to say that we've "returned to our hometown" to tell our own stories through film after receiving our urban education. You might say that we have finally discovered our own voices through better education, that we've found the "tools" to express ourselves.

Another aspect is that rural China is not only our emotional home, but also the part of China most affected by the nation's modernization process. For us, going home to the realities of desertification, depopulation and disappearing village culture is just devastating. The emptiness of village life, the hollowing of people's emotions, these are aspects of Chinese society that we as artists want to capture on the silver screen.

So far, all of your films have been semi-autobiographical and very personal—a trademark of yours. Can you explain why you prefer this format?
It so happened that my childhood as a left-behind daughter is also a social phenomenon shared by many others in rural China. This is why I started my films with this personal experience. My features are different because they're taken from real experiences, so they're very natural. Some films about the same topic may seem a bit patronizing, as they treat children only as victims. But that's

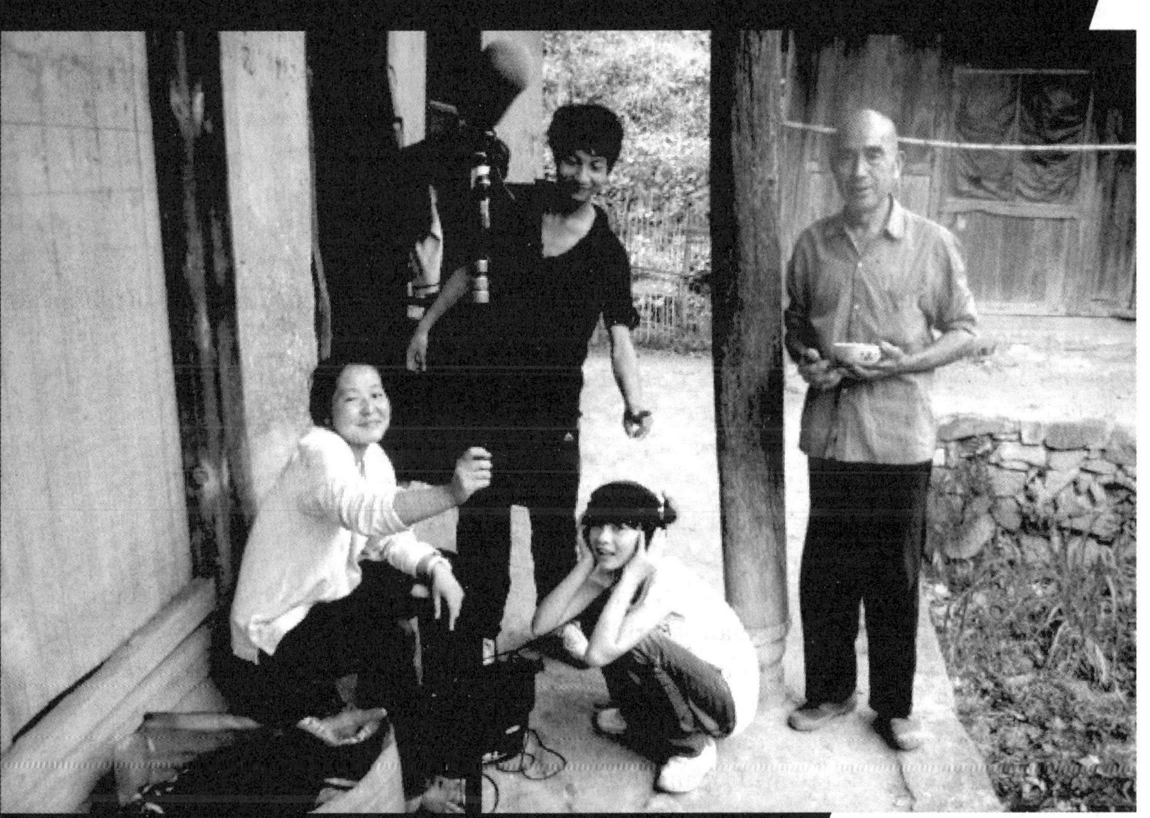

On the set of *The Foolish Bird*, taken in Huang Ji's hometown village in Hunan

not right. In *Egg and Stone*, the lead may not seem like a very likable person, but she has a very strong core and doesn't need other people's charitable sympathy.

I also tell tales from personal experience because I want to minimize the cultural gap for foreign audiences. Personal tales are universal, and I believe they can better connect with audiences even if they don't have any prior knowledge of China or Chinese culture. Although my films focus on Chinese villages, the feelings and emotions they elicit are universal. I think this is why Otsuka, being Japanese, and I, being Chinese, can relate to each other. Or maybe because I'm more of an individual myself—I'm not very Chinese in that way, and my films are not particularly Chinese in character either.

You have been called a "feminist filmmaker" at some of these international festivals. How do you feel about this label?
First off, I don't quite get the concept of feminism, so I don't necessarily like having this label. I also feel there's a fundamental difference between men and women. Biologically, women are very different because they're made to bear children, so I never thought of expressing my ideas from the standpoint of absolute gender equality. I think it's much more accurate to say I make films from a woman's perspective than to say that I'm a "feminist" filmmaker.

Do you think being a female filmmaker has given you an advantage? Or do you think it's an impediment because you're in a man's world?
I'm in a unique position because Otsuka and I are a husband-and-wife team. Between us we can complete all production jobs from writing the screenplay, to recording and cinematography. With *The Foolish Bird,* we've added a recording artist and an assistant director to the team, which is still really quite small. In contrast with mainstream films, ours are small-budget productions. So we don't run into the sort of complicated personnel problems you face with a big film crew.

As for the cast I work with, I think being a female director gives me certain advantages because I can use my feminine touch and emotions to persuade people I need to work with. For example, if I didn't do a good job or somehow made a mistake, I can get away with it a bit more because they're more willing to forgive me, especially if I become a bit teary. I take advantage of people's inclination to want to protect me as the so-called fairer sex.

What about being a working mom? Has that posed significant challenges for you as a filmmaker?
Yes. When I was growing up, my parents weren't around. This left emotional scars, which is why when I had my daughter, I promised myself that I would be different as a mother and that I'd take her wherever I go. After completing *Egg and Stone*, I focused on being a mom for quite a while until my daughter turned three. After that, I began preparing to shoot *The Foolish Bird*. But my years spent away as a mom meant that I'd become a little rusty as a filmmaker. And while we were doing the shoots, I was also a mom chasing after my daughter. My dual roles as both filmmaker and mother made it difficult for me to be good at either job. So it was very challenging.

Here's a question about financing. Are your films mostly self-funded?
Yes, all of the films I've worked on so far are self-funded, most of them with Otsuka's money. We use our money on pre-productions and look for other resources to help pay for post-production costs. *The Foolish Bird*, for example, was made possible with a post-production grant from the Hong Kong-Asia Film Financing Forum.

Some say China's rapidly expanding film market is good for the future of all Chinese films, including independent films. Others are less optimistic. What's your view on this?
I'm neither optimistic nor pessimistic about the future. I'm not so close to independent film circles because of my family's situation. I also don't feel the need to be a part of any circles because I fear it would limit my expression. And increasingly, I find there are many other independent filmmakers who don't feel the need to join any groups. They're just doing their own projects and finding their own voice. This is a very encouraging trend because it's an indication that we young filmmakers are becoming more individualistic.

On the other hand, I feel that because of the digital revolution, we now have more affordable tools for filmmaking, which also makes it much easier and faster to produce a film. But the speed afforded many filmmakers means the quality of film is also going down. This is a pity. I think it's important as a good independent filmmaker to tap into your own feelings. In today's fast-paced life, many of us aren't really in touch with our own feelings. Authorities and private organizations don't encourage us to explore our independent thinking. Yet, without thought or reflection, how can we tap into our own emotions?

Many people in China have become wealthy, yet they aren't able to problem solve. Often times they don't know how to communicate with their parents or children, so they end up handling problems in a very immature way. Then again, if they've never experienced a healthy family environment, it's difficult for them to know what to do. This is why I think it's important that independent filmmakers make it a priority to get their own lives and emotions in order first before rushing to make their films.

Have you considered making commercial films in the future?
I think the filmmaking process is closely related to the life experience of a filmmaker. Now that I've completed both *Egg and Stone* and *The Foolish Bird*, I may feel a little different about life than I did before. I might feel a bit happier now, and this feeling may be an element I will incorporate into the next film, but that's it. It would never occur to me to take a more commercialized approach to my next film.

Take *The Foolish Bird*, for example. This film is about a young girl who cannot talk about sex, or at least doesn't know how to begin talking about it. Because the protagonist cannot find a voice to talk about sex, nor about the sexual abuse she has suffered, I've chosen a very indirect way to put the story together on screen. If I were to use a very commercial approach, or a very blunt way to tell the story, then the film would no longer be *The Foolish Bird*. That's why I feel the question shouldn't be "should you or should you not make a more commercialized film," but rather, "how does the film reflect the filmmaker's feelings and attitude towards life."

After I released my two feature films, many young women with similar experience (of being sexually exploited) came to me saying how, for many years, they never told anyone about their ordeal. But my films gave them courage, and they opened up to me by telling me their stories. These encounters encouraged me a great deal and made me believe the films I've been making have been very meaningful.

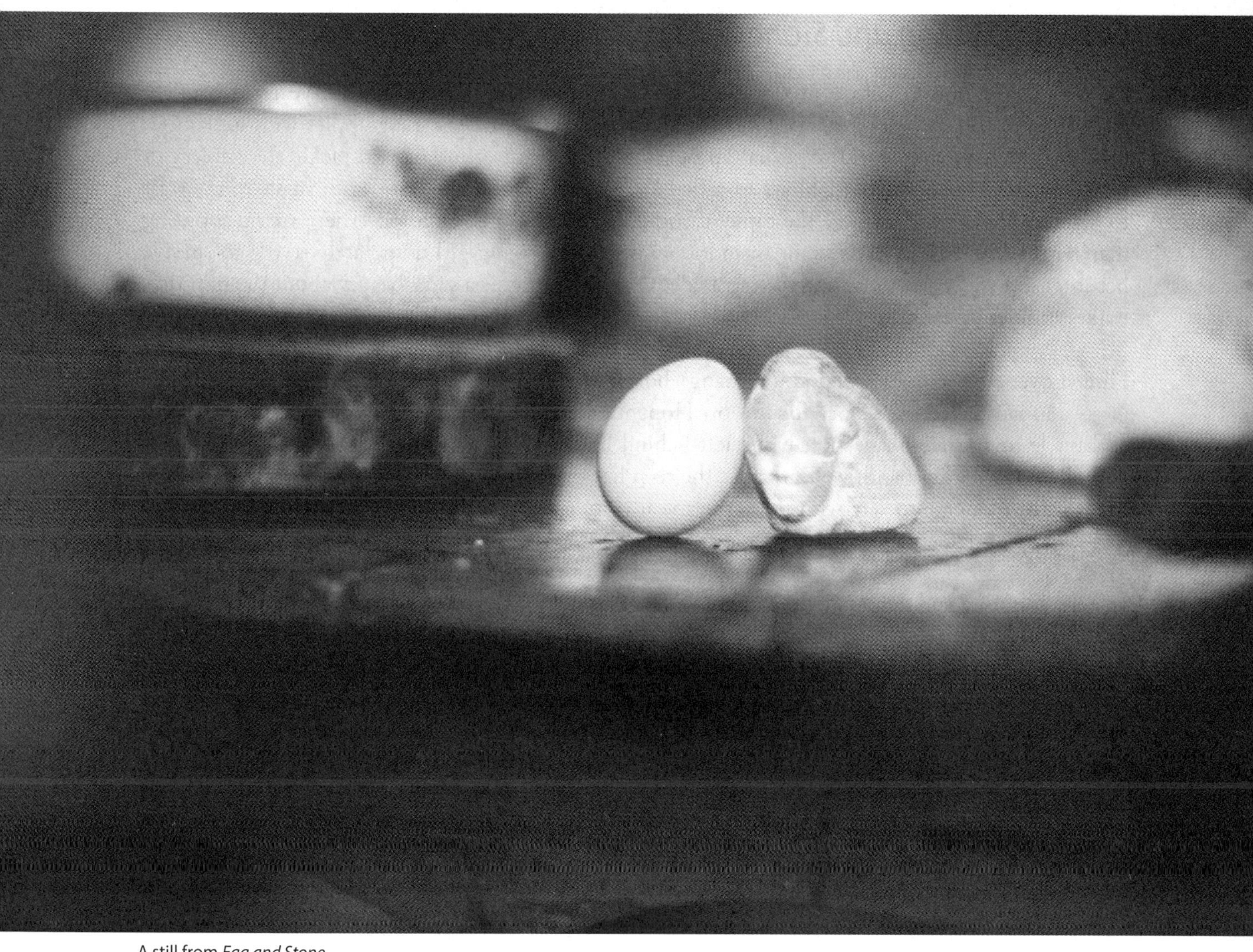

A still from *Egg and Stone*

Case Study: *Egg and Stone*

Huang's feature directorial debut *Egg and Stone* is a compelling portrait of a 14-year-old country girl's attempt to come to terms with her emerging sexual maturity as she grapples with loneliness, fear and the terrifying world of sexual abuse. The 2012 feature, the first to tackle the subject of sexual exploitation involving China's so-called "left-behind children," stands out in sharp contrast to Western movies that explore the topic of sexual violence against children. There are no shouting matches or accusations, no tears or melodrama, just a shy young girl desperately trying to survive her intense anxiety and loneliness during a cold winter. Yet there's a stark beauty about the film that makes it quietly powerful.

Filmed over a three-month period in Huang's hometown of Yiyang, with the entire dialogue in the gritty Hunan dialect, the story focuses on Honggui who has been living with her maternal aunt and uncle in a small village after being left behind by her city-bound parents. Through the aunt's complaints to her husband, we learn that the teen has overstayed her welcome. The initial arrangement is for Honggui to stay with them for a year or two while the parents make some fast money, but seven years later, they still haven't returned to claim her.

Lonely, confused and desperate for some attention, Honggui tries to call her mother but her mother is too preoccupied to pick up the phone. There's a vague promise of a returned call, but Honggui never receives the call back. Worse, she runs into sexual troubles that she doesn't fully comprehend or know how to handle. One day, she realizes she has missed her period. Panicked, she sits alone in the dark, dingy toilet, her hands clutching her panties.

Egg and Stone relies heavily on visual and non-verbal cues to convey the protagonist's sense of fear and anxiety, including hints of Honggui's suicidal thoughts through recurring images of funerals and portraits of the deceased. For a film trying to expose the sexual abuse of a young teen, the muted treatment can seem strangely non-confrontational and even ineffectual. The film also comes off rather like a 'who dunnit' feature, with the audience kept in the dark for much of the time about who got Honggui pregnant. Yet it's precisely this quiet treatment, meant to reflect the victim's anguish and silent cry for help, that makes the film unique and personal.

The Director's Take

Do independent films need to have a social function?
Yes, independent films should reveal feelings and emotions that have been overlooked in our everyday lives.

What's the first film you ever saw and what were your initial thoughts?
The 1988 film "My Beloved" by Taiwanese director Chu Huang Chen. At the time I was only 5, and my entire family and I traveled some distance to a theater in a local town to see this film. It was very moving, and we all cried. It was the first time I felt the power of a good film.

What is your favorite film of all time?
"Tokyo Story," by Yasujiro Ozu.

Who's your favorite director of all time?
Iranian film director Abbas Kiarostami.

What's your best quality as an independent director?
My deep interest in individuals and how they, particularly women, see and feel about their world.

Name one Chinese film you've seen lately that you consider great and why?
"Mr. No Problem," (2017) by Mei Feng, which was adapted from a novella by renowned Chinese novelist Lao She.

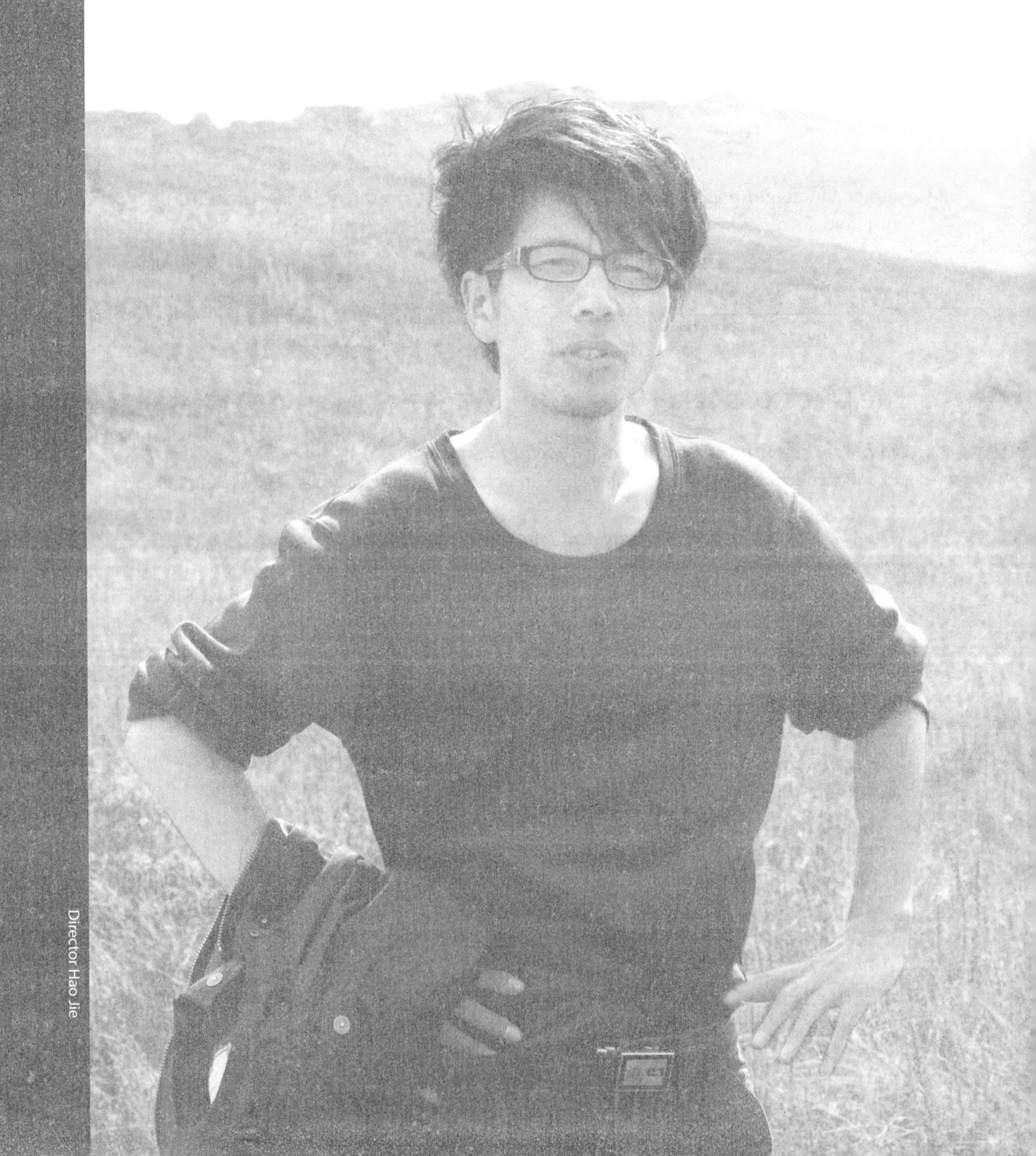

Director Hao Jie

HAO JIE

Sex, Romance and the Village Bachelors

A Short Introduction

HAO JIE is a bold, ambitious but slightly controversial indie filmmaker who repeatedly tackles the highly taboo subject of sex and romance in rural China. Born in 1981 as the son of a local bureaucrat, Hao grew up in a remote, mountainous village in northeastern Hebei, a province bordering Beijing and Inner Mongolia. Despite his rural background, Hao managed to ride out of his humble roots through the "higher-education expansion policy" enacted in the late 90s aimed at helping poor students attend college. From there, he found his way to the Beijing Film Academy (BFA) where he eventually took a year-long certificate course for directors.

Unlike most other indie filmmakers who tend to start their careers by making shorts first, Hao went directly into making feature-length movies. He also wrote his own screenplays, which started with his directorial debut, *Single Man*—a comedy looking at four ageing bachelors from a small village and their antics looking for sex and love in all the wrong places. On its completion in 2010, the film was screened at several festivals to great acclaim, including the Tokyo FilMex 2010, where Hao won the Special Jury Prize. Due to its politically sensitive sex theme, particularly because the film exposes the problem of how difficult it is for most rural bachelors to find a bride, *Single Man* was never released commercially, even though it gained huge popularity on such sites as Douban (China's version of IMDb.com) and Youku (China's version of YouTube). Hao went on to make *The Love Songs of Tiedan* in 2012—which won Best Asian Film at the 49th Taipei Golden Horse Film Festival, Best Director and Best Screenplay at the 7th Xining FIRST International Film Festival—as well as *My Original Dream* in 2015. Both are romantic comedies set in Hao's hometown of Gujiagou and were later released in cinemas. The three films have been linked together as Hao's "Hometown Trilogy."

The protagonists in Hao's first three films are all restless rural males driven by their basic instincts—their libidos and their drive to procreate. These films, however, are not pornographic, despite some promoters presenting them as such to boost sales. Rather, they tend to focus on the harsh reality of village life as a bachelor. Rural China's large gender imbalance, created in part by China's "one-child" policy in the late 70s, means sex and marriage are often privileges many poor peasants cannot afford.

Mostly tongue-in-cheek, Hao instills in his films a rare sense of vigor, an ethnographic richness and an unmistakable absurdity. Very regional in flavor, these features also evoke a strong sense of nostalgia for the earthy, colorful Northeastern Chinese popular culture. Although some critics say Hao's films are crude and vulgar, there is also something honest, humorous and even joyful about his narratives—qualities that are rare among China's indie films. For this reason, Hao is welcomed by many in an industry constantly looking for new talent and a fresh approach to filmmaking. Hao became one of the first indie filmmakers to break into the mainstream when he made *My Original Dream* in 2015 with Wanda Pictures (Qingdao)—one of China's largest private film production companies—as its main investor.

Filmography

Single Man 光棍 (feature film, 2010) - director, screenwriter, editor.
The Love Songs of Tiedan 美姐 (feature film, 2012) - director, screenwriter.
My Original Dream 我的青春期 (feature film, 2015) - director, screenwriter.

Interview:

I arranged to meet with Hao Jie in Beijing in the spring of 2017 at a downtown café, having been introduced to him by friends. I recognized Hao right away when he came into the coffee shop sporting a ponytail and an infectious smile. My immediate impression of him was that this is a "bad boy" with a big heart. Hao was animated and talkative, and although we agreed on a two-hour interview, we ended up spending over three hours talking about various aspects of his filmmaking. He was patient, and cheerfully answered all of my questions, including several follow-up inquiries we exchanged by email.

You have a very unusual background coming from a very small village. How did you manage to beat the odds and make it to Beijing?
My hometown Gujiagou is a tiny Hebei village near Zhangjiakou, which borders Beijing. It is a far-flung village in a mountainous area that used to be very poor. There were probably only about 80 families living there, with an overall population of roughly 200. The place was so remote we were pretty much cut off from the outside world, so I grew up a bit like a wild child in a very primitive environment. In those days, going to a nearby county town was a big deal, and it wasn't until I started middle school that I began to visit bigger cities. The drawback of this kind of upbringing is that I didn't receive a good education. In fact, we didn't even have a library in our village for a long time, so I didn't read many books. But the upside was that I wasn't affected by what some refer to as a "bad (Chinese) education."

I sometimes also wonder how I ended up a filmmaker, having come from such a remote village. Looking back, I think it comes down to two

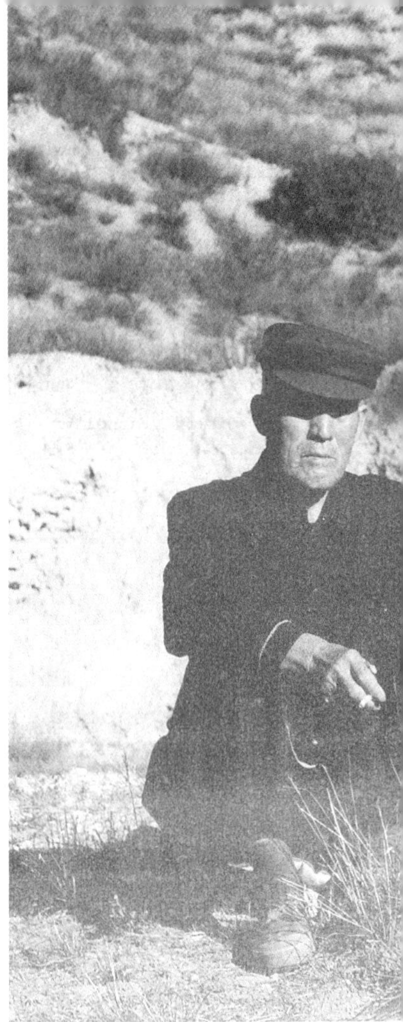

"

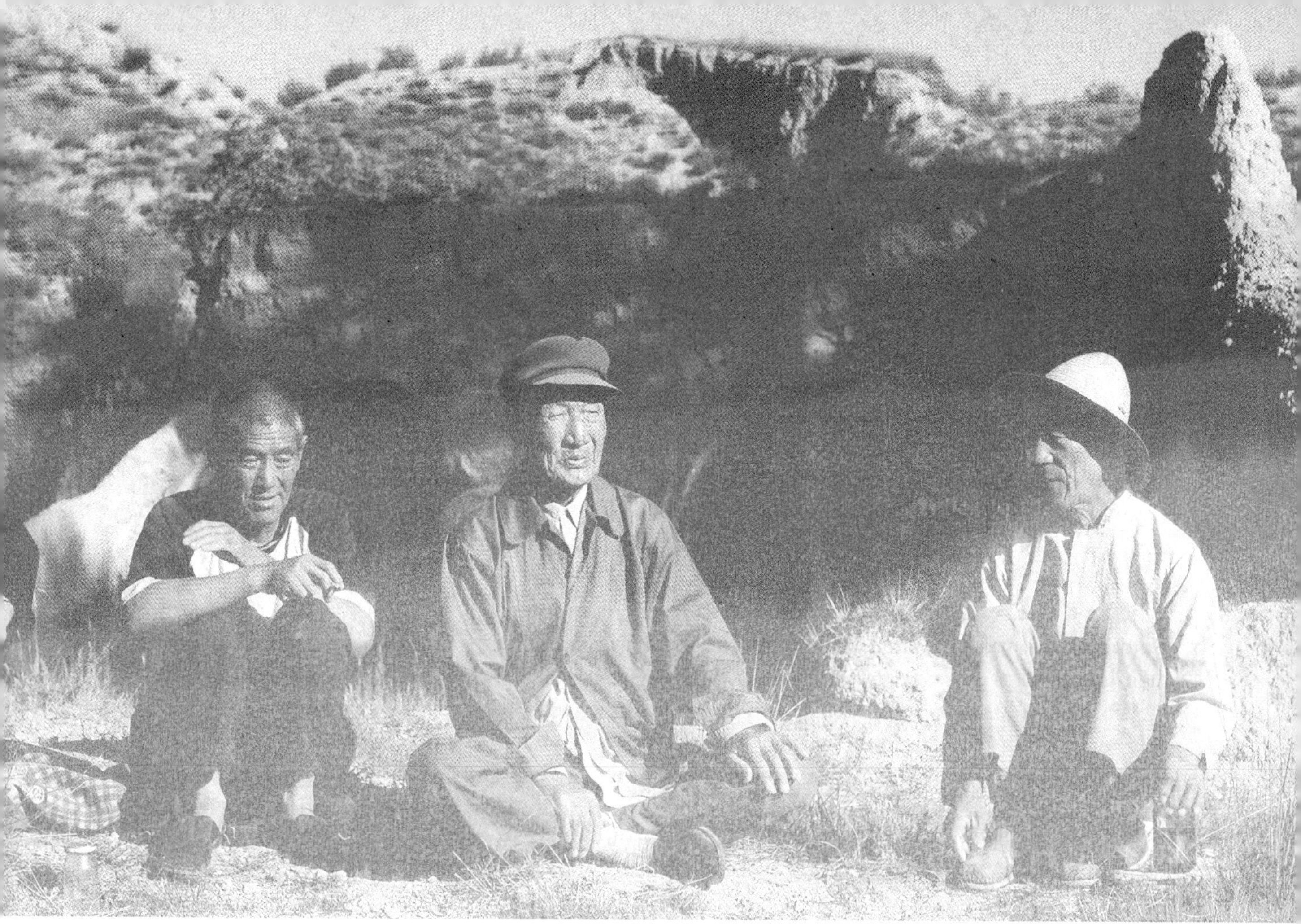

Single Man—a feature about four elderly bachelors from a remote village

reasons. The first one has to do with my father being the secretary of the local party branch. He essentially had the most important job in the village, which made me feel special and privileged. This was a huge confidence booster. Okay, I was raised in a tiny place but I was [treated like] the son of the "emperor." This sense of being "special" really helped made me feel I could pursue whatever dream I wanted to.

The second reason has to do with my village teacher and mentor. Now in his eighties, my teacher was an award-winning educator and a learned scholar who was dispatched to our village under the socialist policies of the late 1970s. The teacher taught elementary school for many decades and had both my Dad and I as students. He was humble, energetic and very encouraging of us in many ways. He was particularly big on creative writing, and would tirelessly help us to improve our written work. He even urged us to send our personal essays to local newspapers. So even though I didn't have a formal education, I was very inspired, and as a result, was admitted to a very good county middle school. My elementary teacher believed in me and with his help, I won a literary prize for one of my stories. I learned a great deal from him about the basics of good writing, which was a big help for my screenwriting later. He also nurtured in me a love for observing people—he really was a *rare* teacher.

When did you realize you wanted to be a filmmaker? And why?
I didn't do so well in middle school and I took someone's advice to focus on fine arts during my high school years as a way to avoid difficult subjects. But, later, I discovered art classes weren't for me either. The major, however, led me to an art program at Hebei University where I was exposed to computers for the first time. That was in 2001, when many Chinese first started to use the Internet. While there, I found many of my friends were downloading films to watch. We watched many films by Zhang Yimou and Jia Zhangke, and later, films by overseas directors, including *Maléna* by Giuseppe Tornatore. This experience was life changing for me, and I was hooked. I started asking around for filmmaking schools and heard the name BFA for the first time. I immediately traveled to Beijing and began attending classes there as an auditing student. I was so broke at the time I couldn't afford a place to stay so I convinced a barbershop owner to let me sleep at their shop after they closed at midnight, then I'd get up at 5 in the morning to go to class at BFA.

Life wasn't easy then but I was elated because I realized I'd truly found my calling. I probably audited classes there for just over six months before signing up for the full-year certificate program designed for directors. The school fees were very expensive, and by the time you added living expenses, it came to about 50,000 RMB ($7,845), which was terribly expensive at the time for folks like me. I felt lucky though because my father wired all his savings, originally intended for my future wedding, to use as my tuition. He understood the importance of a good education. Those two years I spent at BFA were extremely important to me. After that I stayed put in Beijing and earned a living as a contract filmmaker for various web companies and television stations, much of which involved making hideous entertainment programs. I did that for three, four years until I couldn't take it anymore. After I quit my jobs, I poured all my energy into making my own movies, having come to the realization that that was the only thing I wanted to do.

I heard somewhere that you and a few other filmmakers with a similar rural background have benefited from China's educational reform of the late 90's. Is this true?
Yes, I was amongst the first to benefit from the so-called "higher education expansion" policy (meant as a way to address rising unemployment) first enacted in 1999. The policy involved building a large number of new universities, which gave high school graduates many more opportunities to attend national colleges. And as a result, the number of new students admitted to college in 1999 jumped over 40 percent from the year before. It really was a massification of higher education, and without this new policy, bad students like me with poor grades would never stand a chance of earning a place at college. Some critics say this policy has brought down the quality of China's education, but without it, many rural youngsters would never have been able to find their way to the bigger cities.

How difficult was it for you to make your first film as a new director?
I started out by writing the screenplay for *Single Man*, which took over six months. I took it to Xu Haofeng, one of my teachers at BFA who directed the martial arts flick *Judge Archer*. Xu was very encouraging of the project, but because it was my first feature, I couldn't get any investors interested in it. To make matters worse, *Single Man* is technically an underground movie because of its [explicit sexual] content, and there's no way I could talk anyone into investing in a film that had little chance of turning a profit. I know some of my peers made their debut films with their own savings or their parents' money, but I didn't have those options because shortly after my script was completed, my father passed away in an accident. This harsh reality forced me to refocus, and I became even more determined to find money to make the film somehow.

I tried everything I could think of, asking everyone in sight for help, and this took almost two

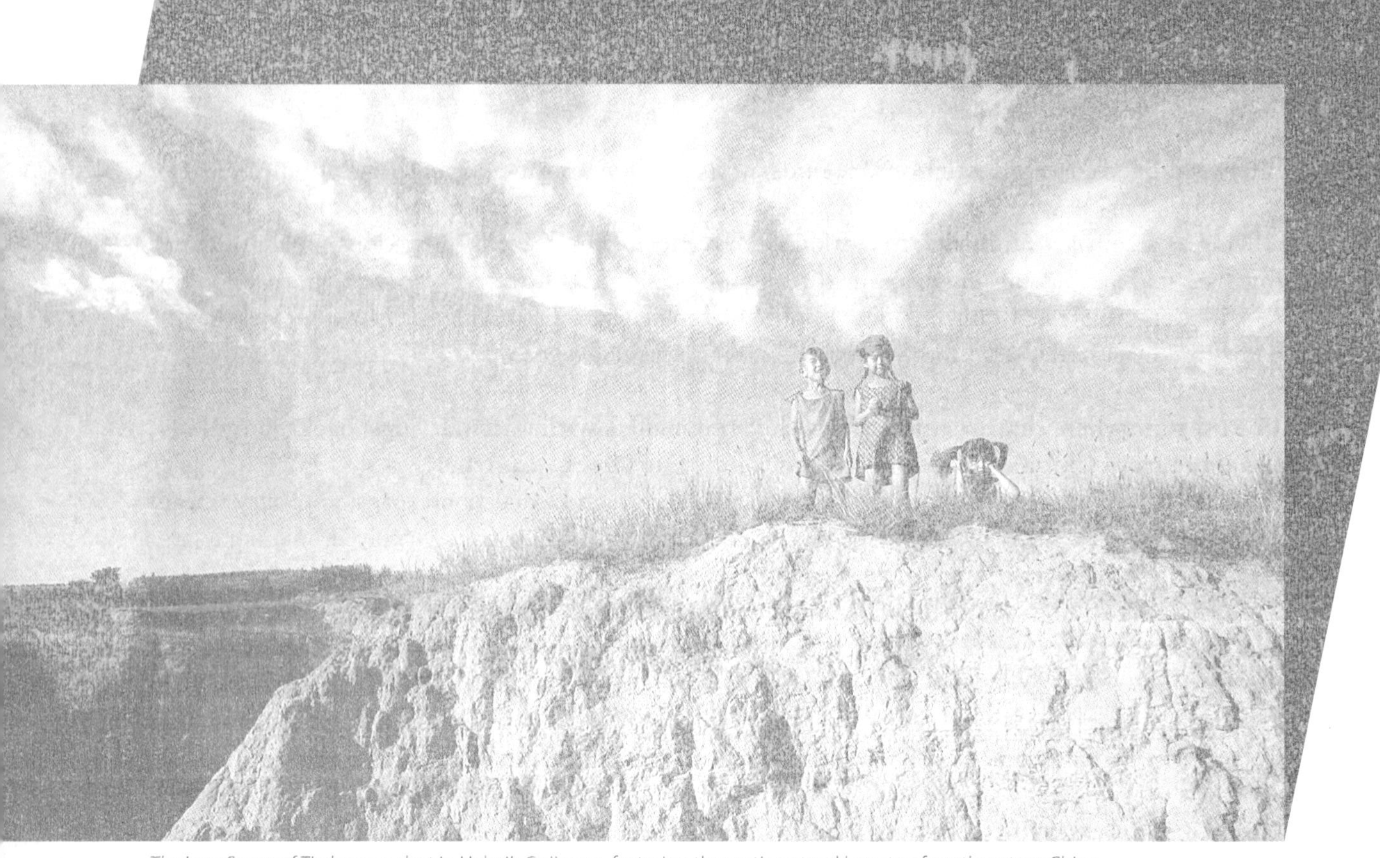

The Love Songs of Tiedan was shot in Hebei's Gujiagou, featuring the rustic natural beauty of northeastern China.

years. Then in 2008 I got a break when I met Mr. Lou Weihua, the head honcho of *Heaven Pictures*. Lou agreed to invest in *Single Man*, eventually pouring 300,000 RMB ($45,000) into it and finally making it possible for me to make the movie.

Was it true that your meeting with Mr. Lou was quite by chance?
There's a backstory here. Before I met Mr. Lou, I'd tried everything, including wining and dining wealthy coalmine owners and big shot businessmen, but all to no avail. At that time I was working

on a TV program that required me to hire several extras. One of the extras, a female college student studying in the US, told me she was only doing it for fun and that she planned to return to the US after the summer. I handed her a copy of my screenplay for *Single Man* and told her about my dream of making the film. Once in the US, she gave it to her boyfriend to read, and the boyfriend ended up showing it to his professor, a Professor Zhu. Professor Zhu really liked the screenplay because it reminded him of his days living in rural China, and he in turn asked his long-time friend Mr. Lou to offer me some financial backing so I could finish making the film.

It turns out Lou is a connoisseur of films because he used to be a technician specializing in film screenings in rural China when he was young. Zhu knew Lou had an interest in getting involved with cinema again and that's why he contacted him. Lou contacted me and asked me how much I needed for the film. I told him the amount, and he said, "No problem, it will be wired into your account tomorrow." Just like that, my problem was solved. Later, Lou forked out another 200,000 RMB to buy cameras and other equipment and started *Heaven Pictures (Beijing) Culture & Media Company*—a non-profit organization aimed at helping to finance young filmmakers' independent projects. *Single Man* became the company's first project. *Heaven Pictures* went on to invest another 600,000 RMB in *The Love Songs of Tiedan*, my second film, but we were still a bit short, so another company stepped in to help fill the shortfall.

My experience goes to show how, if you keep trying, things will work out in the end. At the time everyone was laughing at me, thinking I was crazy for bothering an extra with my screenplay. They thought it was a total waste of my time. And yet it was precisely this non-stop trying at every turn that allowed me to finally meet Mr. Lou.

You've made three films so far, namely, *Single Man*, *The Love Songs of Tiedan* and *My Original Dream*. Of the three, which are you the proudest of and why?
I'm most satisfied with the outcome of *Single Man*, and the least happy with my third film, *My Original Dream*. When I made *Single Man*, I had total control of the movie because *Heaven Pictures* gave me absolute freedom to do whatever I wanted with it.

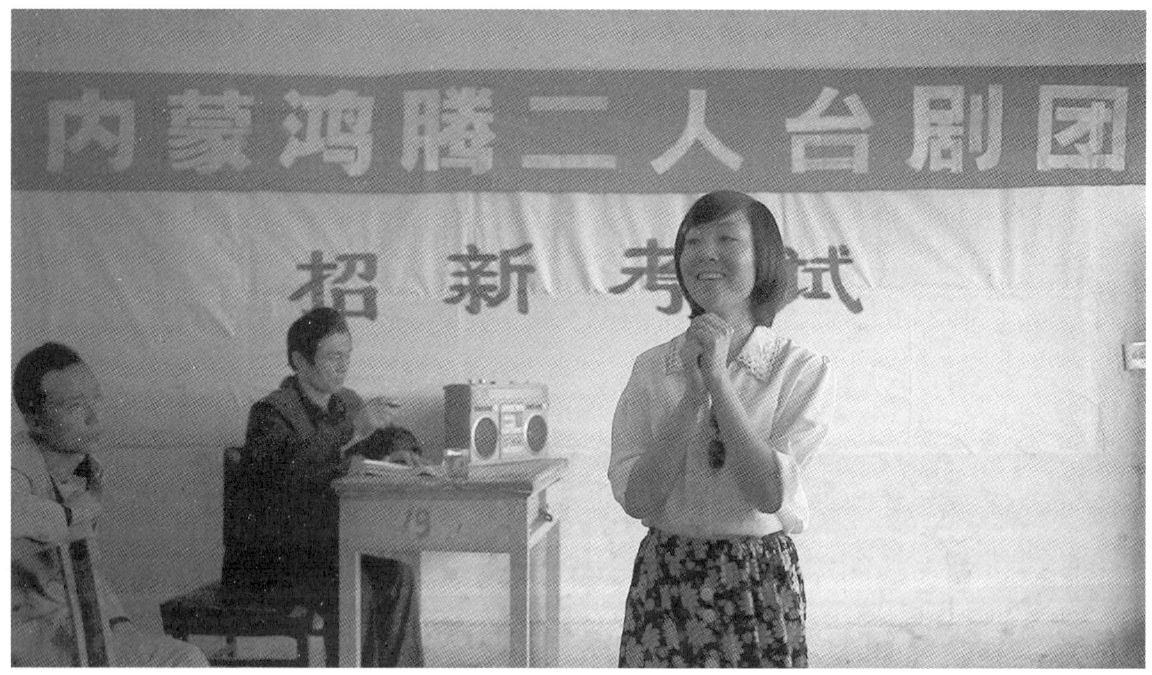

The Love Songs of Tiedan is a love story and a tribute to a regional music tradition.

What about *The Love Songs of Tiedan*?

By the time I started shooting *The Love Songs of Tiedan,* which was a co-production between Heaven Pictures and another firm called Beijing Yuan Qi Culture & Development Company, (each company invested 600,000 RMB in the film) I ended up acquiring a 60-member film crew I'd never worked with before. This meant I wasn't free to make all the decisions on my own, and I needed to spend a lot of time getting to know the team. Because I was young and inexperienced, many crew members didn't take me seriously. In the end, the collaboration was quite a challenge. We originally planned to spend 60 days shooting the film but, for various reasons, I was forced to finish everything within 40 days. In hindsight, I felt there were many things that I could have done a lot better.

I understand *My Original Dream* is the most expensive and perhaps the most commercialized film you've made thus far. How did you end up working with a big company like Wanda Pictures? And how much was the budget?

The budget was 8.5 million RMB (roughly $1.3 million) for production costs alone. If you add promotional expenses, we're easily looking at 15 million RMB (about $2.3 million). I came to work with Wanda because I met one of their representatives at a film-financing meeting in Taiwan, and the company ended up becoming my investor. I have to say working on the project with Wanda was the toughest experience I have ever had in my filmmaking career. The movie took me two months to shoot, but if you add the time needed for pre and post-productions, then it was about a full year. *My Original Dream* wasn't cheap to produce, but I'd say about 90 percent of the money was wasted on disagreements over priorities amongst my crew.

When I made *Single Man*, my budget was a mere 300,000 RMB and I pushed very hard to get the most out of the budget. The production of *My Original Dream* was a totally different story. The problem wasn't entirely on Wanda's side because I also bore part of the blame. Needless to say, a lot of compromises were made in the process. But over time, I learned ways to make the most of every penny when shooting films, having seen how much money was wasted while filming *My Original Dream*. I also learned valuable lessons about how to make a commercial film with a large production company. The best part is that because of this experience, I have ended up receiving more invitations and contracts to work with other studios. The film allowed other would-be investors to see that I was able to get the job done working with a major film operator like Wanda.

Your films all seem to have a common, connecting thread, which is the sexual frustration of the village bachelors. Can you say why this theme is so important to you?

I would call these three films my "Hometown Trilogy", which essentially is motivated by the love and nostalgia I have for the village I grew up in. The three films speak to many true events that had taken place in Gujiagou. All of the characters you see on screen are based on real people. You have to understand, to many male peasants, and especially the poorer ones, getting married and having children is their single most important life goal that borders on being a lifetime obsession. When I made these films, I didn't consider whether they would pass censorship. All I wanted to do was to express myself in my own way. These films that talk about the sexual frustration of single men or younger boys may seem vulgar, but they are very honest portrayals and something you would come across often in rural China. And the songs that are sung by *er-rentai* [performers] are full of sexual innuendos. Some audiences may find it shocking because they've never seen anything like that before. My films, at least these three so far, are different from movies produced by many other filmmakers my age because they are very primitive and elemental. It's rather like I discovered a bunch of radishes in the field and my first instinct was to pull them all out, up to the surface. Many people are actually surprised to find that the [films] were produced by a young man born in the 1980s, not someone who's in his forties or fifties, especially given that the central themes in these films are about rural culture and the livelihoods of older men.

I noticed that you have written the scripts for all of your films. Is this a model you will continue to use in the future?
Actually, I'm in the middle of changing my approach. In the upcoming film, for example, I will be collaborating with other filmmakers on a movie about Chinese students studying abroad. So far, I've written my own screenplays, but those were my own stories. Now, I'm at the second stage [of my career] where I feel I can gain a lot more by collaborating with more experienced people in the industry. In fact, I'm ready to go back and read and watch all the literary masterpieces and classic films that I've missed out on before. I can afford a more leisurely pace at this time in my life because *Hehe (Shanghai) Pictures* has invested a fair amount in me, allowing me to do research in London ahead of my next film. *Hehe* decided to invest in my next project after seeing *My Original Dream*.

Looking back, which directors, either those from China or beyond, do you think influenced you the most when you first started your career?
Without a doubt it's Jia Zhangke. I like Jia's debut film *Xiao Wu* more than his *Still Life* because *Xiao Wu* is an intimate story about one individual's life and it is very moving. But more than the story I think what Jia gave me was the courage to give filmmaking a try. He made me, and many filmmakers like me who are originally from rural China, realize that in front of the silver screen we

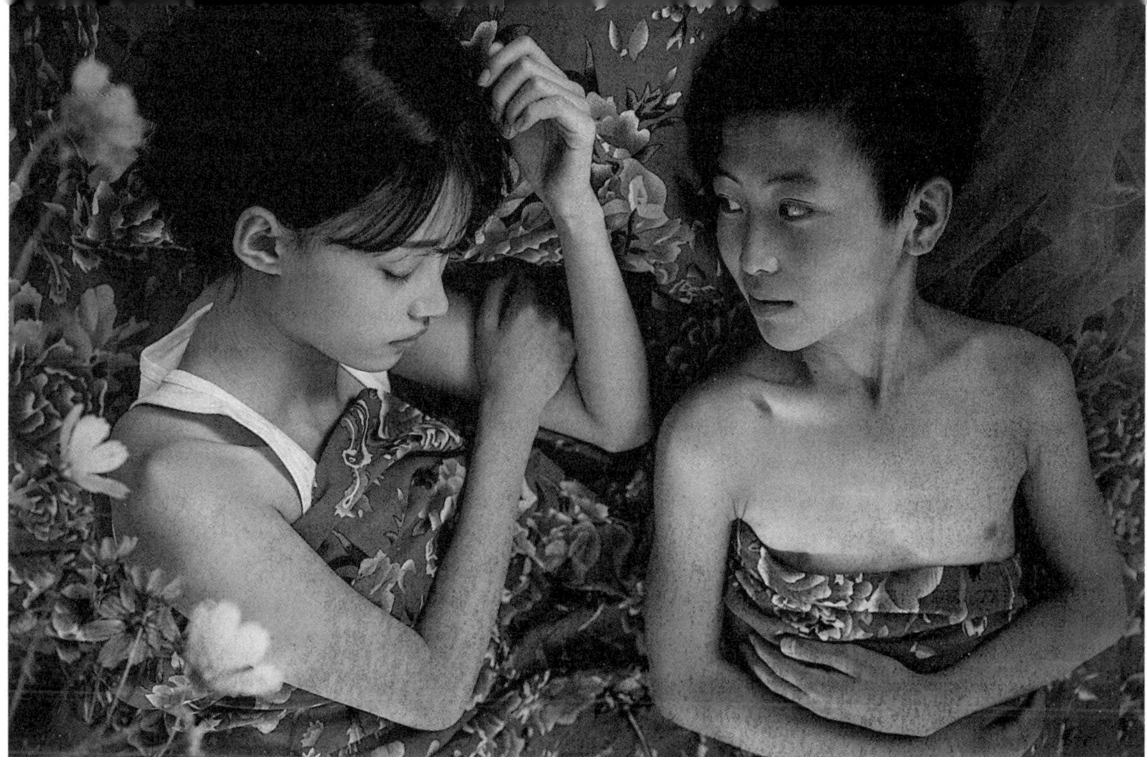

My Original Dream retells the director's own unrequited love experience.

are all equal and that we all have the right to express ourselves. Before watching Jia's films, I was very embarrassed about my rural background. It was Jia's *Xiao Wu* that gave me the idea and inspiration to make *Single Man*.

My Original Dream is a commercial film. Have you considered the option of making more commercial films in the future?

I don't want to limit myself to making any particular type of films in the future. What I do know is that from now on, I will only make films I love without worrying about other things. Honestly, I don't think I have what it takes to make commercial films in the true sense of the word because what I'm interested in capturing are narratives about human feelings, human hearts and human nature. One thing I have finally figured out is that, as a filmmaker, I should never try to cater to anyone else's taste. When I was filming *My Original Dream* I was still quite muddleheaded about what kinds of films I should make. Now, I finally have a clearer idea of how to proceed. In fact, I've made a decision to focus on female protagonists in my next three films. Having come from the countryside, thus far I've only featured male protagonists from a rural background. And my thoughts behind these films can even be labeled as "chauvinistic." But I want to correct my backwardness by trying to understand women better, by tackling themes about women and having women as central characters.

You said your next film is about a group of Chinese students studying overseas. Can you explain what inspired you to tackle this film, and how close you are to completing it?
I've heard a lot about overseas Chinese students and their encounters, as quite a few of my crew members have had the experience of studying abroad. I was always fascinated by their descriptions of living overseas, which seemed so different from what I'd experienced growing up in a small village. I became curious and started researching cinematic works about their experiences, only to discover that there aren't that many films about the subject. This despite the fact that a large number of Chinese students, both rich and poor, have gone overseas in the last ten, twenty years since China's open-door policy. So, I feel as a filmmaker, I have the responsibility to give voice to these students because what they have experienced represents a changing China and where China and the world have intersected. My new film will be about youth and urban Chinese kids' experiences of cultural conflicts and their love troubles while living overseas. At this stage, we're still hammering out the screenplay, which is being written by several writers who have studied abroad. We haven't started shooting yet because I want to make sure the script is up to standard and completed to my satisfaction. The biggest hurdle right now is that the film is about a group of people I'm not familiar with. I need more time to understand my subjects. I also need to reach deeper to understand what it is that makes us all humans. I feel this is something I haven't quite managed to fully reveal in my previous films.

Some people say as China's film industry continues to expand, that this is not only the best of time for commercial filmmakers, but also for indie filmmakers and art- house directors. Others disagree. What are your thoughts?
Speaking from my limited perspective, I'd say we're living in a moment that can be called both "the best of times and the worst of times." On the upside, we're living in a time when a lot of new

opportunities have opened up to people from all walks of life. This is made possible not only by new sources of funding that have been pouring into the market, but also because of the advancement of technology, the rising numbers of film channels and streaming platforms brought on by the advent of the Internet. Suddenly, ordinary people from very humble backgrounds, who historically would never have been given the chance to engage in intellectual discourse, are now being given a voice through filmmaking. The resources we have now are so readily available that anyone who dreams of making a film can try their luck with ease. And even if you can't secure funding to shoot your film the traditional way, you can still do so on your iphone. Younger would-be filmmakers sometimes come to me making excuses about why they haven't been able to make a film and I tell them if you can't make a film given the resources now, then I'm afraid you will never be able to do so in the future.

But of course, all these great resources have a downside as well. We live in a time when people are very impetuous and impatient, and investors all want to see an instant profit. Couple that with ever tightening government censorship and you will realize that despite the opportunities, many of us will end up losing our original vision, or we will be hemmed in by different limitations. So, in the end, we *can* make films, but not always the kind of films that will allow us to leap and bound very far.

Case Study: *The Love Songs of Tiedan*

Hao Jie's second feature, *The Love Songs of Tiedan,* is both a love story and a tribute to a regional music tradition. Told through the eyes of an ordinary man from a small village bordering Inner Mongolia, the story focuses on a folk music genre called *er-rentai* (performed by a male and female duo singing and dancing to the accompaniment of a two-string instrument) unique to the Northeast. A celebration of the region Hao grew up in, the film also captures the earthy and rustic beauty of an area roughly spanning the provinces of Shanxi, Shaanxi, Hebei, Ningxia and the western area of Inner Mongolia.

In the late-1950s in a remote Hebei village with stunning plateaus, wide, expansive fields and cave dwellings, eight-year-old Tiedan has a childhood crush on a grown woman neighbor named Sister

Mei—a beautiful and sexy singer who pairs with Tiedan's father in the duo singing and dancing of *er-rentai*. Sister Mei is soon forced to move to Inner Mongolia with her husband and their three young daughters when the musical genre is banned during the Cultural Revolution. Over a decade passes, and Mei returns to the village with their attractive grown daughters in tow. A new story begins to unfold as the life of the now-adult Tiedan, a traveling *er-rentai* folk singer in his own right, becomes romantically entangled with Mei's three daughters, as if his early affection for Mei has cast a spell on him that he cannot shake off.

On one level, the 110-min long feature, which spans three decades from the 1950s to the 1980s, is an ambitious attempt to mimic earlier classics by older directors. Chen Kaige's *Farewell My Concubine*, a saga chronicling China's recent history through the tale of a love triangle and the art form of Beijing Opera, is one such example. To be sure, *The Love Songs of Tiedan* lacks both the polish and gravitas of Chen's masterpiece. This is due in no small part to the fact that Hao's film was a modest independent production shot on a shoestring budget with a cast made up of mostly non-professional actors. Yet the feature exudes great energy through Hao's enthusiastic showcasing of a colorful music tradition rarely, if ever, featured on screen before. The film draws on themes of love, sex and life of the Northeast, featuring at its center the art form of *er-rentai,* which uses titillating language as part of the entertainment. *Er-rentai* was not only a widely popular form of country entertainment, but was often the only sex-education that many rural youngsters received until its popularity faded in recent years.

Due to its explicit references to sex and desire, *er-rentai* wasn't seen as a worthy subject for cinema until Hao decided to focus on it. In fact, in the past, both Chen Kaige and Zhang Yimou tended to treat the subject of rural-based sex and marriage with suspicion and criticism, viewing them as backward or colored by exploitation. Take for example, Chen's *Yellow Earth* and Zhang's *Ju Dou*, both set in the early part of the 20th Century. In these films, marriages are not about individual love or desire but are transactions in which women in abject poverty eke out their existence as de facto sex slaves and reproductive tools for much older men.

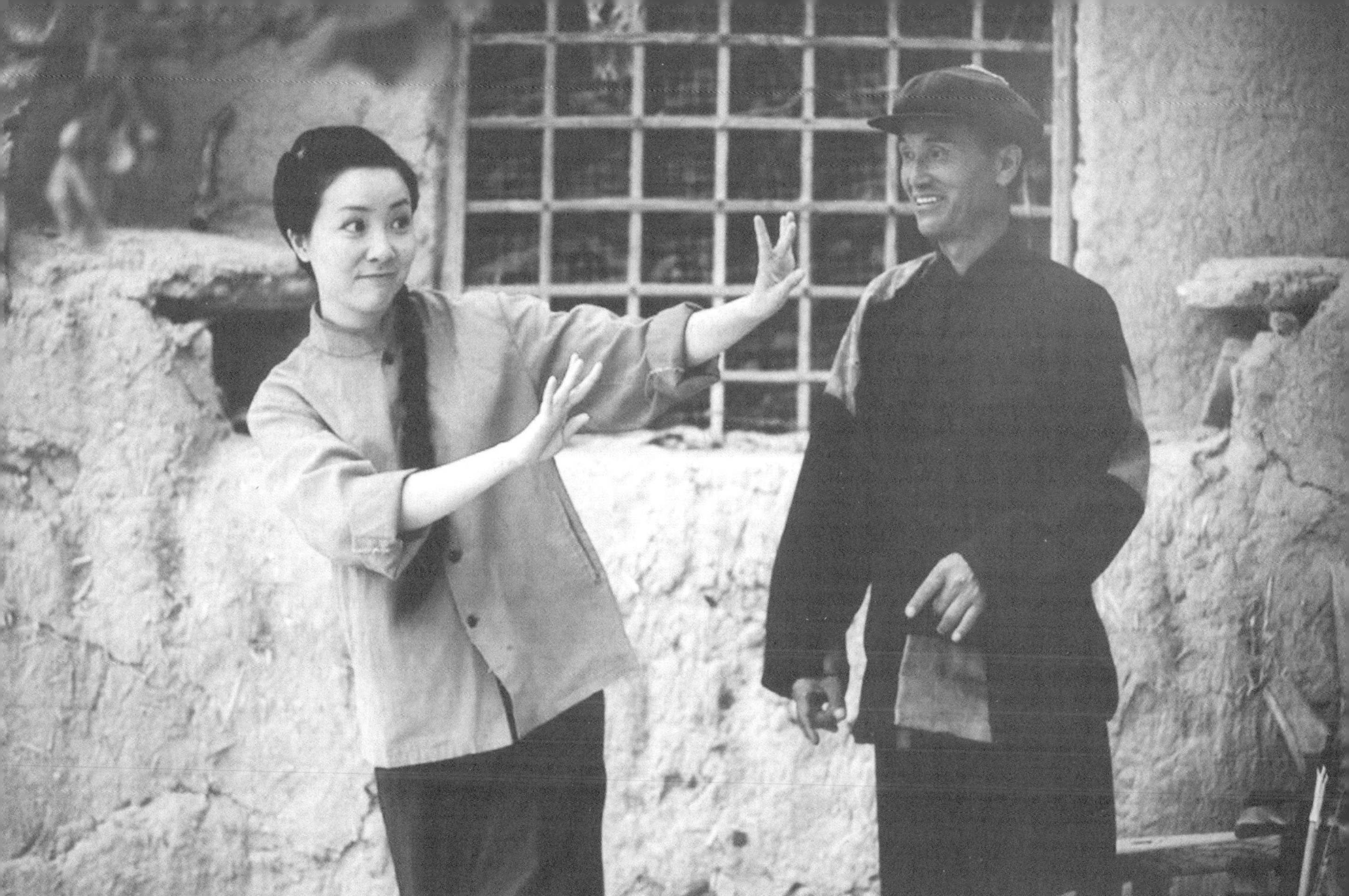

The Love Songs of Tiedan features the Northeastern folk music tradition *er-rentai*

Critics say this often very dark view of rural marriages and romance is in part because Chen, Zhang, and the generation of directors who immediately followed them, are largely urban-based, BFA-trained elites preoccupied with criticizing history and society. When these high-minded film-makers tackled topics such as rural marriages, they tended to look down on them as being fundamentally wrong, backward, vulgar or even perverse.

This is in stark contrast to *The Love Songs of Tiedan*. As with his debut film *Single Man*, Hao peppers his second feature with humor and zeal about desire and love, highlighting the songs and dance of *er-rentai*. As such, he lends a fresh voice and a more positive perspective on China's regional culture, previously seen mostly in a negative light. This fresh approach reflects not only Hao's nostalgia for his rural upbringing and deep love for the Northeast, but also sheds light on the individualistic nature of Hao's generation of filmmakers. *The Love Songs of Tiedan*, after all, is less a didactic feature film about China's feudal society than nostalgia, a romantic memory drawn from Hao's childhood.

Another thing Hao seeks to offset in the film is city people's squeamish attitude towards sex in general. Hao is very unapologetic about his celebratory enthusiasm for sex and desire, which he sees as not only a distinctive part of our human needs, but also a key source of motivation in life. As such, the film is a story about a man's coming of age, his sexual awakening, and the motivating force behind his childhood dreams in a part of China rarely seen on screen.

The Director's Take

What's an independent film?
Independent films are freer, the content is purer and they're full of possibilities. Filmmakers don't have to worry about the box office, censorship or audience taste. In some cases, some directors don't even consider if their films will ever receive a theatrical release.

What qualities must independent films possess?
They need to be unique and the best ones are one of a kind. This is something all artists will strive to achieve, but something that's extremely hard to do.

Why do you make films? And who's your audience?
Initially, it was because I wanted to express my feelings about my first love—which I eventually made into a film (*My Original Dream*). Then I discovered filmmaking is a good way to convey sentiments that I can't express in words. It satisfies my emotional needs and provides me with an outlet.

What's the first film you ever saw and what were your initial thoughts?
Jia Zhangke's *Xiao Wu (Artisan Pickpocket)*. My first impression was one of surprise—that you can make a film so closely related to your own life and your own background.

Which single movie made you realize that film is an art form?
French director Robert Bresson's *Au Hasard Balthazar*, about a donkey and its unfortunate encounters with different owners.

What is your favorite film of all time?
I haven't seen enough films yet, having come from a small village. So I can't say. But I'll continue to educate myself by watching more films.

Who's your favorite director of all time and why?
Robert Bresson, because of his use of film language, which masterfully captures the unspeakable truth about human nature. This is something I really admire.

What in your opinion are some of the qualities that all best films share?
Films that are about human nature. Films that communicate the message that we're all alike and have the same needs, no matter where we come from.

What's your best quality as an independent director?
My continued interest in pursuing the question: "What really makes us human?"

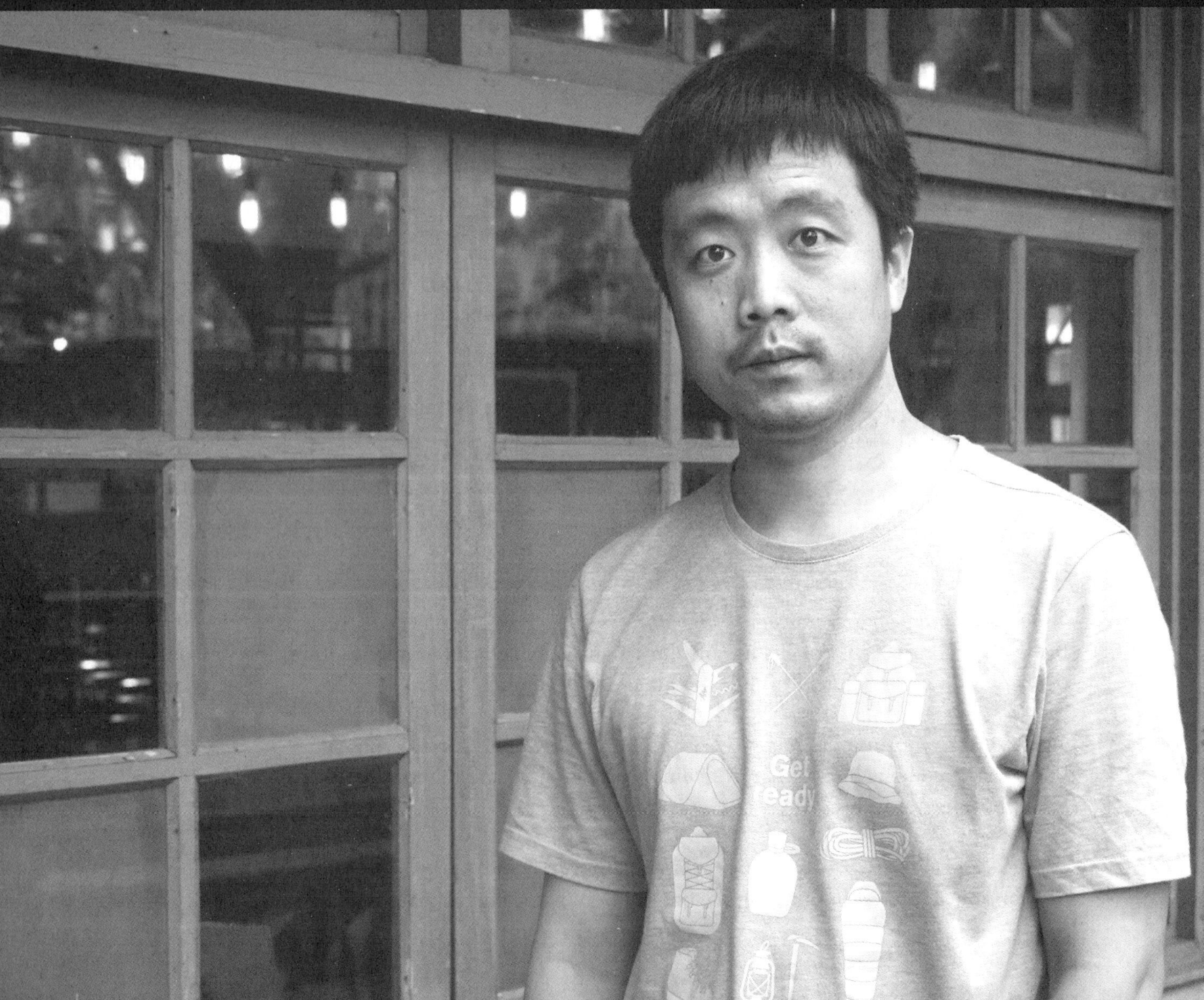

Director Yang Jin

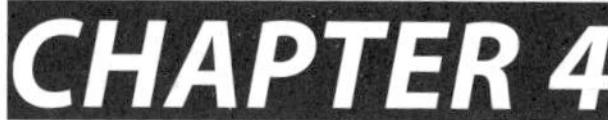

YANG JIN
The Grim Lives of Country Youth and Children

A Short Introduction

YANG JIN is a soft-spoken, understated filmmaker who has a distinct artistic vision devoid of allegiance to trend or profit. In part because he has close ties to rural Shanxi, Yang has been committed to making budget films about people and the lives they lead in the countryside of Shanxi, particularly focusing on children and young people, even if it means his films may have limited appeal to the audience. "If it weren't for my father, who got out of the countryside and worked in the city, then surely I'd have been destined to be a country youth just like my cousins," Yang says in a statement about his second film, *Er Dong* (2008). "I know (my cousins) work very hard, and they have to spend a good part of their youth shouldering the burdens of life. Already, they talk about the hardships of life, and there's a sense of helplessness in their tone of voice…"

Yang was born in 1982 in Shanxi, and enrolled in the Shanxi Film School's photography program in 2000. In 2003, he switched to the College of Art and Communication at Beijing Normal University, where he received a BFA in film directing. In the early days, Yang made documentaries and short features. But he soon showed his talent both as a screenwriter and director with his directorial debut, *The Black and White Milk Cow,* (2004). Shot in his father's hometown of rural Shanxi on a micro-budget, the film is a bold look at the starkly limited prospects for young people stuck in China's poorest regions. Although the feature, which also touches on the taboo subject of AIDS, won him the Ecumenical Jury Award and the Don Quixote Prize at Switzerland's Fribourg International Film Festival, it was never released in Chinese theaters because it was an underground film.

In 2008, Yang followed up with his second feature, *Er Dong*, which was a recipient of the Hubert Bals Fund at the Rotterdam International Film Festival. The film, also written by Yang and similarly produced with a shoestring budget, was another underground affair depicting the life of a trapped youth left behind by the times in a remote village. What makes this particular film unique, however, is that it underscores how important Christianity and churches have been to many rural villagers—something not really seen on screen before.

It was not until his third feature, *Don't Expect Praises* (2012) —a Tom Sawyer-esque story about two naughty boys who spend a summer fishing together and plotting to run away—that Yang made a deliberate choice to clear the censorship process, which helped him secure a release in Chinese theaters for the first time.

Yang's reputation as a director well-versed in the subject of country childhood and youth was quickly established, and he was brought in to direct other people's film projects, including *When I was Eight Years Old* (2017) and *Patrolman Baoyin* (2018), written by Lin Heping and Cao Kou respectively.

Filmography

(As director and screenwriter)

The Black and White Milk Cow 一隻花奶牛 (feature film, 2004) - director, screenwriter.

Er Dong 二冬 (feature film, 2008) - director, screenwriter.

Don't Expect Praises 有人贊美聰慧，有人則不 **(feature film, 2012) - director, screenwriter**

When I was Eight Years Old 那年八岁 **(feature film,** 2017) - director

Patrolman Baoyin 片警宝音 **(feature film, 2018)** - director

(As cinematographer)

My Fair Son 我如花似玉的儿子 **(feature film, 2005)** - cinematographer, for Director Cui Zi'en

Only Child 独生子 (experimental film, 2007) - cinematographer, for Director Cui Zi'en

Fairytale 童话 (mixed media, 2007) - photographer, for Artist Ai Weiwei

Boxed Lunch 盒饭 (feature, 2007- cinematographer, for Director Zhang Chi

Queer Queen, Comrade China 志同志 (documentary, 2009) - cinematographer, for Director Cui Zi'en

The Old Donkey 老驴头 **(feature film,** 2010) - cinematographer, for Director Li Ruijun

Fly with the Crane 告诉他们，我乘白鹤去了 **(feature film,** 2012) - cinematographer, for Director Li Ruijun

My Original Dream 我的青春期 **(feature film, 2015) - cinematographer,** for Director Hao Jie

Interview

I first managed to get in touch with Yang Jin via a friend's introduction. I arranged to meet with Yang and his wife, Zhang Jun, also Yang's producer, at their fourth ring road Beijing office on a May morning in 2017. Yang, with attentive eyes and boyish good looks, struck one more as a college student than as a man in his mid-thirties. Easy going but cordial, he thanked me for making the trip to his office and asked me to join him and his wife in the conference room. Yang was patient and answered all of my questions during our two-hour plus interview. Later, the three of us went downstairs to a shopping mall and shared a meal together as we continued our conversation. We kept in touch and did several follow-up Q and A exchanges by email. The following interview is a compilation of those conversations and interviews.

Can you explain what brought you to Beijing and why you wanted to become a director?
I was born in Pinglu County in Shanxi Province, and in 2000, I enrolled in Shanxi Film School and majored in photography. At that time, I had no idea that I would end up being a director. It was three years later, after I went to study at the College of Art and Communication at Beijing Normal

University that I found my calling. At the university, several Shanxi directors who were slightly older than me, including Ning Hao and Han Jie, were particularly inspirational as they were able to make inexpensive DV films for just several tens of thousands RMB. I was especially influenced by Han Jie who at the time was working as an assistant to the famed Shanxi director Jia Zhangke.

How did you get started with your first feature, *The Black and White Milk Cow*?

At university I met a couple of really good teachers, Professor and filmmaker Cui Zi'en and the documentarian Situ Zhaodun. After my course work at Beijing Normal University, I made my first feature film, *The Black and White Milk Cow,* which was based on a novella by the author Wang Xin-jun. The film was part of an assignment given by Professor Cui for that summer. I really liked the novel and I asked Cui to help me write a letter asking Wang for the screen rights. Wang, who knew Cui, ended up giving the rights to me for free. I quickly adapted it into a screenplay and completed the shoot by the end of the summer.

But why this novella? What attracted you to Wang's writing?

I was moved by the story about a young man having to face very difficult life choices all alone after his father's untimely death. In order to take care of his ailing grandmother who lives in the country, this city-based young man suddenly has to return to his hometown to assume the position of a rural teacher. The village is so poor that the mayor cannot afford to pay the man's salary. So, in the end, he's given a milk cow as compensation. Soon, the cow becomes the comic focal point of the story. I was drawn to the story because I could relate to the protagonist's life experience. In 2002, my father passed away suddenly at the age of 48 and I had to make some really tough choices. With my father's death, his job assignment became vacant and the government originally offered his job to me as a way to ensure my family's livelihood. At the time I was studying at Shanxi Film School in the city, and I was really confused about what to do. The teachers at my school were very keen for me to stay on, reminding me of the many opportunities to travel abroad, so the thought of leaving school to work in the country was unbearable for me. In the end, the job went to my mother, and this is what made it possible for me to eventually travel to Beijing to complete my film studies.

I have heard that many filmmakers not originally from Beijing have to take on odd jobs to support the high cost of living in the capital city. Did you have a similar experience?

No, I didn't have to because I was able to live on a couple of grants I received from two film festivals. At that time, my tuition at Beijing Normal was also relatively inexpensive—about 10,000 RMB a year (roughly US $1,600 in 2004), and my mother helped me pay for most of that. Of course, after graduation there were days when I was without work, but I refused to touch anything I didn't like. I insisted on doing things that were related to art films, including helping out at film festivals or working as a cinematographer for other filmmakers. The pay may have been low but at least I was happy.

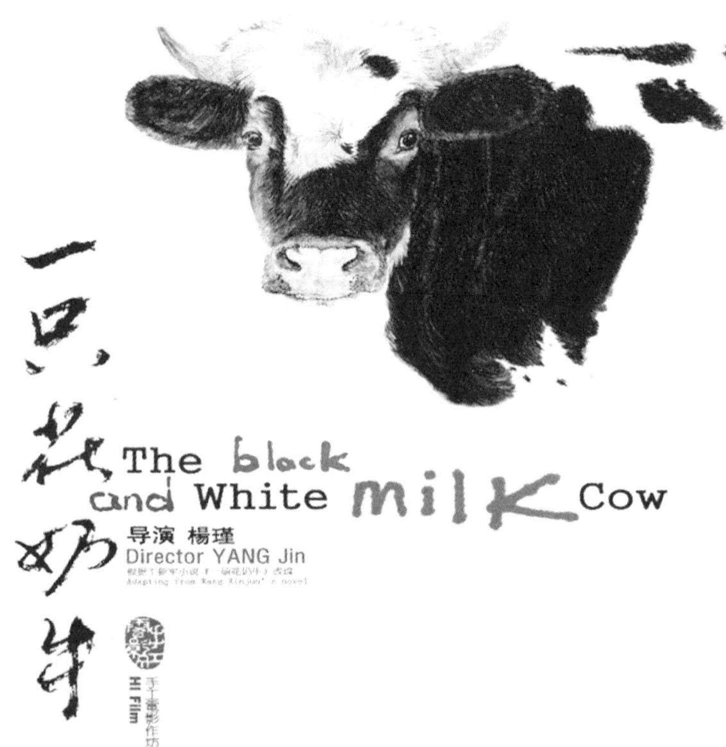

A Poster for *The Black and White Milk Cow*

How was making your first feature? What were some of the challenges?

Because Professor Cui was a sponsor for *The Black and White Milk Cow*, he contributed 10,000 RMB as capital money for the film, so I was very lucky. We had a production team of only three people, and the shoot took just 18 days. It was a DV film and I used a SONY 150P that belonged to my then girlfriend, now wife, to complete the shoot. For the cast, originally, I found a young man attending Shanxi Agriculture University as the main lead, but he quit after only one day. In the end my sound engineer stepped in as the lead, so I reshuffled the team and found another person to do the sound effects. I worked both as the cinematographer and director, and my wife helped out as the producer. We were able to find the rest of the cast from my village, and they were all related to me either as relatives or friends of my parents.

The costliest part of the film came from renting a dairy cow, which came to 2,000 RMB ($320) for seven days. It was pricey because local villagers weren't used to drinking milk, so there weren't any dairy cows around that I could rent. In the end, I had to bring the animal from a factory near the city. For the filming, I also asked my great grandmother to play a part. She was already 93 years old at the time, but her hearing was still very good. She also had a sharp mind—you only needed to tell her the lines once and she'd get it. Some of the other elderlies I worked with weren't so easy. They got distracted easily and had a harder time memorizing their lines.

Post-production was another story. Originally, I did the editing at school, but the machine was so old it kept getting stuck. Finally, my classmate Situ Zhixia (son of Professor Situ Zhaodun) invited me to his house and showed me a really great set of editing equipment his dad had purchased. So, I was able to stay at his house for an entire month to finish the editing job.

Your second feature *Er Dong* is also set in your hometown Shanxi. Why did you choose this locale? What is it that you wanted to express about your hometown?

The first reason for the locale was familiarity. It helps if you know the place well and how people live. Another reason had to do with my shock over some of the drastic changes that have taken place in my hometown. Take for example, the rapid increase in the number of Christian believers in Pinglu County since the year 2000. Seemingly overnight, a lot of people I know, including my grandma and several of my aunts, all became believers. At first, I didn't understand the reason behind this phenomenon. But later, I realized this increase (in numbers of Christian believers) has something to do with the many youngsters departing the countryside for better jobs in town, leaving the villages in rapid decline. Many of the older folks suddenly find themselves without mental support or sustenance. I remember helping my wife Zhang Jun film a documentary about Christian believers and we learned that in our village of Caochuan (in Pinglu County) alone, there were three large churches. These churches were built since the early 1990s with money donated by the villagers. They are very basic churches built from bricks, though they tend to be quite large in size. Believers usually gather every Wednesday in the village churches. And on Saturdays, they will travel together to larger municipal towns to visit the much bigger churches. For important religious holidays such as Easter and Christmas, these believers would travel even further afield to churches in major cities. These changes really touched me and I wanted to record them through film.

Er Dong is a film about a troubled youth trapped by his environment. Can you explain why you're drawn to this theme?

With _Er Dong_, I was particularly motivated to capture the story of my female cousin and her husband. In the film, the characters Chang'e and Er Dong are based on the true story of my paternal uncle's daughter and her then boyfriend. They are uneducated, and both are sent to a free Christian art school to study the bible and music and both are groomed as future village missionaries. But they fall in love and elope instead, before eventually getting married. The film is based closely to their real-life experiences. Those were the days (around 2002) when the school was open to taking very young students in their teens as apprentices, though they stopped the practice after realizing the youngsters tended to be very rebellious. One of the things I wanted to highlight in the film is how difficult the rural environment is for the "left-behind" youngsters. Society is changing rapidly around them and a lot of their peers with means have left the village for better job opportunities, leaving behind older folks and youth with fewer skills or means. Without a marketable skill, many of these youngsters feel trapped. Some fall into an impossible dilemma—they don't want to work in the fields as farmers, yet they don't know what else they can do. That's why my cousin and her husband got into all kinds of trouble. The year they eloped; they were only 19 years old. Life was very tough for them after they got married. It took another ten years, when they reached to their thirties, for their livelihood finally begin to improve.

In the movie, there's a shotgun that Er Dong hides. Was it very common to own such weapons at the time in the village?
Yes, until the 90s, it used to be relatively common for farmers to own a shotgun to hunt animals. It was a way for people to subsidize their food sources and income. But later, the local government banned the possession of guns, making ownership illegal.

Can you explain why your cousin never went to college and was forced to live in the village with a difficult life, while you were able to attend college in Beijing? Where did the gap come from?
My uncle was not well educated and he had always worked as a farmer in the village. The village was very remote, and access to the nearest school required at least two hours travel on foot. My cousin attended school until the second year of junior high. She decided to quit school after that, complaining that school was boring. My father, on the other hand, was much better educated than my uncle and had a good job as a physician, which allowed my entire family to live in a municipal level city. My father was also very different from most fathers because he acted like my friend. He also disliked drinking. While other men went out drinking together, he would stay home and play chess with me. He was an avid reader, and would relate what he read by telling me stories. Under his influence, I became a bookworm. When my father took me to visit his friends, I'd find a book from a shelf and read it under a bed, before nodding off for a nap. A couple of times my father left without realizing I was still under his friend's bed.

What about funding? Was it hard to raise money for *Er Dong*?
After making the first feature I did a few odd jobs here and there, including getting involved in Ai Weiwei's *Fairytale* project. It was a documentary with a thousand-plus hours of material, and I was one of ten cinematographers he used. I earned about 90,000 RMB ($14,400) and I poured all of it into the preproduction work for *Er Dong*. In 2008, I took my rough cut to Rotterdam's IFFR and

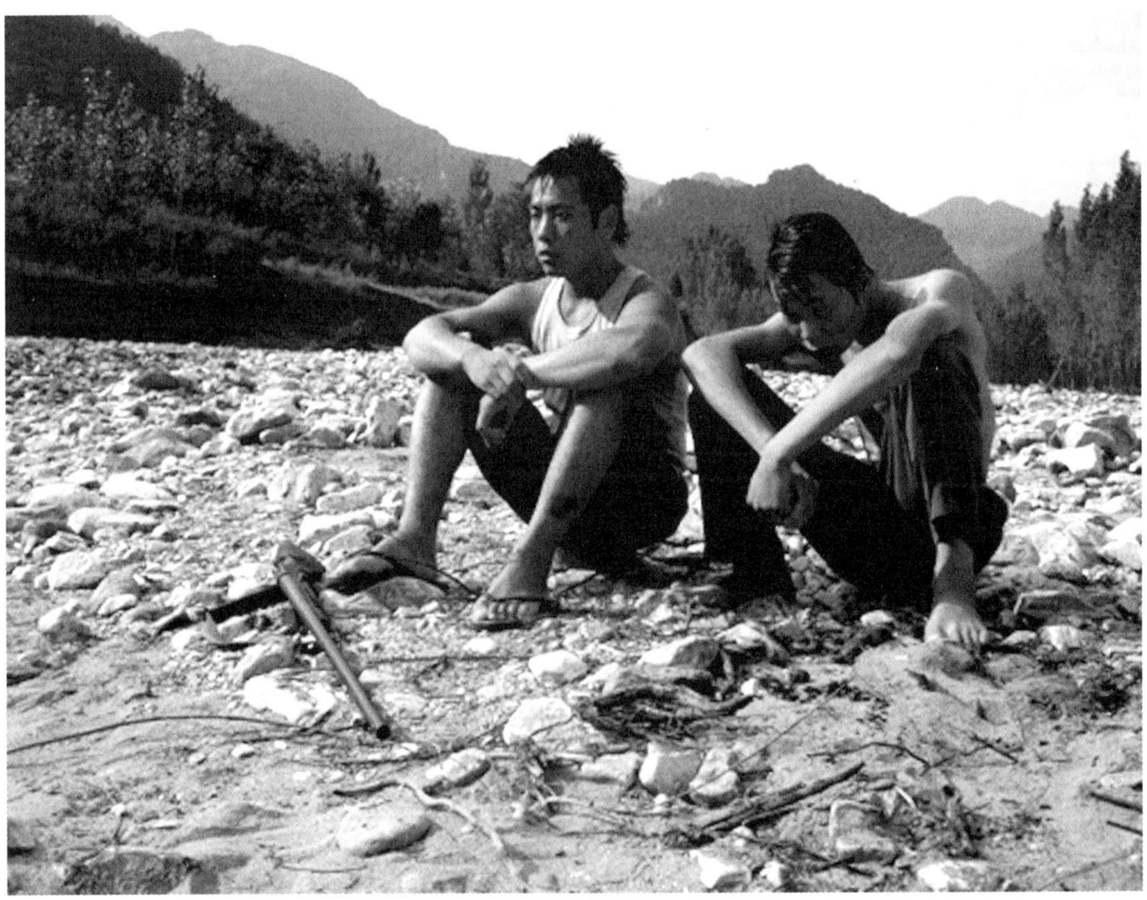

A scene from *Er Dong*, about a troubled youth trapped in rural Shanxi

was able to win 20,000 euro in film grant (from the Hubert Bals Fund) for the post-production work of the film. For this project, I had a team of seven people. They were all classmates from Beijing Normal who contributed their time for free, including Situ Zhixia, who worked as my cinematographer. The docudrama was shot mostly with a handheld camera, which helped intensify the restless mood of the main character. The cast, all non-professionals, was recruited locally from my village, including my cousin and her husband, who played themselves as Chang'e and Er Dong.

On Douban, (the Chinese version of Imbd.com) some critics say _Er Dong_ feels a bit flat and blame this on the performance of the non-professional cast. Do you think by hiring non-professional actors, you had inadvertently sacrificed the quality of the acting?
No, I don't because I feel in real life, that's how the villagers really are—you don't see them getting very excited. Everything is internalized, and they carry on life without making much fuss despite the difficulties. In the film I did have to use a few long shots for the fighting scenes because I didn't want to add pressure to the actors. But that didn't affect the overall outcome of the film. I never considered hiring professional actors for the film because I feel such actors would not have been able to accurately capture the essence of a farmer or a coalminer. Their facial expressions alone would betray them.

The actor who played Er Dong, although he's not a professional, has something about him that really makes the film come alive. How did you instruct him to play that role?
Originally, I tried to find someone else to play that character, but a couple of the actors we tried out were either too young or too inexperienced about rural life. In the end, I asked Bai Lijun, husband of my cousin in real life, to play himself in the film. Bai is a smart guy and he understood what I wanted quickly without requiring a lot of instruction. Like the character in the film, Bai did all sorts of odd jobs in real life, including transporting metal ore for miners and logging as well as selling motorcycles on the side. Motorcycles were very popular in my hometown because they were essential for getting around the countryside or going to town, so they were a much-coveted item as a wedding gift. Of course, Bai also got into a lot of trouble in real life, many of which I recounted in the film. Cutting down trees for money, for example, was one of them. In real life, he had to pay a hefty fine for that. So, Bai was perfect for the role of Er Dong

In the film you also touched upon the theme of children, seen in Er Dong's visit to a large "baby-selling" stone, where people supposedly buy or sell children. Is this partly based on the past history of your village?

The selling of children described in the film is more metaphorical than real. I included the part about abandoned babies because in the 90s when I was in my early teens, I remember there were a lot of discarded babies. Those were the one-child policy days, where families who were trying for a boy but ended up with a girl would give up on the baby so that they could try their luck again. If they decided to keep the girl, they had to pay a hefty fine before trying for another baby. I remember my father, in his role as a physician, was given the responsibility of birth control in town. Because of this position, he had to figure out ways to save many baby girls from abandonment by procuring families willing to adopt them. The film is a reflection of those days.

And you keep coming back to Er Dong's struggle for identity, or at least for a sense of belonging in the film.

Yes, Er Dong struggles to decide what he wants from life. Does he want to become a Christian believer or remain a farmer? In the end, he rejects both choices and opts to leave the village to start life anew in the town.

Er Dong's rejection of Christianity may have come from his sense that the religion feels like another kind of control. But what sorts of people does the religion tend to attract in real life and why?

Actually, Christianity is practiced slightly differently in rural China, where many of the so-called "local churches" are likely to be the homes of villagers. These home-style churches started to pop up in China during the 1970s. Of course, in the 70s, such churches were banned, so many believers would practice together in secret. In the 80s and 90s (when the government relaxed its policies on religion), local villagers would congregate as small groups at these home-style churches every Wednesday. On Saturdays, they would form larger groups to visit real churches in the city by bus, and the commute might take them a couple of hours each way.

I've interviewed dozens of Christian believers both in my uncle's village and in a provincial town

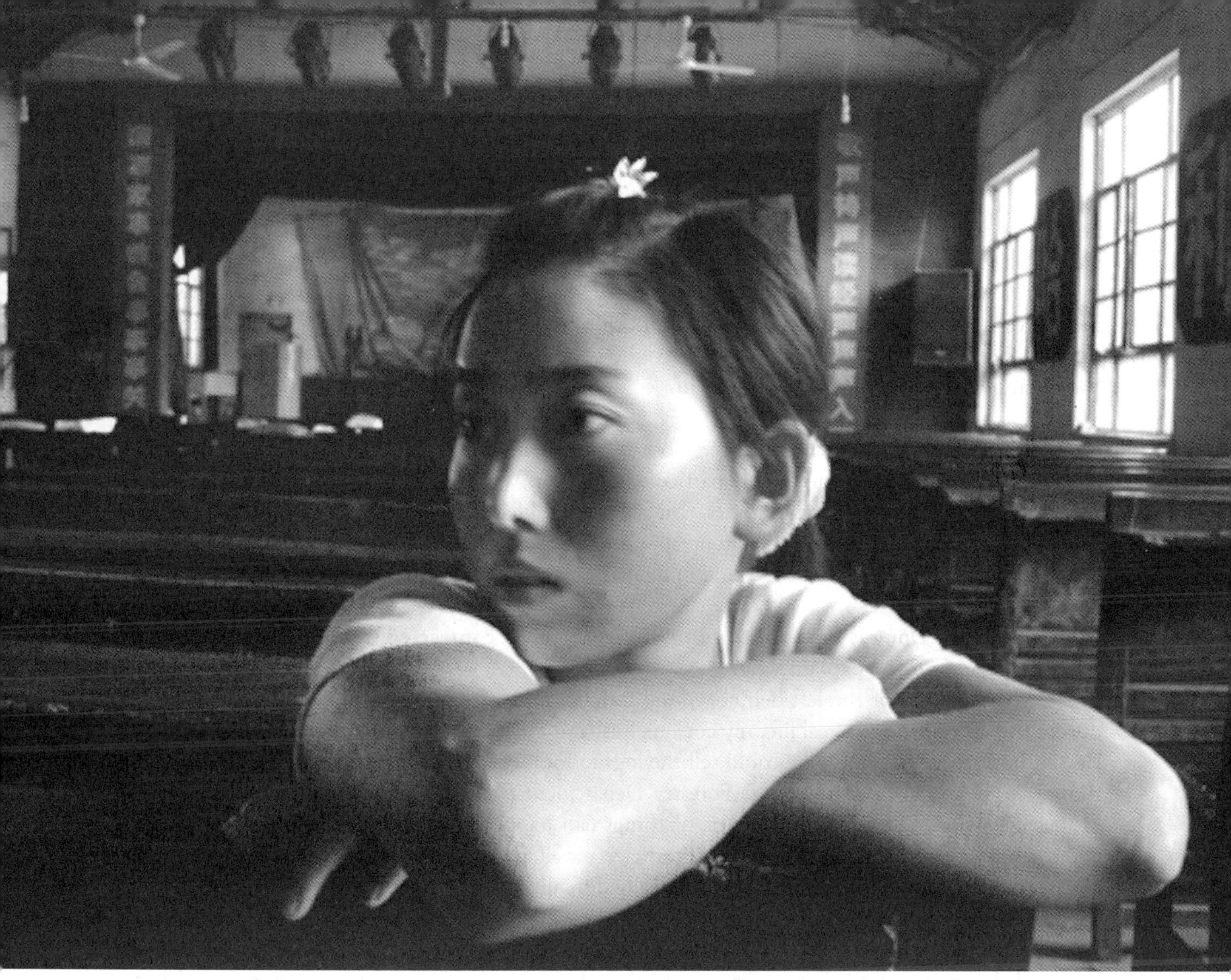

A church scene from *Er Dong*

nearby for a film project, and I found that over 60 percent of my sample believers tended to be older folk who were either suffering from long-term illnesses or who had endured some sort of misfortune in life. Their decision to become Christians had a lot to do with their desire to relieve themselves of their pain and sense of isolation. One woman, for example, lost her child and was suffering great emotional pain from her loss. Others were either living with long-term sicknesses or had a family member who was terminally ill.

I found the thing that attracts believers the most to Christianity is the collective nature of the religion. The "sharing sessions," for example, are particularly popular. When people gather together, they learn to sing hymns and share the bible stories. They also share life experiences, exchange encouragement and tips to solve their problems. The group support and the chance to express themselves, which are very important to many, offer them a kind of mental strength they cannot find elsewhere.

In the movie, Er Dong is fined for logging in a small forest contracted to him for development by the village. Can you explain why?
In the village, many of the left-behind young farmers must do odd jobs to support their living during the slow seasons. In real life, my cousin's husband Bai purchased a wooded area from the village authorities for logging so he could sell the logs to local coalmines as kiln columns. Technically, those trees belonged to him, but the Forestry Department from the larger township accused him of illegal logging. Essentially, these sorts of things can happen because village-level management and town-level ownership of land tend not to be very well defined. And arbitrary charges can occur whenever it suits local officials. It makes life really difficult for many local farmers who want to get ahead by making some extra money.

Your third feature, *Don't Expect Praises*, is also about rural China, this time with two boys spending a summer together as the main story. Can you explain how you got started with this movie?
There are a lot of reasons, but it all started with a trip I took back to my hometown in 2007. On a bus, I bumped into a childhood friend—actually, my very best friend from elementary school—

but I couldn't remember his name for the life of me. When we finally caught up with each other, I found out that one of his father's private coalmines had been submerged underwater due to the construction of the Xiaolangdi Dam which impounds the Yellow River in Jiyuan, Henan Province (The dam was completed in 2001). The submerged area covers a good part of a village that used to be our stamping ground as childhood friends, and the news shocked me. Suddenly I felt my childhood was gone, now forever underwater, and I wanted to find a way to bring back my memories of childhood. And that was what led me to making this film.

So, the story is based on your experiences with your childhood friend from school?
Yes. My friend, whose parents' house was in the mountains in rural Shanxi far away from our city school (this friend was a boarder at our school), always told me how much fun his hometown was—how you could go swimming out in the open, eat fried fish, etc. So, one year, I made up an excuse and went to stay with him in his country home for the whole summer. The film is a way for me to commemorate this very pure friendship from my childhood. In the film, the main character Yang says he has to go home. But when Yang turns his tricycle around to leave, his pal Xiao Bo repeatedly begs him to stay longer. So, in the end, Yang changes his mind and ends up staying. This is the one part that touches a lot of people. It goes to show how deep the two boys' friendship is.

Can you explain the title _Don't Expect Praises_? What's the meaning of the title?
I wanted to say that kids are all beautiful, even if they appear to be very naughty and don't get praised by adults. When I was in elementary school I always sat at the very back of the classroom and I was buddies with several naughty kids. I think the naughty children tend to be the ones who will go far in the world when they grow up. Those who are praised, the ones who behave well at school, however, may not necessarily be very competent in society in later years. As a child, our education was all about memorization of the text we had studied the day before. Not only that, we had to recite the entire text as a small group of about five in class. We only had three chances to get it right, so as a kid I quickly learned to do a lot of guesswork if I couldn't remember the text. Sometimes we had to stay behind at school to copy the text, and we weren't allowed to go home until we got it right. That was really painful.

For this film, your entire cast was made up of non-professional actors, including the two boys who play the leads. Was it challenging to teach the boys how to act?

No, I didn't have any trouble teaching the two boys. They were selected from a local school and we picked two of the youngest and the most rambunctious boys from a large group of students because I really wanted to convey the authentic sense of innocence. Both were very smart, and I only spent about twenty days training them.

***Don't Expect Praises* is a children's film. Was it difficult to find investors for such a film?**

When I started out, a friend gave me my first lump sum investment. Later, two companies also promised to make an investment but they soon pulled out after I started shooting. My wife helped me by borrowing 200,000 RMB (roughly $30,000) from her parents, and I also received some grants from a different source, so I had about 600,000 RMB to finish the shoot. However, it was not until I signed a contract with *Heaven Pictures (Beijing)* that I was able to finally secure investment for the animation segment of the film and the post-production costs. Eventually, another firm came forward to help me with publicity. So, all in all, the budget for the entire film came to about 1 million RMB.

You have made three films based on your own experiences or those around you. Why are you partial to these types of stories?

I like to make films about real people because these kinds of stories are the most honest and authentic. Stories about the common people, about their very ordinary, everyday lives, are what move the audience the most.

Of these three features, which would you say was the most difficult to make, and why?

Definitely the third one because I added a segment of animation to it! As a filmmaker I'm usually quite self-sufficient and I can do a lot of things myself, including writing the screenplay and doing the cinematography. I can even do English subtitling in a pinch. But the animation bit was the only thing I couldn't do. For that, I had to hire a professional artist to finish the job, which took a full year. The film was also the costliest to make. Of the 1 million RMB budget, more than a quar-

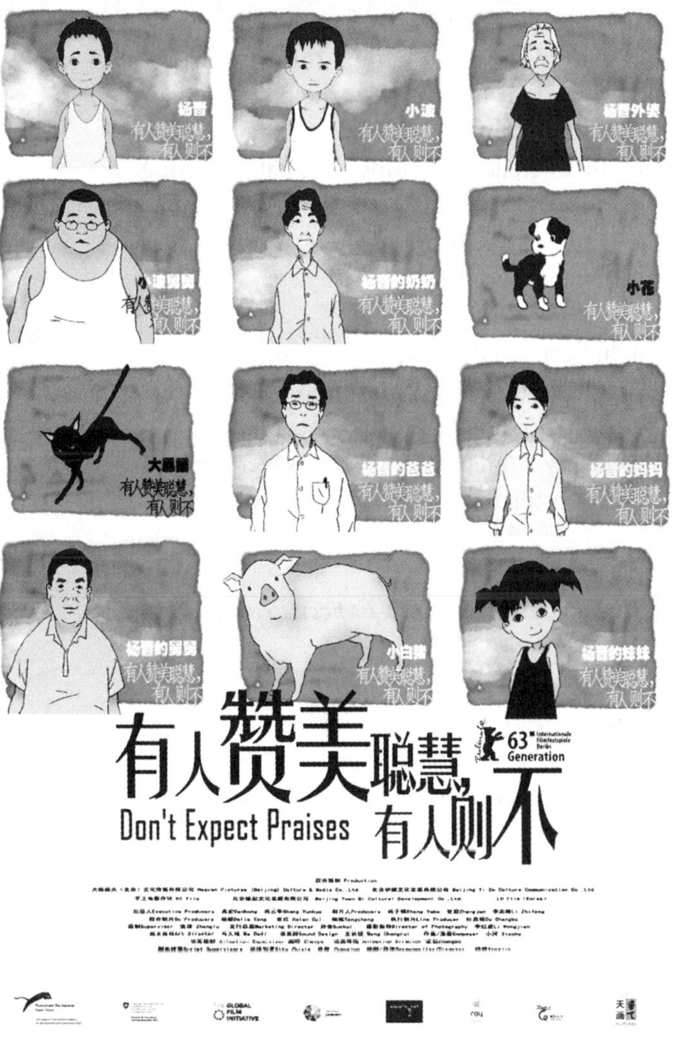

A Poster for *Don't Expect Praises*

ter went to making the animation. I wanted to include the animation because it helps to separate reality from Yang's daydreaming as well as his memory of the past and his long-deceased grandma. So, the animation part represents anything that's not in the present tense. *Don't Expect Praises* is also my first feature to receive a screening permit, which made the theatrical release possible.

Your fourth film is also a children's film called *When I Was Eight Years Old*. What is it about?

I made this film [in 2016], but it's not my own project. The film was written by the TV screenwriter Lin Heping, and came ready with investment money. I was merely hired as the director. It's a tale about a country boy sold to a blind fortuneteller as his helper and guide because the fortuneteller needs to go from door to door to conduct business. In the old days in northern China, this sort of profession was relatively common, and poor families would sell or rent their kids to the blind as their "seeing-eye dogs" for survival. The story is based on Lin's own childhood experience growing up in a village in Liaoning Province during the 60s. In real life, fortunetellers not only read palms during the day but most of them also engaged in the retelling of history or literary classics at social gatherings in the evenings in exchange for lodgings. Famous serial works such as *Outlaws of the Marsh* and *The Romance of the Three Kingdoms* were all part of their repertoires.

Mr. Lin, now in his sixties, served three different fortunetellers when he was a boy, and this gave him a wealth of knowledge about the classics even though he never finished high school. This familiarity with the serial-novel format was what helped Lin become one of the best-paying TV screenwriters in China because today's TV series tend to be very similar to how stories were told in the traditional serial-novel style. They always leave you waiting for more in the next chapter when the story reaches a crucial moment.

In a way, *When I Was Eight Years Old* is told quite differently from *Don't Expect Praises*. And would you not say even the themes are quite different?
Yes, *Don't Expect Praises* is about an innocent childhood friendship, whereas *When I Was Eight* is about a young child's relationship with a grumpy blind old man. In *When I Was Eight*, the old man and the young boy don't get along at all in the beginning—one is mean, and the other is very rebellious and naughty. But over time, the old man and the boy find common ground and develop a close relationship not unlike that between a grandpa and a grandchild.

Was it difficult for you to direct *When I Was Eight Years Old*, since you didn't write the screenplay and the story wasn't based on your personal experience?
Not at all, because it was a script I really liked. And if I ran into something or a part of history I wasn't familiar with, I would go talk to the writer to ask for his opinion. Or else I would consult books at a library, or do research online to better understand the issue.

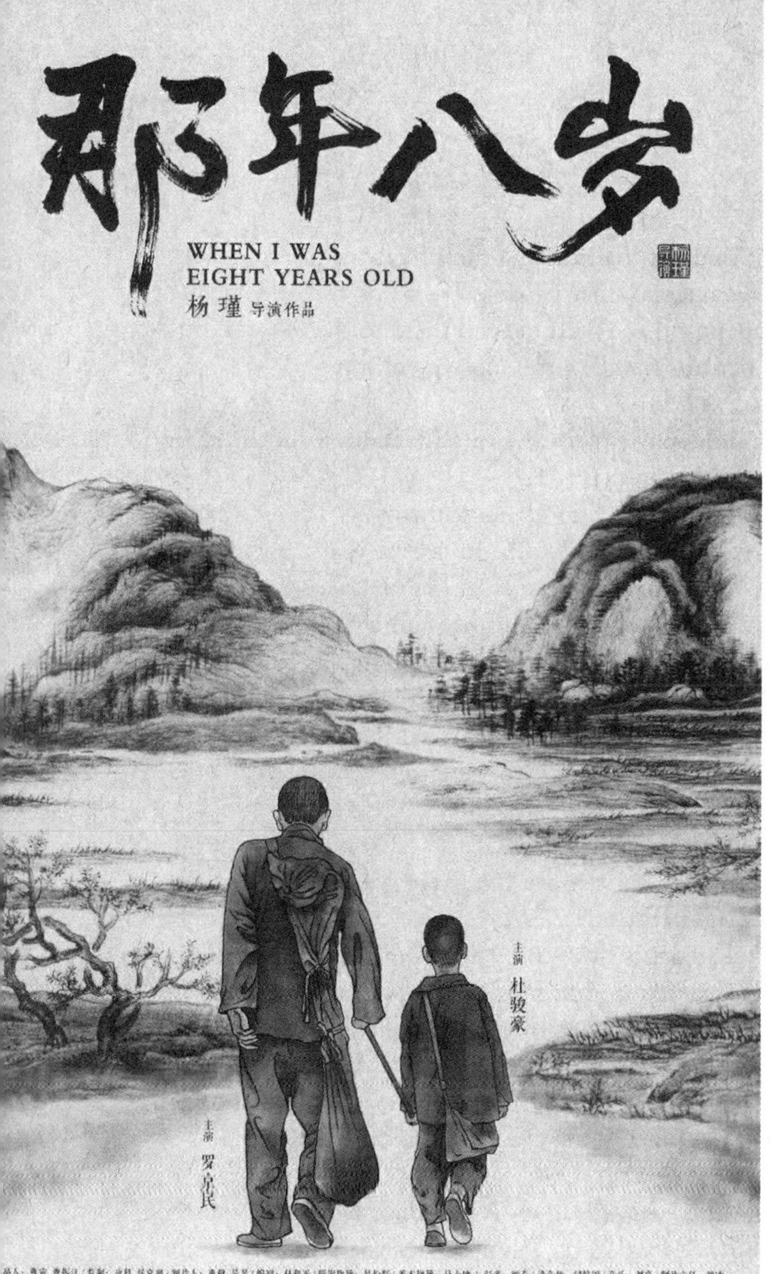

What projects are you working on now?
I have just finished shooting a film about a frontier policeman in Western Inner Mongolia called *Patrolman Baoyin*. Based on a true story, the film is about how the patrolman, with an assigned patrol area as vast as 1,672 square kilometers, helps various people in the zone adjust to the harshness of life while also trying to solve tough criminal cases. Again, it's not my original project, but I was approached to be the director.

Some Chinese filmmakers call themselves independent filmmakers; others call their works art films. How would you describe your films?
Personally, I like to use "art films" to describe my works because in my understanding, independent films refer to movies that have yet to receive a stamp of approval from

the censors, or works by filmmakers who, in the name of maintaining their freedom of expression, deliberately refuse to subject their movies to censorship. When I made *The Black and White Milk Cow* and *Er Dong*, I was too inexperienced to understand the need to send them to the censors. But since *Don't Expect Praises*, I've been applying for permits for all of my subsequent films.

Given today's political climate, do you think independent films can still claim a foothold in China in the near future?
These days, I think it's much more difficult for us to see a film as hard-hitting as Tian Zhuang-zhuang's *Blue Kite*, which is a very thought-provoking, critical work. In recent years, but particularly in the last three years, young filmmakers, lured by the readily available cash provided by investors, become muddled-headed and are easily persuaded to make movies purely for profit. They don't bother with their own independent thoughts, or ponder about the happenings in our society any more, which is why it's becoming extremely rare to see films that can truly be called independent, or at least hard-hitting. The only exceptions are documentaries. As far as feature films are concerned, 6th generation directors Jia Zhangke and Wang Xiaoshuai are perhaps the only ones still very committed to making films expressing their independent thoughts.

Speaking of 6th generation filmmakers, what would you say are the main differences in their approach to film versus those that are from your generation?
In terms of style, I think the biggest difference is that artists from our generation made films mostly with a digital camera, whereas those from the 6th Generation shot movies using the traditional film-based method. Between 2003 and 2005, a large number of directors made their debuts with DV, including Ning Hao and Ying Liang, Liu Jiayin and Peng Tao. In terms of content, I'd say those from my generation tended to focus more on stories about our own lives, like memories of our childhoods, which were more individualistic. But for the earlier filmmakers, their focus was more on society.

As a young filmmaker, which established directors' films would you say have impacted you the most?
When I was a student, I watched a lot of films by Edward Yang, Hou Hsiao-hsien and Imamura Shohei. I like many of Imamura's films, including *Black Rain, Warm Water Under the Bridge* and

The Ballad of Narayama because they are about the lives of ordinary people, especially people on the very bottom rung of Japanese society. But my favorite is *Dr. Akagi*, which was dedicated to his trained physician father. The film is about a country doctor seeking a cure for hepatitis in 1945 Japan. My father was also a physician, so I can really relate. Imamura used to be Yasujiro Ozu's assistant and Ozu once said to him, "You shouldn't make so many films about dirt and filth." But Shohei insisted that he would continue to make films about people who live like "maggots." That's why I like him the best.

Case Study: *Er Dong*

Fatherless urban youth growing up in the shifting sands of a seismic economic transformation in the 20th century China is a common theme featured in many of the works by 6th generation directors. *Beijing Bastards* and *Beijing Bicycle,* by the Beijing Film Academy-trained Zhang Yuan and Wang Xiao Shuai respectively, are just two examples. In *Er Dong*, Yang Jin's second feature, the director picks up where the earlier filmmakers left off, but is given it a new twist by zooming in on a stray youth in the countryside. By using the docudrama technique made famous by another famed 6th generation director Jia Zhangke, Yang brings forth a detail-rich, quietly moving portrait of a doomed youth lost in a 21st century Chinese village.

Er Dong is a restless 18-year-old who lives in a small village in rural Shanxi with his widowed mother. Growing up, he always has a nagging sense that somehow, he doesn't belong, that perhaps he's not his mother's real son but the product of a cash transaction. Because he keeps getting into trouble by messing about with a shotgun, riding around on his motorcycle and getting into fights, his mother—a devout Christian—decides to leave him at a Christian boarding school in the hope that he will find God as well as a new direction in life. Instead, Er Dong finds a girlfriend there named Chang'e. When he gets expelled from the school, he elopes with Chang'e on his bike with the dream of starting a new life somewhere else.

It's not that Er Dong is deeply in love with Chang'e: he himself is still a child in some ways. It's just that having been abandoned first by his birth parents, then by God and finally by society, he has nothing else to claim as his own. Chang'e happens to be another lonely soul he has found along the way with whom he knows he can create something close to a thing called "home."

In the film, Yang aptly captures the rebelliousness and recklessness of a misguided country youth running wild in the absence of a male role model. At the boarding school, Er Dong meets a vocational teacher who is willing to teach him the skills to become a proper repairman. In many ways, the teacher is the only father figure in Er Dong's life. Yet the lost teen, not fully appreciative or understanding of the opportunity at hand, chooses to skip classes and eventually gets expelled from school, thus missing out on an important chapter in his life. After he becomes a father, he is forced to grow up quickly by taking on backbreaking jobs at a brick factory and a coal mine. Ahead of him is an exhausting cycle of temporary employment, hard labor, poverty and a future of little hope. In this way, Yang sheds light on a rarely discussed social problem—the grim prospects for undereducated rural youth coming of age in 21st century China.

Another interesting phenomenon Yang has captured in this film is rural Chinese people's strong reliance on Christianity and God for strength and support during the very turbulent years of a fast-changing China between the late 90s and the 2000s. People of different ages, but particularly those who're getting on in years, talk about God in their everyday lives. They thank God for everything and consult God on important decisions, including such things as setting a wedding date. What is striking is that some of the choir scenes at church captured on camera by Yang bear an uncanny resemblance to the charging youngsters singing revolutionary songs during the Cultural Revolution days. Just a few decades ago, people sang Maoist songs to draw inspiration and comfort. Now, rural people seem to have traded Mao's portrait for that of the cross to arrive at the same purpose.

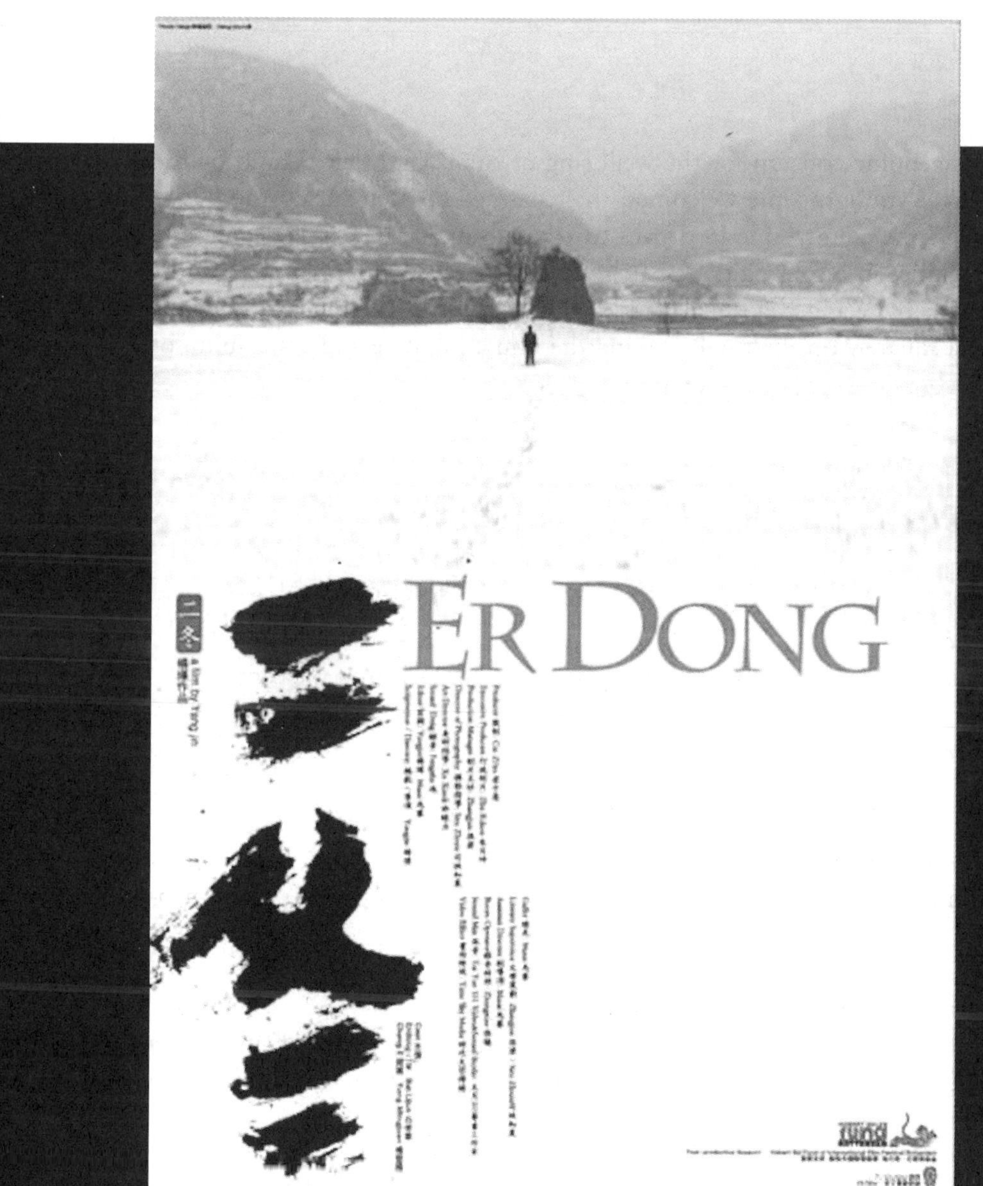

A poster for the film, *Er Dong*.

Er Dong is inspired by Yang's genuine concern for the wellbeing of rural youth left behind by the times in the countryside. These young poeple welcomed their passage of rites during the 90s—a time when many parents left the countryside in droves to take advantage of China's economic boom and better job opportunities in bigger cities. As such, *Er Dong* revives the "fatherless youth" theme of the 80s made famous by Wang Xiaoshuai and Zhang Yuan. The difference is that this time, Yang focuses his camera squarely on the rural, making the film an update and continuum of this earlier theme.

The Director's Take

What's an independent film?
Independent films refer to movies that have yet to receive a stamp of approval from the censors.

What qualities must independent films possess?
Critical Realism.

Why do you make films? And who is your audience?
I want to use film to communicate with ordinary people and to tell tales about what's really happening right now.

What's the first film you ever saw and what were your initial thoughts?
When I went to kindergarten, I saw a film with a ghost character called Zhongkuai. It involves a woman painting her face black, which is quite scary. Later, I learned it was a feminist film directed by Huang Shuqin under the title *Woman, Demon, Human*.

Which single movie made you realize that film is an art form?
The Phantom of Liberty and *That Obscure Object of Desire* by Spanish filmmaker Luis Bunuel.

What is your favorite film of all time?
Dr. Akagi by Imamura Shohei.

Who's your favorite director of all time and why?
Imamura Shohei because his films are all about the lives of ordinary people, especially people on the very bottom rung of society.

What in your opinion are some of the qualities that the best films all share?
An attitude towards life itself.

What's your best quality as an independent director?
I always have a lot to say about my feelings towards life.

What's the title of the best Chinese film you've seen in recent years?
The Elephant Sitting Still (2018) by Hu Bo.

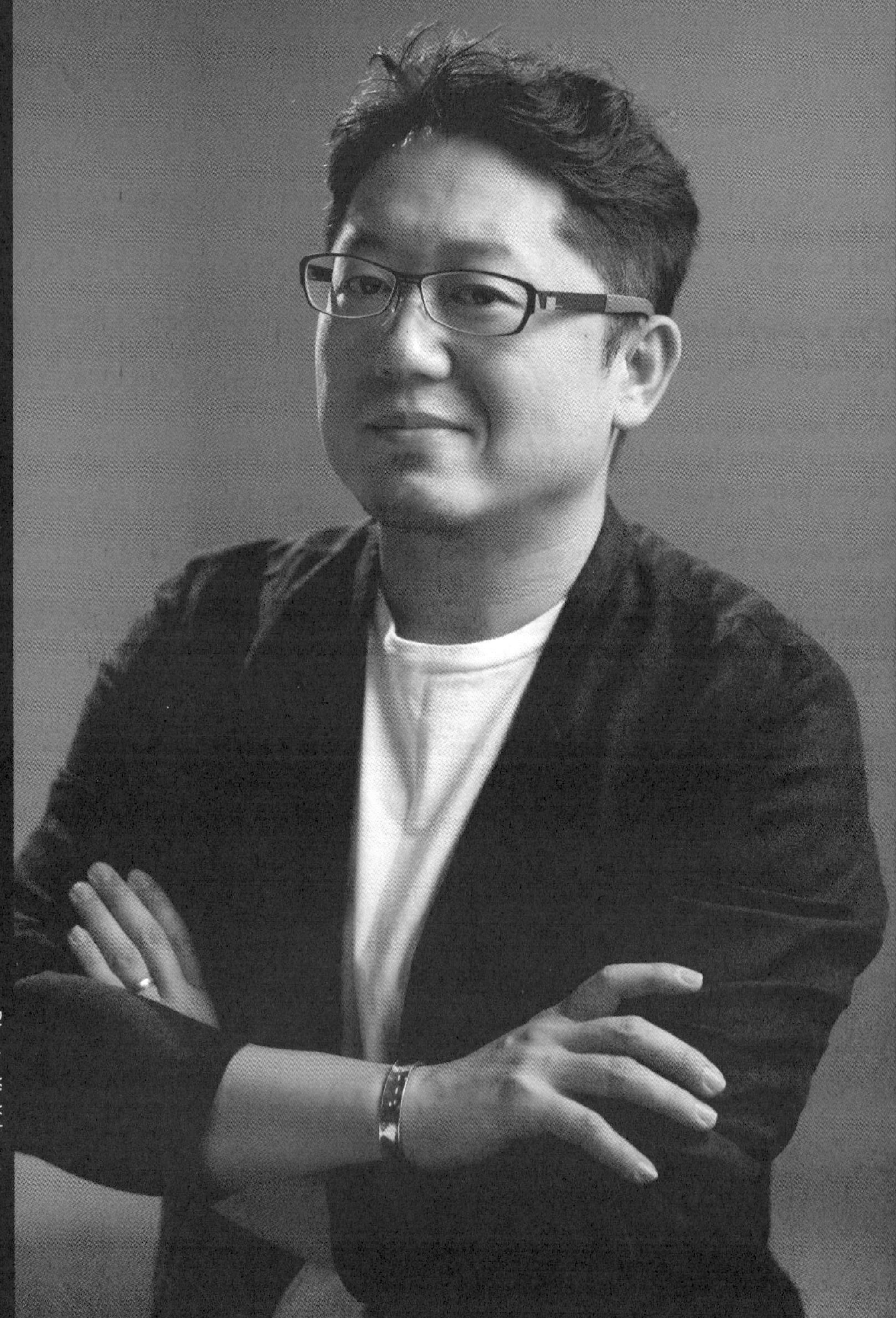

Director Xin Yukun

CHAPTER 5

XIN YUKUN
The Shady Side of China's "Wild West"

A Short Introduction

XIN YUKUN is a film wizard who has seemingly appeared from nowhere. Born in Baotou in Inner Mongolia in 1984, Xin is from a family with no ties to the film industry. (Both of his parents worked as non-management level bank clerks.) In 2015, he rose to fame with the commercial release of his directorial debut, *The Coffin in the Mountain* (aka *Deep in the Heart*)—a critically acclaimed crime thriller set in a deserted Chinese village. The film was a surprise hit at the box office, yielding 10.66 million RMB (roughly US$1.5 million) when its production costs were a mere 1.7 million RMB (roughly US$ 243,000). The feat was a first for a newcomer. Xin's second feature, *Wrath of Silence*, was another popular film, which established Xin as a gifted storyteller who has found that rare balance of being critical of his time while still managing to be successful at the box office.

Xin, who never went to college, grew up addicted to crime and suspense genre films. He likes to call himself a movie-fan director because he is a great admirer of many world-renowned directors, including Steven Spielberg, the Coen brothers and Christopher Nolan. At the age of 17, Xin decided to quit high school in order to study at a film school attached to the well-known Xi'an Film Studio. He didn't stay in Xi'an for long though, and soon left for Beijing with the intent of enrolling at the prestigious Beijing Film Academy (BFA). Although he failed the entrance exam several times, he was able to sign up eventually as a student for the one-year cinematography certificate course in 2008. After that, he made his way into the film business by doing odd jobs here and there with different film crews.

Xin got his break when he submitted his directorial debut, *The Coffin in the Mountain*, to Xining's FIRST International Film Festival in 2014. He brought home both the best film and best director awards for that year. The noir-rich drama is a cleverly plotted, mystery crime drama about a coffin left in the mountains of a central Chinese village with no claimers. It went on to win many more prizes, including the Grand Prix at the Warsaw International Film Festival in Poland the same year, and the best screenplay award at Beijing Youth Film Festival the following year. Lauded for its intricate plotline and its takes on crime and punishment with a maturity and confidence befitting a veteran, *The Coffin in the Mountain* was eventually released in Chinese cinemas in 2015, to rave reviews. The surprise success was particularly poignant given that it came at a time when the crime genre was experiencing a slump in the Chinese market, and the cast was made up of mostly unknown amateur actors.

Xin, who sees himself as a half-commercial, half-auteur filmmaker, completed his second feature, *Wrath of Silence,* in 2017. The film, which critics say bears a striking resemblance to Korean director Na Hong-jin's *Yellow Sea*, is a powerful but fatalistic crime story that sets a mute but vengeful miner against a world of corruption in China. Like *The Coffin in the Mountain*, this film is also set in China's "wild west," (in this case, the rural north of China's Inner Mongolia) though the plotline is much less complicated this time around. Xin, who makes it his goal to "uncover the darker side of humanity in rural China," made a point of illustrating in this follow-up attempt that China remains deeply divided in terms of how its wealth is distributed. Although *Wrath of Silence's* box office takings were not as high as expected (even though the accumulated revenues were still about $7.6 million), the film helped establish Xin as a successful young director who knows how to game China's strict censorship system while still managing to deliver his personal messages about the shady side of China's rural society.

Filmography

Force of Seven, 七夜 (short film, 2010) - director, screenwriter.
The Coffin in the Mountain 心迷宫 (feature film, 2015) - director, screenwriter.
Distance 再见，在也不见 (anthology drama film, 2016) - one of three directors (the other directors are Tan Shijie and Sivaroi Kongsakul).
Wrath of Silence 爆裂无声 (feature film, 2018) - director, screenwriter.

Interview

In the summer of 2017, I arranged to meet with Xin at a local café near the second ring road in Beijing. Xin, who appeared with his young wife, was bespectacled and clean-shaven, looking more like a post-graduate university student than a director. He spent almost three hours with me and answered all my questions patiently and politely. From our conversation, I got the sense that Xin is a very solid young filmmaker who has strong ideals, and that he wants to do his best to leave a mark as a successful crime film director who excels at storytelling. In the spring of 2019, I had a follow-up interview with Xin via email after the release of *Wrath of Silence*. Again, Xin answered all my questions promptly and patiently. The following interview is a compilation of my two interviews with him between the years 2017 and 2019.

Your road to becoming a director is rather dramatic—you quit high school in order to go to a film school. Can you explain what it was about film that attracted you in the first place?

It has a lot to do with the early films I saw as a teenager, which greatly inspired me. In the early days I was a huge fan of Steven Spielberg's films, particularly *Jurassic Park*. It was simply magical and I was awed by his use of special effects to make extinct animals come alive on screen in such a compelling, mesmerizing way. The film made a huge impact on me, planting a seed in me as a future filmmaker. Later, through reading magazine articles, I learned more about the background work of various movies, and how they were made with so many people working together behind the scenes. Of course, the core of a film's artistic expression comes down to the director, so I knew if I were to get involved in filmmaking that I would want to be the director.

I must also admit that I was a so-so student in high school because school just wasn't that interesting to me. And by the time I got to my freshmen year in high school, my grades had started to slip. That's when I knew I wouldn't be able to do very well with *gaokao* (China's national college entrance exam). Meanwhile, I became more and more enamored with watching and reading about films. It so happened that my mother was very encouraging of me pursuing my own dreams because she felt as a young girl, that she wasn't able to do it for herself. So, she really wanted me to

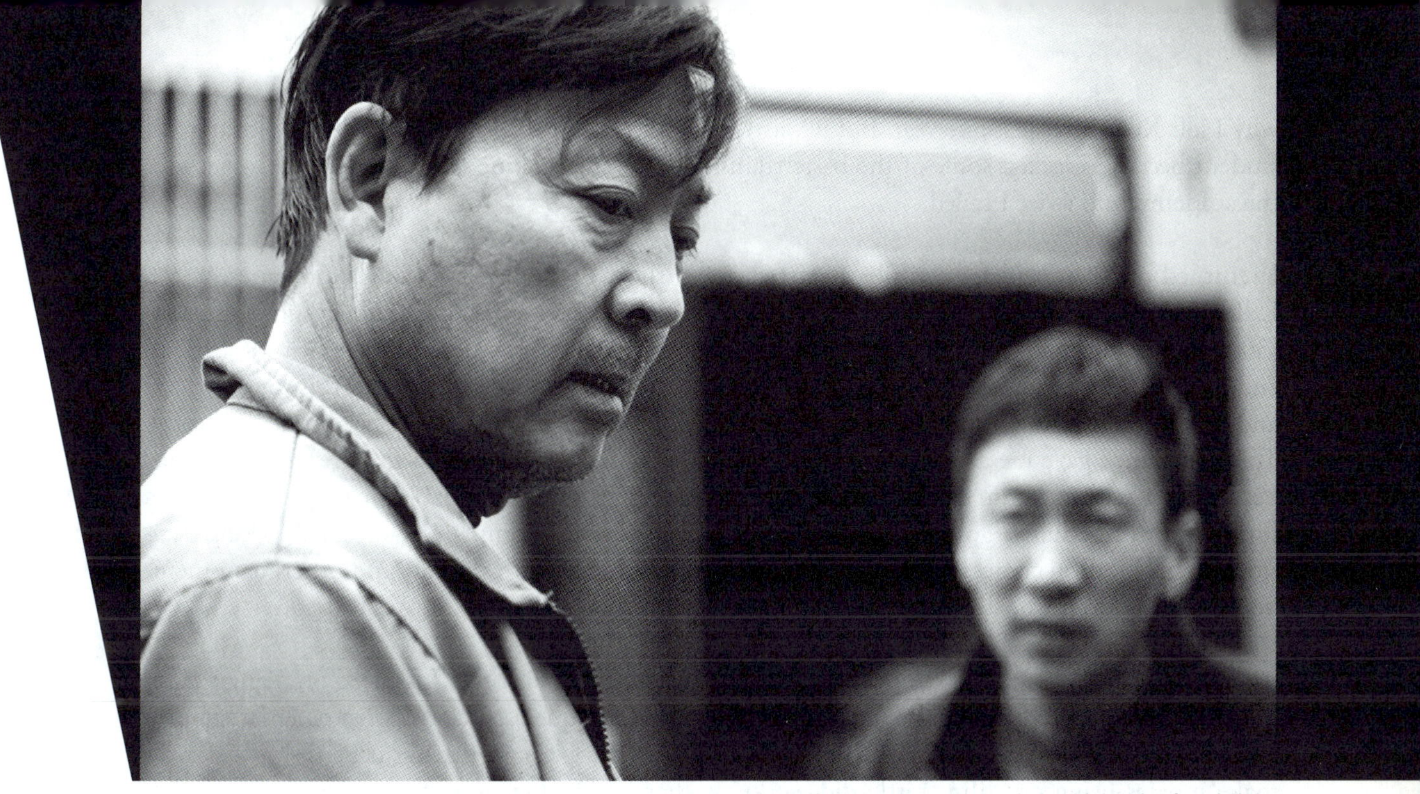

The Coffin in the Mountain reveals the shady side of rural China

be able to fulfill my own ambitions. That's why, when a friend of mine mentioned that Xi'an Film Academy was recruiting new students, I went ahead and signed up for the school without any hesitation—this decision was something most people from my town couldn't understand at the time.

You went through a lot before making your first feature film. It took you something like a decade after you had received your training in filmmaking. Can you talk about your experience?
When I was studying in Xi'an, I met a few teachers there who told me if I were serious about making films, I should study it more systematically and that I needed to go and study at BFA. This was

why I left Xi'an after just one year. But it wasn't easy for me to get into BFA as a regular [four-year] student because I lacked some of the basic training they were looking for. Twice I tried to get into the academy, and twice I failed.

I returned to Xi'an, and for a while, I started doing short PR films for various companies, which I did purely as a way to earn a living. When I was about 22, I began doing "column dramas" (30-minute-long mini-TV stories about people) for different companies with the help of a friend and, over time, I got quite a reputation as someone who's very good at this. I did this for two years and made about 20 such mini dramas, and eventually worked my way up to becoming a director. This experience gave me a boost of confidence, allowing me to hold on to my dream of someday becoming a serious filmmaker. In retrospect, this experience was invaluable in preparing me as a future director because I got a real taste of what to expect as the commander-in-chief making decisions about location choices and learning how to communicate with the cast and other team members. It really was my on-the-job training.

After some time, I left the job to try my luck again with BFA. This time, I focused on being a cinematographer because I love all the equipment and the techniques associated with cinematography. I got on to the (one-year certificate) program in 2008, and I was in the last class to learn how to make movies using real film. Little did we know that RED One camera, the first generation of high-definition digital cinematography camera, was to debut around the same time, and that the technology I learned would soon become obsolete (in part because of the cost of developing the film). ARRI also debuted a few years later.

But the BFA training did help me learn about filmmaking in a very systematic way, such as how to categorize things, and what are the many different rules in making a film, etc. This experience proved very useful to me in the post-production work of *The Coffin in the Mountain*. For example, knowing that this was a realist film, I knew immediately that I needed to use medium shots for the shoot, and that using handheld camera would help make the viewing experience more intimate for the audience. I also knew to avoid making use of wide-angle shots, which would have made the film seem more dramatic. It took me a long time to get where I am, but the richness of my life experiences was all necessary in my preparation for becoming a director. I believe as an artist, you really need to accumulate a wealth of experience in order to have enough material to work with for your creative expression.

And how did the idea of your debut film, *The Coffin in the Mountain,* come about?
One of my friends—a client whose company produces promotional videos—introduced me to a producer named Ren Jiangzhou. The introduction was crucial because Ren was later to become the producer of *The Coffin in the Mountain*. I worked with Ren closely for a while on promotional videos for his company, which he really appreciated. Later, we became good friends. One day in 2011, I showed him a short horror film (*Force of Seven*) that I'd made with several friends of mine from the film school. Ren was very impressed, and sometime later, he told me a true crime story that had taken place twenty-odd years ago in his hometown in Henan. It was an account passed down by his mother. A light bulb immediately lit up in my head because I'd been saving money thinking it was time for me to write a screenplay and make my first movie, and this story seemed perfect for me. The tale not only has the elements of noir and humor but it also tells us a lot about our humanity.

Ren told me that if I were interested, I could turn it into a screenplay. But I didn't take action immediately. I was actually hoping to make another film (this later became my second film, *Wrath of Silence,* which Ren also helped produce), but Ren had different ideas. He spent the entire year of 2012 working on his own script based on the true story. He also started approaching potential investors, and initially, no one seemed interested. It wasn't until early 2013 that a business friend of his agreed to invest 2 million RMB (roughly US 281,800 dollars) in the film. Ren told me about the news and urged me to help him rewrite the screenplay. That was when we decided to work together on the film, with the end of 2013 as our deadline for completion of the film. With Ren working as the production manager, we received 20,000 RMB seed funding to start the pre-production work, and I put aside all my jobs at the time to focus on the project. The original true-life tale that took place in Henan in the 1990's became the basis for *The Coffin in the Mountain,* though we changed a lot of the setting and background in order to make it more current and affordable (a

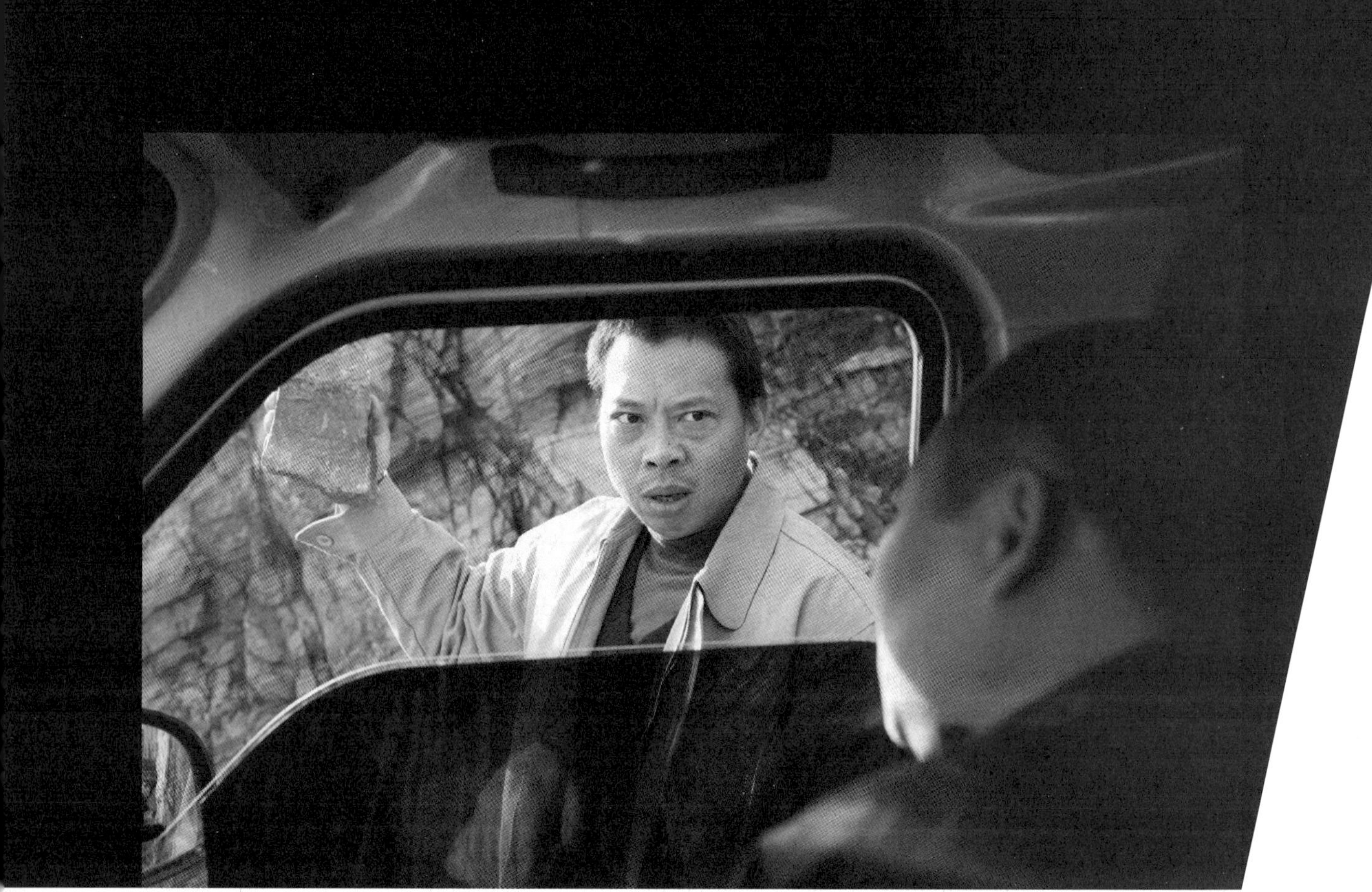

The Coffin in the Mountain is a murder mystery that emerged in 2015 as a surprise hit.

period film would also require a collection of items unique to the time period, which would raise the cost of production) so it would be more of a relevant story reflective of our own times.

What were some of the difficulties you encountered, this being your first film?

I was extremely lucky with *The Coffin in the Mountain* because I already had a ready sum of money to work with. So many first-time directors that I know of had to sell their cars and houses, some even had to borrow money to make their first films. But this project came with investment and a fully written account of a story. All I had to do was to focus on writing the screenplay. I was also lucky because over time with all my experience producing promotional videos, I'd accumulated enough of a network of talent who were eager to learn new skills alongside me. So, when I announced my new feature project, many were happy to be on my team to help me make the movie. Finding the location also went smoothly—Ren simply led us to his hometown village in Henan, the site of the original crime scene. We found the setting ideal for our story because it had all the elements we needed: water, mountains, forests, the remoteness and a sense of isolation. From the perspective of production costs, this was a huge saving because it took away the need for us to find other locations for the shoot. But we did encounter some serious problems after we decided on the location towards the end of 2013. In fact, it wasn't until most of the production team members had already arrived on location that we learned the main investor of the film decided to pull out at the last minute. At the time, we were about one million RMB short in funds (roughly 140,000 US dollars). Ren and I spent the days like years for a while, not knowing what to do. Worse, I had to keep this awful news a secret from my crew for weeks, until Ren finally managed to borrow some money from friends to tide us over. Ren was gone most of the time during our filming and didn't return until he finally found enough money for us to finish all the shooting. That was a really painful experience.

I heard you also had a crisis with the lead actor you had originally picked to play the village chief character, Weiguo?
Yes. We originally picked someone that was perfect for the role as the village head. Although he wasn't a professional actor, he had that rustic, peasant look, and we had high hopes for him. The problem was, he triggered a spinal problem and badly injured his lumber vertebrae during his train ride to Henan. Although he was still keen to play the role, saying after some medical help, he should be good to go, we decided it was best to find a replacement for safety reasons. We were in a bit of a crisis because this happened just two days before filming was to begin. In the end we found Huo Weimin, a professional actor from the local area. Huo looks less like a farmer and more like an intellectual from the city. But he was very devoted to the role and very professional. So, it all worked out in the end.

What happened to the original screenplay written by Ren, your production manager?

What Ren wrote was more like a draft, a written account of the incident that took place in his village. You can't call it a screenplay because Ren wasn't trained as a screenwriter. But my partner Feng Yuanliang and I were able to rework the draft and turn it into a professional script. Ren's original vision was also quite different from ours. He was thinking more of a social realist approach in line with the early films of Jia Zhangke, presenting the story exactly as it happened without any twists or turns. Feng and I decided to add some mental challenges to the narrative to make it more entertaining, but more importantly, to fictionalize part of the story—a key to obtaining a screening permit from the authorities. We knew our bottom line was to make a film that would pass censorship and at least make some kind of profit for the investors, which we were able to achieve.

Where was your second film, *Wrath of Silence,* shot on location? And was it also a story based in part on a true event?

It was shot entirely in my hometown in Baotou, Inner Mongolia. The story is entirely fictional, although the inspiration had come from various news stories. The script was something I'd worked on, off and on, by myself for five years, and I completed it long before I started working on *The Coffin in the Mountain.* This was the project I'd hoped to start out with as my directorial debut, but it didn't work out that way. I had to put it aside until I'd completed *The Coffin in the Mountain.*

***Wrath of Silence* is set for the year 2004. Is there a special meaning to this particular year?**

I chose 2004 because around that time there was a lot of illegal mining of rare metal minerals in Inner Mongolia. In those days, the market prices for minerals were very high and the laws were lax, so these conditions really fit well with the background of my story.

What would you say were your greatest challenges in making *Wrath of Silence*?

[That would be] myself! When I made *The Coffin in the Mountain,* critics and the audiences were very forgiving because they gave me the benefit of the doubt as a newcomer, plus the fact that the film was produced with a very low budget. As a result, it received a lot of good reviews, perhaps better than it really deserved. But I knew for the second film, people would be less forgiving and take the film for what it was. That is why I really wanted to outstrip my first film and do a better job.

In order to do this, I first decided to change my style of narration—rather than using the previous circular narrative style, I opted for a simpler, more straightforward linear narrative. I also spent a lot more effort on the characterization of people, which helped develop the story greatly. In *The Coffin in the Mountain,* the characters are rather one-dimensional because the focus is on the plot. In *Wrath of Silence,* we have three main characters and I felt each of them was interesting in their own way, so a strong build up was needed. And because we were able to secure more investment funds for this project, it allowed us to spend more money and effort on the cinematography using more traditional methods, such as using a fixed camera position rather than a handheld camera like we did in *The Coffin in the Mountain.*

I heard that it took you quite a while to find the proper location for this film.
Yes, it took us 66 days to complete the shoot because it was very tough to find the perfect location. We wanted to avoid the snow season, and there was a real rush to complete all the shooting before the snow came. But it all worked out.

How much was the production cost of *Wrath of Silence*? And did the added costs give you more pressure?
It was roughly 10 million RMB (1.5 million dollars) in production costs alone. When you include publicity, perhaps twice as much. (Chinese website Huxiu.com estimated in April of 2018 that the cost of the film was closer to between 3 and 4 million US dollars.) We didn't intend to jack up the costs so much in the beginning, but because we had a lot of fighting scenes, which prolonged the filming time, it meant more money. We also used a lot of special effects in the feature, adding more costs to the budget.

I was lucky enough to receive some foundation money, so the pressure wasn't too bad, though the pressure was definitely there. I had communicated my concerns to all of my investors, and they

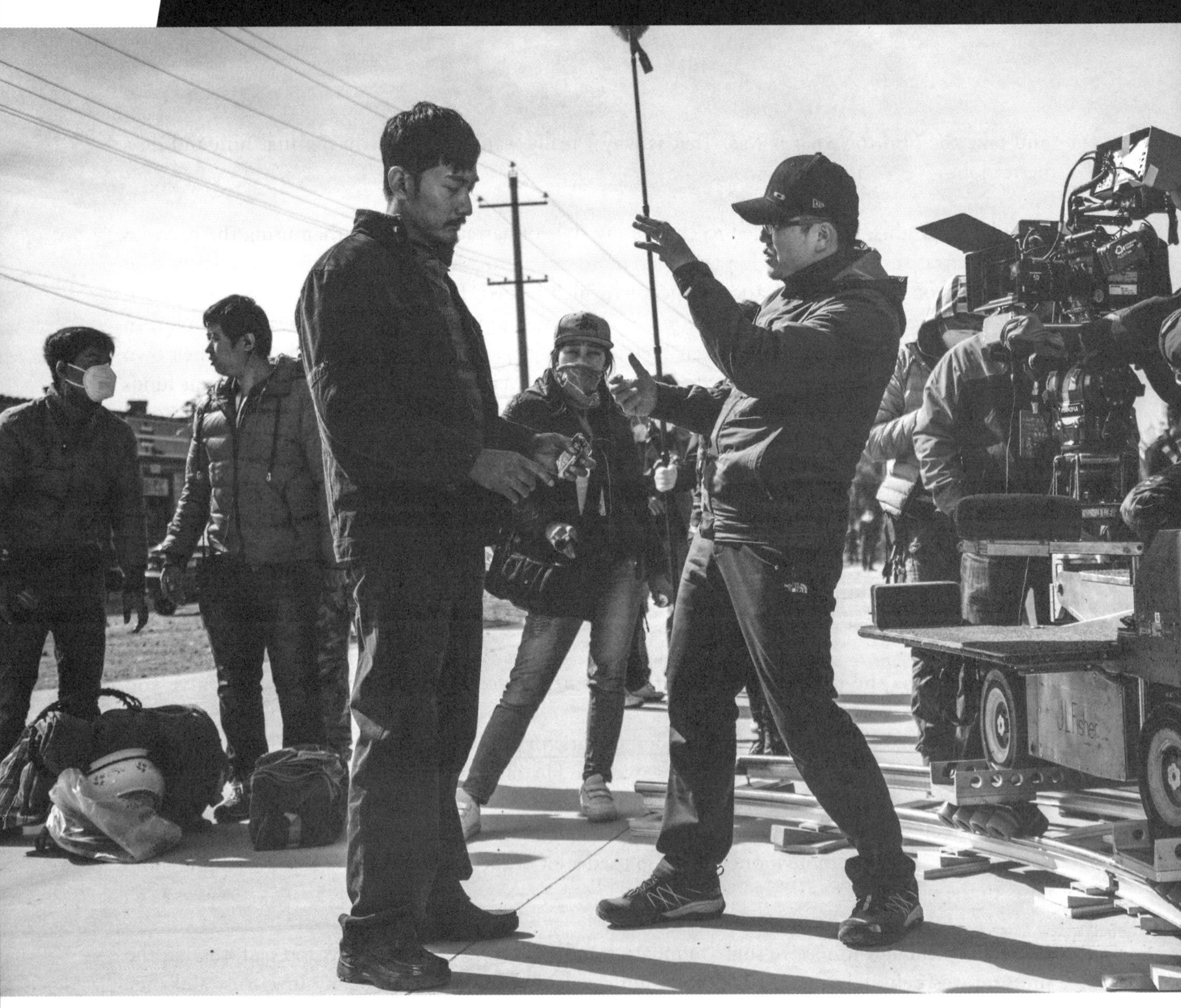

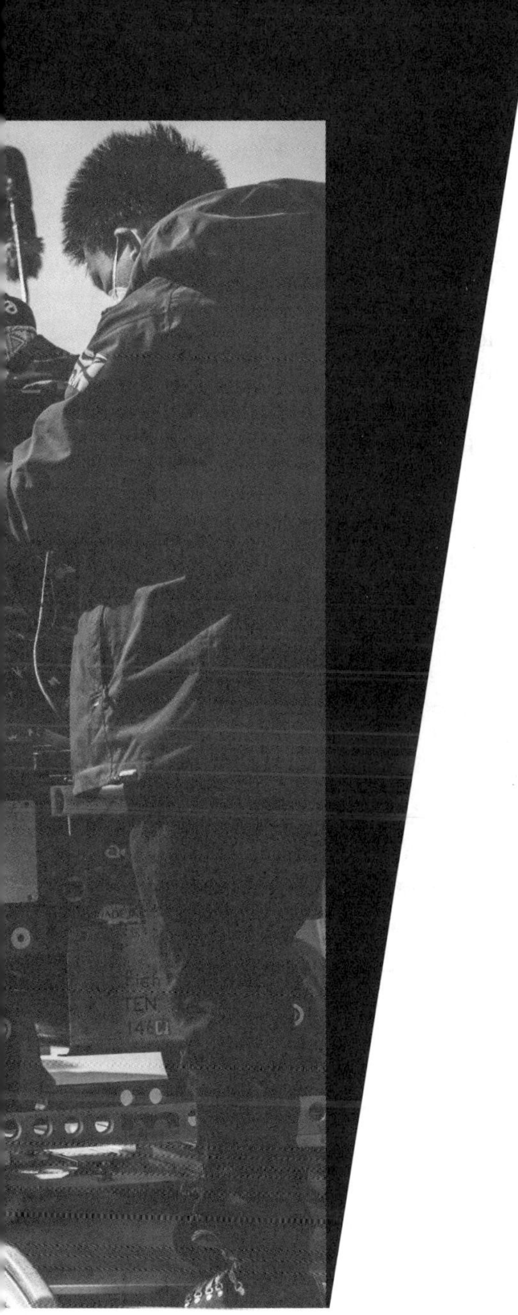

knew this kind of film has a more limited market, [this being a genre film], so they were aware of the limitations. In the end we were happy with the box office (estimated at about $7.6 million) because we didn't lose money.

Unlike your first film, in *Wrath of Silence* you made use of a professional cast to play the characters, including action star Song Yang and award-winning actor Jiang Wu. Did this pose more challenges for you?
Yes, it was definitely more challenging for me because these stars have a lot more film-related experience than me. The chance to work with them helped me learn a lot. From the start, I tried not to be too controlling so I could allow the actors more personal space to be creative in their own ways.

You chose to have your lead character Zhang Baomin be a farmer who is also a mute, and yet he is also a 'Rambo-like' personality capable of fighting off a dozen bad guys all by himself. Do you not think that this set up is a bit far-fetched?
Zhang Baomin is not really a mute, but a person with some form of speech disability. He's a lone character who

A still from *Wrath of Silence,* starring action star Song Yang (left) doesn't like to communicate, and has been prone to violence ever since he was a young boy. In the film, he is able to fight so hard and so violently against the henchmen of the evil boss because he is led to believe that his son has been kidnapped and is locked in the back room of the boss's office. He's desperate and is willing to fight to the bitter end in order to save his son.

Critics and reviewers repeatedly say they can see traces of Korean films in your works. Can you talk a bit about the influence of Korean films?

In the beginning as a young filmmaker, I was more curious about mastering techniques and learning as many skills as I could through actual practice. But as I matured and after having watched more classic films by masters such as Kurosawa and Antonioni, I discovered the different cinematic theories as well as the many types of cinemas that are available out there, including the crucial elements that make a film truly attractive. And yes, as a more mature filmmaker, I've been more influenced by Korean films, especially crime and noir films, which I'm a huge fan of because they are very deft at revealing the darker side of society and humanity, and they feel very real and honest. I became a fan of Korean films when I was around 25 or 26—a time when my values gradually started to solidify and when I became a fully developed member of society. I also became more aware of the many social problems such as social injustice and people who are marginalized. It so happens [the themes of these] Korean films very much corresponded with my own concerns about the Chinese society. So, it gave me great satisfaction to watch films by Park Chan-wook, Bong Joon-ho and Kim Jee-woon. They may present you with a very familiar story, but in the end, you will see a very unusual film. There's something mesmerizing about their movies because no matter how many times you watch them, you'll always discover a few new elements in them.

You have made two crime and suspense films already, and crime is your chosen genre. Do you find it challenging making this kind of film in today's political climate?

It is definitely more challenging, and a bit dangerous [given today's climate] because if you want to make a good crime film, you must dig deep into the inner world of your characters, which involves exposing the darker side of humanity, not to mention the inclusion of images of violence and bloodshed. And the censors have a lot of rules on what is allowable and what is not, so it's not easy.

Yet the challenging environment forces you to become more innovative and come up with unusually creative products.

Of course, it pays to take the time to slowly explain and convince the censors about your creative needs. Then again, I have to say for my first movie, it wasn't as tough as I'd expected when I went to get my screening permit. Essentially, you're given a lot of leeway with the first half of your film. The key is in the second half—how to handle the ending. For *The Coffin in the Mountain*, I added a postscript at the very end saying that father and son both hand themselves in to the police as a way to get around the censorship. You won't see the postscript in my original version, but the Chinese audience in the know will understand that this [extra step] was necessary for me to obtain the screening permit.

You have gained a reputation as a crime genre film director who can make a profit with a relatively small budget. Is this a successful model that other filmmakers can emulate?
When I made my first film, we had no idea we'd eventually receive awards and recognition. In fact, my team and I weren't even sure if we would finish shooting the film. Our strategy was to make the film in stages: first we would finish writing the screenplay, and once we received some initial funding, we would move on to do the filming. But then the money dried up [for post-production], so I took this time to do the editing at home. When I found out about FIRST International Film Festival, I decided to try my luck there, even though I knew most of the films they'd picked in the past tended to be more auteur in style. But *The Coffin in the Mountain* came out a winner, much to my surprise. So, we took the whole process step by step. Later, the film went on to receive a major prize at the Warsaw International Film Festival in Poland, which was an even bigger surprise for us.

The film's success at these festivals helped us find a distributor. Initially, we were approached by several larger distributors, but with strings attached. We felt we weren't ready to make such deals yet, so we ended up with Taihe Entertainment. Taihe was very easygoing, and paid us the cost of the film up front. That was a big help because a lot of investment we put into the film was money Ren had borrowed from friends. So, we were able to pay our debts right away. Taihe also approached

The Coffin in the Mountain not as an auteur film but as a regular drama film because they felt it was entertaining and mentally challenging enough to have a wider appeal, which helped the publicity. The film grossed $1.5 million in box office, so after deducting the publicity costs, Taihe still made a little bit of profit. In the end, we more than broke even, which is the best outcome we could have hoped for.

What is it that you wish to capture in your films?
The many transformations that have taken place in Chinese society in recent years, as well as the metamorphosis that occurs in people because of these social changes. I'd like my work to provide some kind of archival material for future generations, much like the way Chen Kaige's *Farewell My Concubine* did to me. His film allows me to understand what had happened to China at a particular time in history.

Speaking of previous generations of filmmakers, what would you say are the main differences between your generation of filmmakers and the so-called 6th Generation filmmakers?
The earlier generation of filmmakers, despite some individual differences, shared similar grievances against society because a lot of them were trained at one or two of the top schools, and they lived in an environment in the absence of the Internet. But now, filmmakers my age or younger are no longer trained by just a handful of academics because the deregulation of the field means anyone can find a way to get trained as a filmmaker. Meanwhile, the

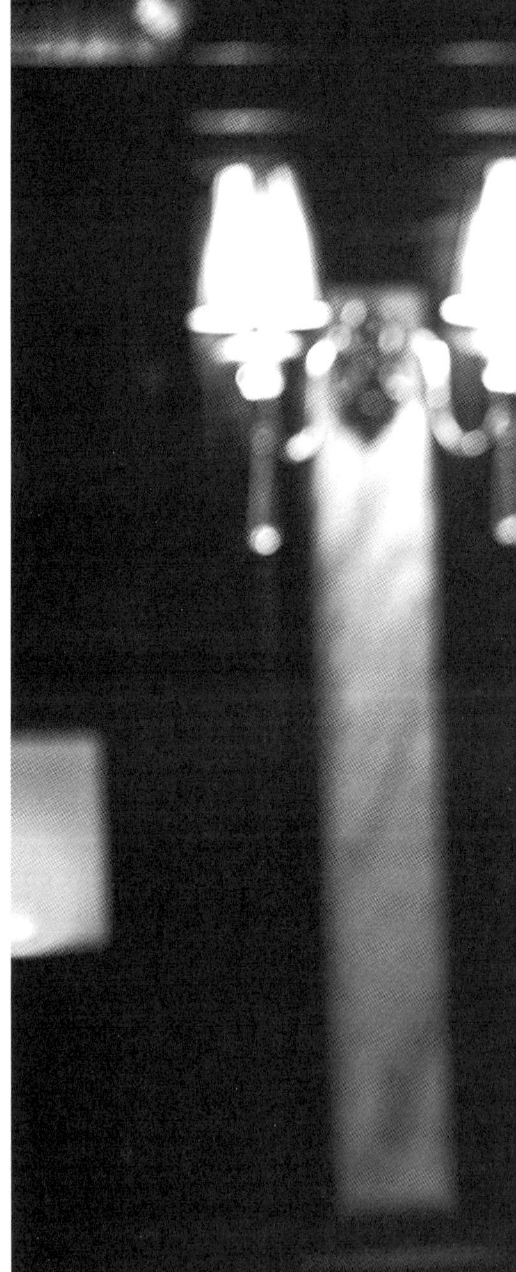

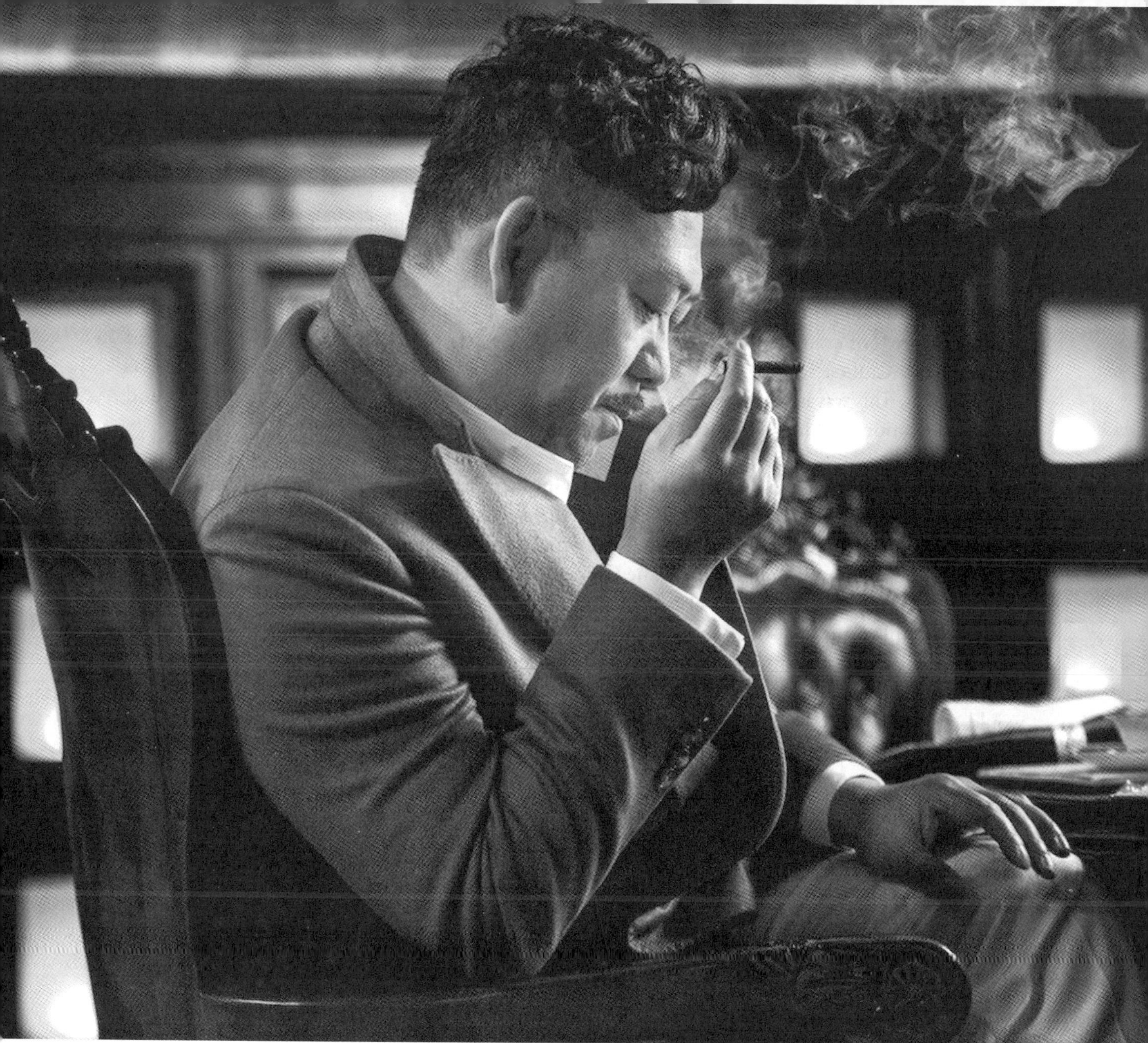

A still from *Wrath of Silence,* starring award-winning actor Jiang Wu.

Internet is now so advanced and the information we receive is so multifaceted that, depending on our interests and individual backgrounds, the differences in our personal tastes have become huge, and the themes we pick can also be extremely varied. We also have more freedom to choose from various types of film genre or medium to express our artistic creativity now, something that was not possible before. For example, Liu Jian's *Have a Nice Day*, a noir film reflective of the darker side of contemporary Chinese society, which was featured in the Berlin Film Festival in 2017, was done as an animation. This was never done before. So, this is why it's very difficult to find common ground in our [generation of] films these days.

And how do you view China's censorship and its impact on the future of Chinese film?
I feel that there will come a day when the authorities must consider making some kind of concessions in order to allow a better future for Chinese film. We've opened the market for foreign films for some time now, and over time, the Chinese audience has acquired a taste not only for the special effects of blockbusters, but also for deeper, human-interest stories created by mid-sized or smaller-sized film studios—this is something foreign studios excel at in making. I feel we cannot compete with Hollywood studios in making blockbusters, and the only way we can try to compete in the future is perhaps through making better human-interest stories. But in order to do that, we would need to relax certain rules to allow more topics and themes to emerge. Otherwise, the Chinese audience may not want to go to the theaters to watch Chinese films.

Meanwhile, there are some Chinese directors who don't worry about passing the censorship at all. They may choose to put their films online for a limited number of viewers, or decide to participate in an international film festival by cooperating with an overseas company, and this will allow them to bypass the requirement of first getting a permit before entering their films in a foreign film festival. This of course will also mean that some of our best talent will be lost to the overseas studios as a result.

Finally, what's your advice to younger filmmakers?
When you make your first movie, you must secure at all costs absolute creative freedom to express yourself. This is your first chance, and perhaps your last chance, to ever do so.

Case Study: *The Coffin in the Mountain (aka Deep in the Heart)*

Xin's debut film is a suspense crime drama in the style of the Coen brothers' *Blood Simple*. Set in a remote village in rural Henan—a province in central China's Yellow River Valley—the story begins with the death of an unlikely thug, which, due to a strange combination of circumstances, links up three separate rural families, each with its own set of complex human relationships, skeletons in the closet and needs for a cover-up. Divided into three chapters and cleverly told in a non-linear fashion with multiple plot lines, the tale is full of twists and turns, ultimately unveiling the darkest secrets of the human heart.

Zongyao, the son of a famously upstanding village chief Weiguo, is desperately trying to get himself out of the clutches of his very stoic and controlling father who seems to be meddling in every aspect of his life. Zongyao hates Weiguo so much he is not on speaking terms with him. On a brief visit back to his hometown, Zongyao tries to elope with his old flame Huang Huan, but ends up killing the local thug Bai Hu by mistake. Frightened by what he has done, Zongyao decides to hide with Huang in a nearby town after quickly burying Bai in a shallow grave. A few days later, fearful that the remains might be exposed, Zongyao returns to the village, only to run into the funeral procession of the very man he thought he'd slain. Is the case closed? No, but—all is not what it seems.

Before Zongyao's return, a charred corpse shows up in the wooded area of the village. Zongyao's father Weiguo, in his position as village chief, has been knocking on every door for someone to claim the body. Huang's parents, who have been desperately searching for their missing daughter, come forward first, believing the body to be that of their daughter. When they're told the corpse is that of a man, they quickly return the body to the village chief. In this way, the body is claimed and rejected a few more times by a couple more families before the truth is finally revealed at the end of the film.

Critics recognize *The Coffin in the Mountain* is not perfect, with many pointing out that the close-to-two-hour drama is overly long. Admittedly, the dialogue and performances also come across as a bit stiff—a problem commonly seen with first-time directors, given that many can only afford to

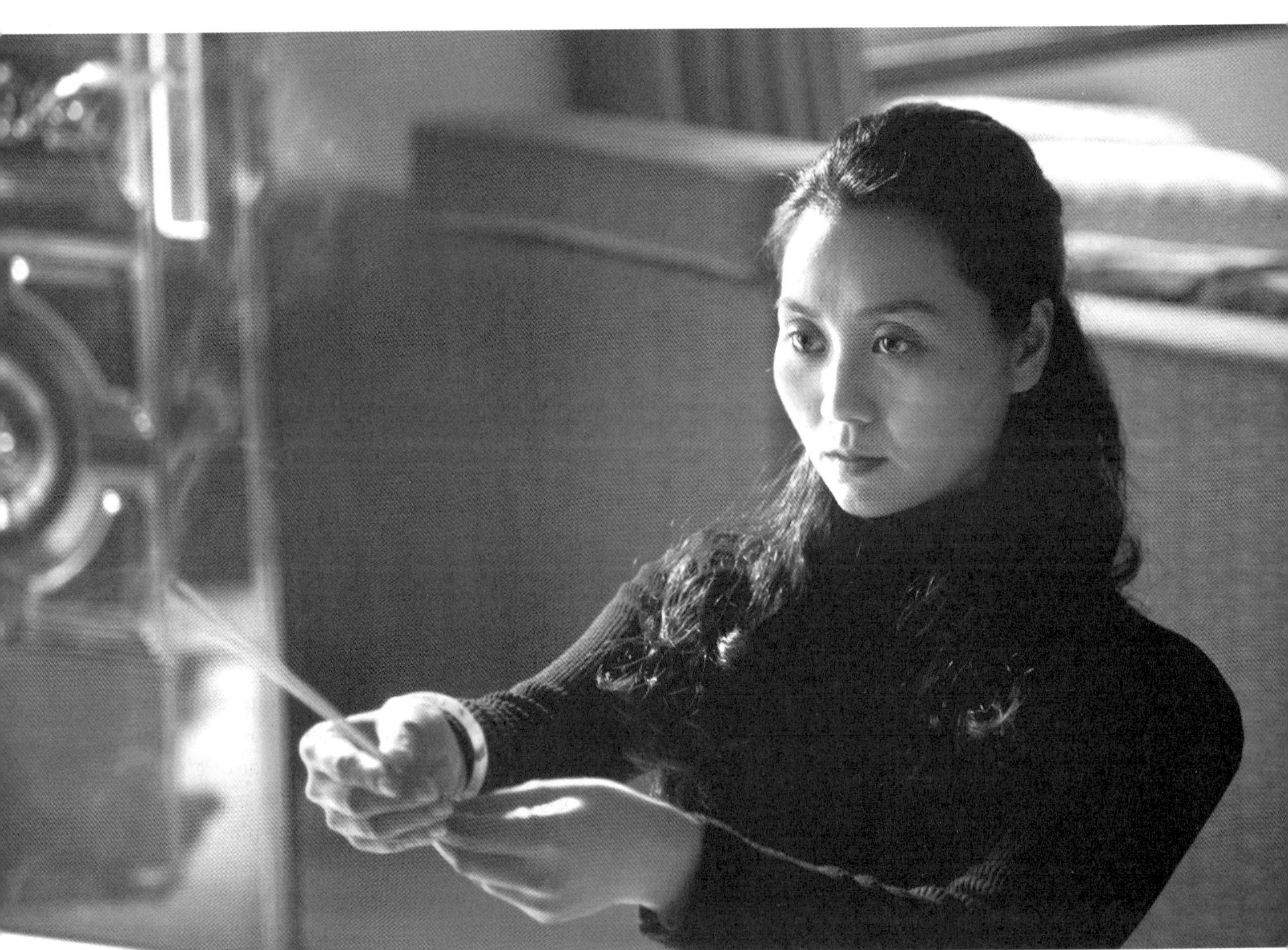

A still from *The Coffin in the Mountain*

pay non-professional actors because of budgetary limitations. Still, the film came as a big surprise to many viewers. What makes *The Coffin in the Mountain* special to many is that Xin has woven an engaging, whodunit film noir by making use of the simple technique of a scrambled-timeline, steering clear of the pomposity and gimmickry that define many newbie, wannabe auteurs of to-day's Chinese-language cinema. Having borrowed heavily from U.S. and Korean crime films, Xin is able to present a narrative that is intelligent and surprisingly coherent, with the characters from each family impacting the fate of the others in intriguing ways. The result is that the ends all tie to-gether neatly, allowing the audience to slowly grasp the bigger picture. This kind of polish is a rarity among Xin's peers from the same age group.

Beyond the central mystery of the coffin, *The Coffin in the Mountain* also skillfully reveals some of the very common archetypes seen in today's rural Chinese society: the overbearing father, the spoilt son, the emotionally battered wife, the cheating husband and the gambling thug—each lurking around with his/her own ill intent. And it is the inaccessible wilderness that has made it all too easy and tempting for normally "good" people to commit selfish crimes. Xin's unadorned docudrama approach allows his characters to become more human and less like caricatures.

Xin, however, openly admitted that he had to make certain compromises to get the film released. The first hurdle was the Chinese title, which had to be changed to *Deep in the Heart* in Chinese from its original *The Coffin in the Mountain* (because the name "coffin" is considered a taboo deemed unsuitable by the censors for use in public) before Xin could secure a screening permit. Xin also had to add a special postscript at the end of the film clearly stating that "those who are guilty decided to go to the police to accept their due punishment" as a way to get around the censorship requirements. To date, the film is still known as one of the most surprising box office miracles in recent years made on a tiny budget by a first-time director.

The Director's Take

What's an independent film?
The work of an auteur, the pure expression of a filmmaker.

What quality must independent films possess?
An independent spirit without the consideration of audience tastes or other people's benefit.

Why do you make films? And who is your audience?
Filmmaking is a way for me to explore my inner world and the world around me. I make movies for those with a similar curiosity about themselves and about the larger world.

What's the first film you ever saw and what were your initial thoughts?
I don't remember the very first film that I saw, but the early film that really left a strong impression on me was *Jurassic Park*. I was blown away by it.

Which single movie made you realize that film is an art form?
Orson Welles' *Citizen Kane*.

What is your favorite film of all time?
Memories of Murder directed by Bong Joon-ho. It's a movie that helped me establish my own film philosophy.

Who's your favorite director of all time and why?
Bong Joon-ho because he has a very distinctive style. Each of his films is full of surprises. They are fun to watch and yet each film takes its subject matter seriously and is executed with great care.

__What in your opinion are some of the qualities that all of the best films share?__
Brave, sincere, independent and pointed.

__What're your best qualities as an independent director?__
Tolerant and focused.

__Name one Chinese film you've seen lately that you consider to be great?__
NeZha by Jiaozi.

__What do you most want to express through film?__
The diversity of the world and the complexity of our humanity.

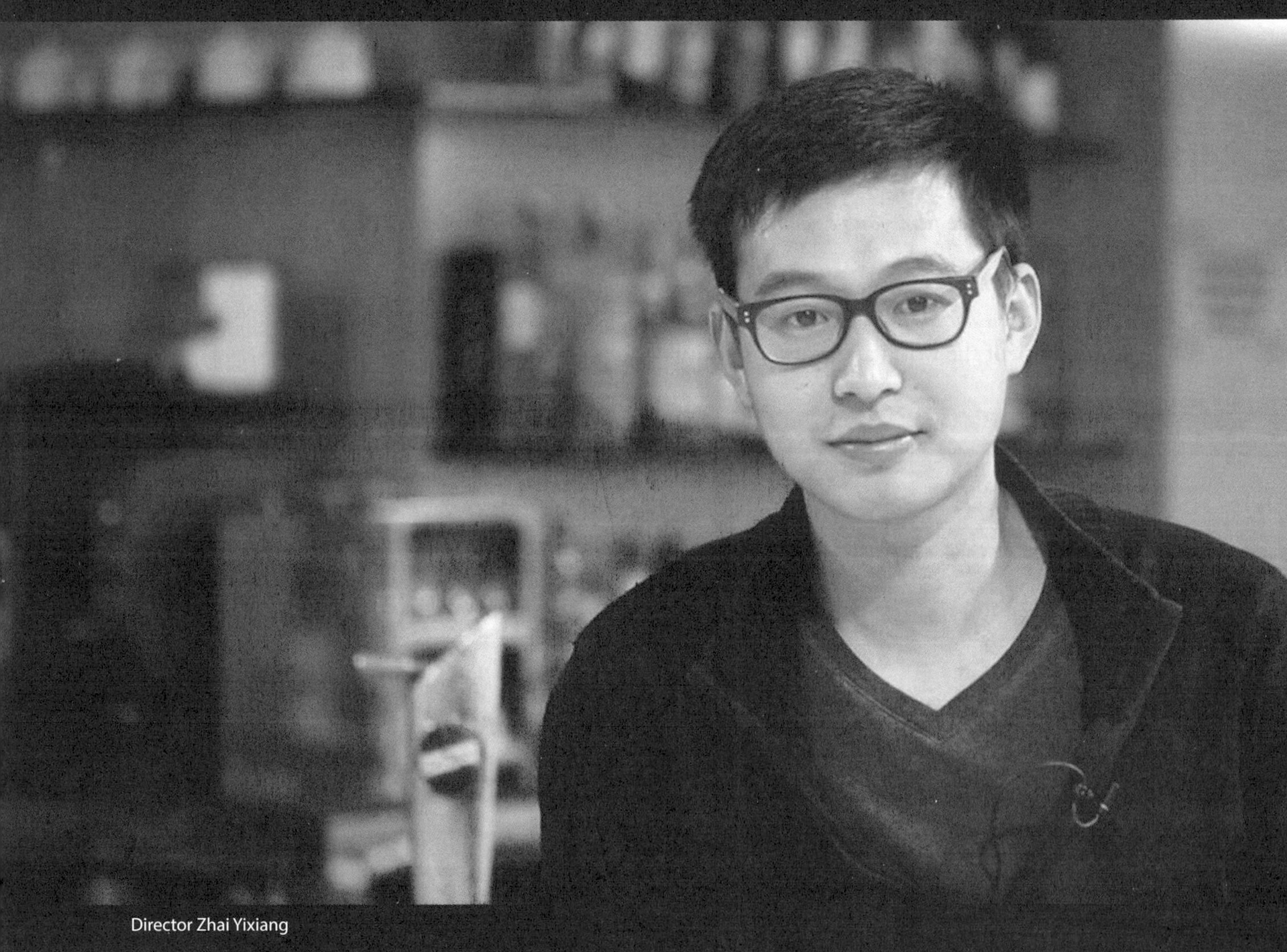

Director Zhai Yixiang

CHAPTER 6

ZHAI YIXIANG
The Conflict Between the Individual and Society

A Short Introduction

ZHAI YIXIANG was born in 1987, in Xuzhou, Jiangsu Province. Zhai trained as a design artist and graduated from the Academy of Arts of Southwest University in Chongqing. As a filmmaker, he was mostly self-taught; his only training was received from a 40-day workshop at Li Xianting Film School (formerly based in Beijing's artist village of Songzhuang). Despite his informal training, Zhai has great ambition for his films, vowing he will let his works reflect the issues of his contemporary society. As a young filmmaker, Zhai excels in using fragments of impressions and moods to craft unsettling stories—a reason why some observers say he has inherited the tradition of the 6th Generation filmmakers.

Zhai is a keen observer and shows maturity well beyond his years, especially in his ability to dissect social problems. The main theme that interests him is marginalized communities caught between rural towns and the big cities. He is particularly adept at using his lens to capture the feelings of alienation and helplessness of rural people. Some critics have compared Zhai's films to those by Edward Yang, and the former admits he has been strongly influenced by Yang's movies, especially *A Confucian Confusion* and *A Brighter Summer Day*. Zhai sees his works as low-budget "auteur style" art films that are reflective of social issues and "our lost values." His narrative approach tends to be much quieter in tone than many films made by his peers around the same age, as he prefers to let contemplative silence rather than blunt words convey his message. "Real life," Zhai says, "is not always as explosive as many filmmakers make it out to be. I want my films to better reflect our real life."

Perhaps in part because Zhai was exposed to a group of very independent-minded filmmakers at Li Xianting Film School, he has a streak of defiance in his use of social realism. This does not always sit well with the authorities. His directorial debut, *This Worldly Life,* about the corrupting effects of materialism on people through the simple tale of a young monk forced to resume a secular life, did not pass censorship and was never released for public screening. (It was eventually made available on a foreign-owned platform for streaming on demand.) His second feature, *Mosaic Portrait,* is an even more hard-hitting tale about rape, patriarchal family values and the unfairness of news reporting, a story based on true life events. The film starts out like a classic whodunit but ends with a Rashomon style of contradictory points of view, culminating into a thought-provoking question that asks, just whose truth, if any, should we believe? This sensitive film hit a nerve with the censors, and his timing for an application of a screening permit in 2018 could not have been worse as China's propaganda department took over the role of regulating the film and television industry in March of that year, and 2019 was a year of many political anniversaries in China, including the 70th anniversary of the founding of the PRC. At the very end of 2020, Zhai still had not received a screening license, and thus far, there is no sign that the film will ever receive a theatrical release in China.

Chinese critics describe Zhai as a gifted emerging filmmaker with great promise. Some observers note that Zhai weaves the damp environment of Guizhou into his visual narrative in *Mosaic Portrait* to help enhance the feeling of "alienation." In so doing, Zhai has created a feature not only rooted in reality but also rich in metaphor.

Zhai has garnered numerous prizes for his films. *This Worldly Life* was awarded Best Artistic Contribution at the 9th FIRST International Film Festival in Xining as well as the K26 Best Feature Film of Hamburg Film Festival. *Mosaic Portrait,* meanwhile, won several significant awards in its earlier stages of production, including the Grand Prize in the 2016 Golden Horse Film Project Promotion and the White Light Post-Production Award in the WIP Lab of Hong Kong-Asia Film Financing Forum. *Mosaic Portrait* had its debut at Karlovy Vary International Film Festival in May 2019, and went on to win Best Art Exploration prize at the 13th FIRST International Film Festival. In January of 2020, it was also screened at Le Festival Allers-Retours in Paris.

Filmography

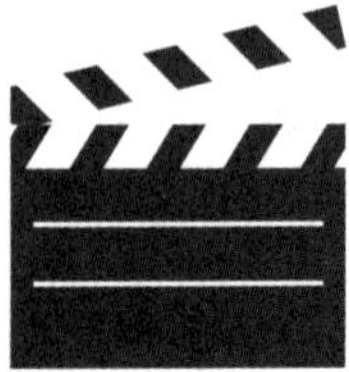

26 Degrees 二十六度 (short film, 2010) - director, screenwriter, editor
My Son Leaves Beijing for America 儿子离开北京去美国 (pseudo-documentary, 2013) - director, screenwriter, editor
This Worldly Life 还俗 (feature film, 2015) - director, screenwriter, editor
Mosaic Portrait 马赛克少女 (feature film, 2019) - director, screenwriter

Interview

I met Zhai Yixiang through the introduction of a mutual friend. We met in April 2017 for an extended interview for the first time at a café in 798 Art Zone—Beijing's hip art district. At that point, Zhai had just completed his script for *Mosaic Portrait,* and the filming was yet to begin. In August 2019, I sat down with Zhai again at a café near Beijing's Third Ring Road, where he updated me on the many trials and tribulations involved in the making of the film. In particular, he highlighted the challenge of working with the censors because the film touched on some very sensitive political issues. Zhai struck me as a slightly shy but confident artist who clearly knows what he wants to convey through his films. During our interviews he did not dodge tough questions. Instead, he spoke with great honesty about the difficulties of working as an independent filmmaker in an increasingly tough political environment, which included the much stricter censorship rules imposed by the new film law in March 2017. The Q and A portion below is a compilation of notes from both of my meetings with the filmmaker and from several follow-up email exchanges.

What was your upbringing like, and where did the idea of becoming a filmmaker come from?
I came from a small town called Subei (in Xuzhou). The place was so small I remember there wasn't even a theater in town when I grew up. Because of school, I went from a small town to a larger town, before eventually ending up studying at the Southwest University (Xinan Daxue) in

Chongqing. At college, I majored in art, and didn't have much contact with film until later. But during my last year of high school, one of my roommates happened to be from a family that video-taped weddings for a living. One day, he showed up at school with a DV camera—an older model that had been handed down by his parents. When I saw it, I just couldn't take my hands off of it. So, the two of us would videotape things around us. We'd storyboard and replay the videos. We started cycling around the neighborhood armed with the camera and began interviewing all sorts of people, feeling as though we owned "a real weapon." We were so excited about these outings we even created makeshift microphones for our interviews. The experience made me recognize the true power of the camera as a tool for expression, and it was hugely satisfying.

I didn't start watching films more systematically until I was in college. It was during my freshman year that I learned how to download a movie. My college would also hold special screenings of films by famous filmmakers at the library, inviting the likes of Wong Kar-wai, Xie Jin and some of the 5th Generation filmmakers to the school. I'd also go over to the film department at my college to watch films every week. Most of the films I saw there were movies by the 6th generation film-makers, including Jia Zhangke's *Still Life*, which had a great impact on me because I felt the film was done simply—it was just the recording of a place, and it gave me confidence that making a film was something that I could handle too. I think the biggest takeaway young people from my generation got from the 6th Generation filmmakers was that making a film was something that was within our reach. Suddenly, I started thinking about film from the perspective of a maker rather than that of a viewer. And from 2008, I started filming a short with a DV camera. It was a film set in my hometown, about a group of children with absentee parents, and how they spent one sum-mer vacation together.

With this short film I started thinking I should enter a local film festival. This eventually led me to meet Ying Liang, who was the organizer of a film festival in Chongqing at the time. It was Ying Liang who introduced me to Li Xianting Film School in Beijing, where they would hold short-course film production workshops. I eventually went for one of their 40-day programs during my senior year. The program helped me realize that film is not defined by any hard rules and that you can make a film in any format you see fit. Ying Liang was one of the instructors at the film school, and he told us anyone could make a film just as long as you're creative. He also taught us how to make films on a shoestring budget, and how to challenge ourselves to tackle difficult topics without fear. The homework I did for that class was *26 Degrees*—a seven-minute-long short film about an embarrassing moment between a man and a woman.

This Worldly Life is about a monk forced to return to his hometown.

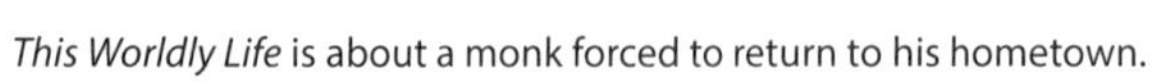

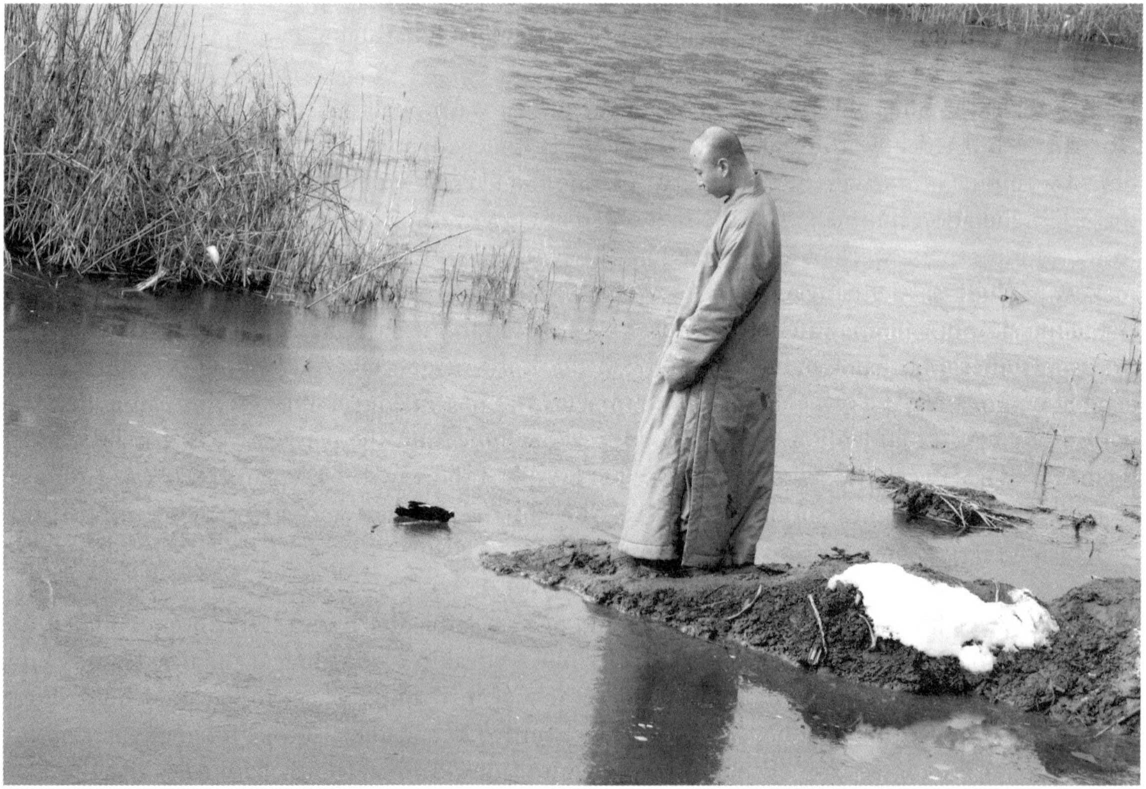

You majored in art and design, but why did you insist on becoming a director? What does filmmaking mean to you?

First of all, a film is made with pictures, and pictures are very direct. I also loved writing poems and listening to music as a student, so when I discovered film was a combination of all of these different art forms, I felt it was the best kind of medium for me to express myself. Once I realized I wanted to make films, I started looking into film schools, though I soon realized I didn't have the basic knowledge to pass the entry exams of these colleges. In China, if you want to get into a profession like filmmaking, you have to start studying the basics during your high school years. I didn't do that, which was why it became really difficult when I finally made up my mind. It was only because I found my way to Li Xianting Film School that I finally got on track with filmmaking.

After you finished your workshop at Li Xianting, did you stay in Beijing to find filmmaking opportunities?

I went back to Chongqing first to finish my last year of college, before returning to Beijing in 2010. I deliberately chose to live right next to the Beijing Film Academy (BFA) [so I might have more job opportunities], and one of my first jobs was working as a film editor for a friend. I started writing the script for *This Worldly Life* while working full time as an editor and director for a couple of new media websites, filming short documentaries about people. I quit these jobs after two and half years, when I finally finished my screenplay.

So, what's *This Worldly Life* about? And what inspired you to write the story?

The film is about a former monk with idealistic pursuits. But the core of the story recounts how the protagonist, after returning to his hometown, slowly loses himself during the process of secularization. The film was half modeled on the disappointing experience of a friend who, after college, had to eventually give up all of his ideals because after returning to his hometown, he was coerced into living a very humdrum life working as a government official, getting married and having children right away, all because this was what his parents had planned for him. I decided to add a little twist to this otherwise, very straightforward story. So, I superimposed my friend's life onto that of an imposter monk I met during a random visit to a fortuneteller's booth.

Is the film's title, *This Worldly Life*, a metaphor about our life struggles—the process of losing our ideals and ourselves as the pressure of everyday life slowly corrodes us?

Yes. It is a film about losing our values, ideals and ourselves. I feel that many young people, including me, start out with dreams and ideals. Yet in our everyday lives, older and more realistic people (including our parents) keep telling us that we ought to be more "down-to-earth" and give up on our dreams in order to adapt to the needs of the market and society. Over time, we become more and more defeated—we follow their advice, get married, have children and buy an apartment. We make compromises and lose sight of our original vision. Personally, I'm in the midst of this process of being "secularized," with many around me advising me to give up on making independent films because of censorship and the demands of the market. It's a real struggle—a very painful process for me in fact. Frankly, I feel our standards and values are very confused right now. We have no religion, and our traditions are cut off from our past. Everything is about what we can get for ourselves—we've become very utilitarian. Even the charity works many people are involved in are all about self-gain.

When you started preproduction work for *This Worldly Life*, were you worried about investment money? And how did you find your initial investment?

Yes, I was. That's why I made sure the theme of *This Worldly Life* wasn't too ambitious—that the story was small enough and easy to understand and that it wouldn't require any large spectacles. I also set the film in Jiangsu, my hometown. This would not only help me save money, but also make my job easier. For one thing, I was able to hire locals to play the characters and rent film sets for less money, not to mention that I know the sensibilities of that society very well. As for investment money, initially, a small firm agreed to put in 80,000 RMB (roughly $11,000) for the film, but they changed their minds at the last minute. It was my parents and my sister who put in the bulk of the money for the film. The film was very low budget—excluding publicity, it only cost about 100,000 RMB (roughly $14,200).

What were some of the challenges you encountered in the making of *This Worldly Life*?

For *This Worldly Life,* I was not just the writer-director, but also the producer because no one was available to do the job. I was about 26 at the time, and I had a real sense of urgency to finish the script and start shooting my first film. Perhaps I was fearful that if I waited too long, I might lose the momentum and the urge to express myself. At that time, my second teacher Peng Tao was very encouraging. I was also lucky that my roommate, Li Chunyu, who was pursuing a master's degree at BFA, agreed to be my cinematographer. Li and I went to my hometown in Jiangsu and completed the shoot in 20 days.

For this film, I hired a lot of local people to play minor characters. I also asked my friend to play the second lead character. As for the main lead, the monk character, I decided to ask Wang Pei to do the job. I discovered Wang from Ning Hao's *No Man's Land*. Wang played a minor character in that film but he caught my eye, and I thought he'd be perfect for the lead so I approached him. Wang liked my script, saying he could really relate to the story because he had similar personal experience and shared the feeling of alienation (after moving back from a big city to teach in a small town), and so he agreed to take part in the film.

But I felt that as a team, we weren't as well prepared as we could have been. I was doing several jobs at once, including scheduling for shoots, scouting for locations, and acting as the art director. And often, we would only begin to look for local actors after we'd decided on a location, which made it really challenging. I was constantly on the phone begging friends and other people to help me find local actors on short notice. Post-production was a lot better. I was able to solicit Zhou Qiang's (producer for Jia Zhangke's *Still Life*) help to finish the job, which was huge. After watching my rough cut, Zhou agreed to help me with toning, translation of subtitles, etc., and all for free. His help was a great endorsement for my film. He said he appreciated the film's quieter temperament and the more nuanced film language, which was a far cry from many of the independent films he'd seen by directors my age, as many tended to be rushed or with melodramatizing.

Speaking of film language, how did you study the language of film? And which directors have influenced you the most?

I think I was most influenced by the film styles of my instructors at Li Xianting Film School, including that of Ying Liang. At the school, there's a strong emphasis on the mood of the main character, the sound effects and the handling of space. [The late BFA professor] Zhou Chuanji's stress on the need for background noise in a film also had an impact on me, though overall, I was mostly self-taught. Initially, I didn't know how to write a script, so I did a lot of research on the Internet, and eventually came to a good solution—using the *zhanghui* (chapter-by-chapter) narrative style of the traditional Chinese novel. It's helpful because it forces me to find the most important points in a synopsis instead of going all over the place with a summary.

The late Professor Zhou Chuanji taught at BFA. Were you ever tempted to go back to study at a proper film school in order to deepen your knowledge of filmmaking?
I did consider going for a degree program at BFA, but after some research, I found the kind of films they require for graduation is all about family and youth—totally not what I had in mind. The requirement just seems so impractical and unrealistic because these themes seem rather empty. I also don't like BFA's stipulation that all cast members must speak standard Mandarin. In real life, people don't talk like that [because many speak in different dialects]. I am more interested in something that is thoughtful, something that honestly reflects reality and helps us better understand our lives and our society, something more in line with Edward Yang's films, especially *A Confucian Confusion* and *A Brighter Summer Day*.

***This Worldly Life* didn't pass censorship. Can you explain what happened?**
At first, we sent the film to the Zhejiang authorities for inspection, and they said the synopsis was confusing and didn't work. We quickly changed our tactics by sending it to the Beijing authorities. Again, they said they didn't like the theme about Buddhism, adding that the religion reference lacked "positive energy" and therefore, was disrespectful to life, so they refused to grant me a permit.

***This Worldly Life* may be a bit dark, but so was Bi Gan's *Kaili Blues*. How was it that Bi was able to eventually secure a screening permit for his, but you weren't able to get yours?**
I started postproduction work of *This Worldly Life* around the same time Bi started with *Kaili Blues*, and we both worked with Wang Zijian, who acted as our producer through Blackfin Productions.

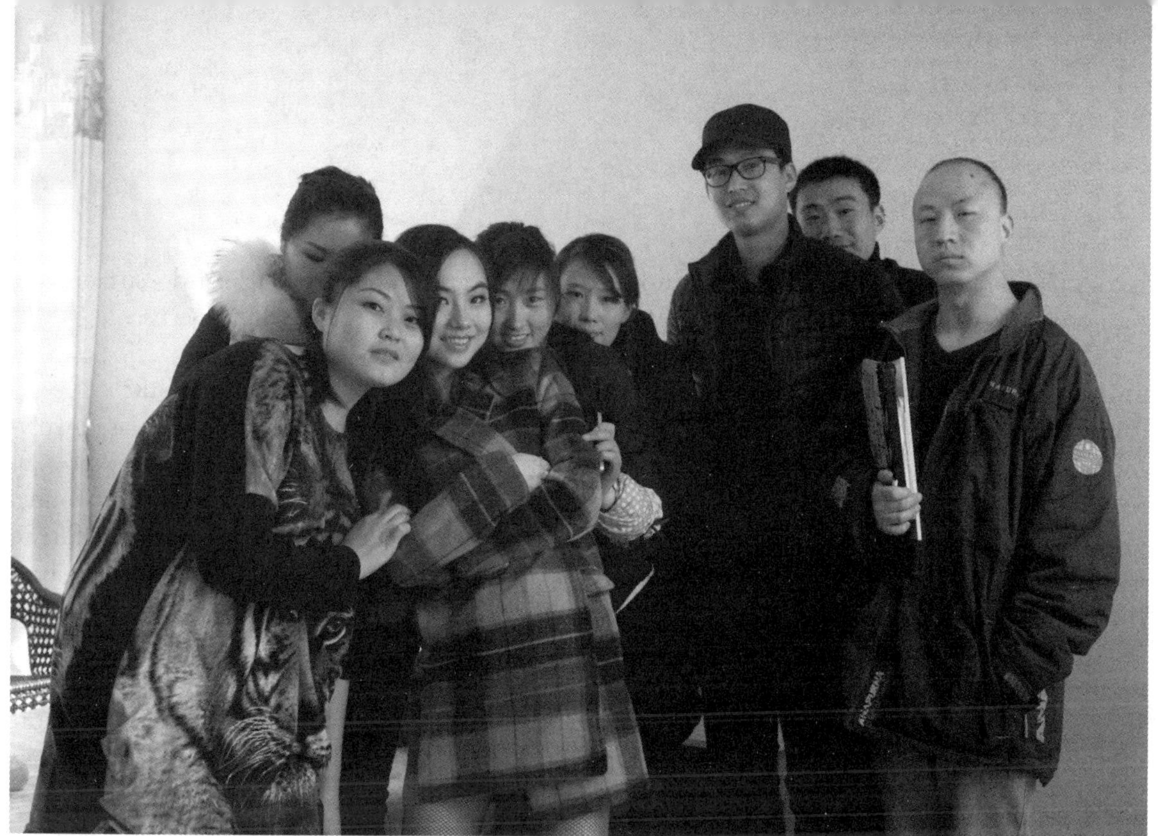

Zhai Yixiang and his film crew on the set of *This Worldly Life*.

We both initially had trouble securing screening permits for our films, but Bi soon left the company to partner with someone (Dan Zuolong) who evidently was much more connected in the film industry. With his new partner's help, Bi soon changed the title of his film and eventually got the screening permit for *Kaili Blues*. I never did receive mine, and as a result, this film never saw the light of day in China.

How did you get to know Wang Zijian and what kind of help did Blackfin Productions provide for *This Worldly Life*?

I was introduced to Wang through a friend I know from my days at Li Xianting. At that time, I had already finished the pre-production work for the film. Wang provided help with film editing, recommendations to film festivals, postproduction work and publicity. Blackfin doesn't provide monetary investment, but does provide help in the form of manpower and film expertise.

You wrote and directed your second feature, *Mosaic Portrait*. What is the film about?
The film is based on a true crime story I read from various news sources—a 2013 rape case involving a girl of 12 living in a remote village in Hunan, but with multiple crime suspects. This case was so unusual that it came as a shock to many people at the time. Not only was the girl very young, the father also made the extreme decision to have the pregnant daughter give birth in an effort to identify the sex offender through the DNA of the baby. The film follows relatively closely to how the real story unfolded, although I added a lot of my own observations through extended research, including interviews with several journalists who reported on the case.

In my research I opted not to approach the victim for interviews for fear I might cause her more distress. Instead, I tried to understand her emotional state by interviewing many young teenage girls of her age. The girls I interviewed expressed a sense of loss and abandonment by their parents once their younger siblings were born, particularly if they happened to be boys. There were a lot of twists and turns to the real crime story, and it took me 18 months to uncover all the hidden facts and the subsequent developments. Towards the end, the male teacher of the young girl—whom she accused as the sex offender, was released without prosecution. An elderly relative of the family already in his mid 70s, instead, became the prime suspect.

A main theme in the film is the relationship between the reporter and the young girl. The reporter is from a first-tier city, and the young girl is from a very remote village. The very different backgrounds of the two form a contrast as well as an echo. In the film, many adults try to help the young girl by imposing their own values onto the teenager, including insisting that the girl give birth to her baby so they can do a DNA test; as well as taking her to a charity organization in the city in order to "heal" her. But to the young girl, none of these are what she really wants. The adults got it all wrong. What she needs is for people to pay attention to her and to see things from her perspective. We often follow our old pattern of thoughts without careful reflection. I think it's more important that we think through things from the standpoint of the victim, not that of society. The end of the film is something many may find surprising because the story is not what it seems.

The title, *Mosaic Portrait*, is an intriguing one. Just how do you understand the concept of "mosaic" in this case?
In real life, and from videos and books, we often come across many visuals that are coded. In my view, a mosaic is a very interesting art piece because it makes us feel like we're seeing the world through a veil—everything looks very hazy. Some mosaic pieces are formed by countless small pixels assembled together. In the movie, the protagonist Xu Ying is a young teenage girl just beginning to develop a sense of self. In her eyes, the world is full of mysteries, and yet her own self-understanding is also very muddled, giving her the sense that she's walking in a "fog." To enhance this mood of fogginess, we used many images of mist and water in the film. As you know, water is a very fluid substance, and full of uncertainty.

The film was shot in Shenzhen and Guizhou. I can understand the choice of Shenzhen, but why did you choose Guizhou?
We spent a lot of time scouting different locations, including Yunnan, Chongqing, before settling on Guizhou. I found Yunnan to be overly bright and optimistic, which is not right for the mood of this film. Chongqing felt a bit too chaotic, and the people there overly positive, which again, is not what I wanted. But Guizhou is wet and rainy, and there's an unmistakable quality of mystery about the place because of the constant hanging fog, so it was perfect for what we were looking for. We spent only ten days filming in Shenzhen, and the rest of the time was spent in Guizhou.

The camera work for *Mosaic Portrait* was superb, which helped your cinematographer Wang Weihua win "best art exploration prize" at Xining's FIRST International Film Festival. Can you explain the photographic technique of this film?
We started the project by spending a lot of time picking out the best locations—we were very picky about the use of space and mood in the natural environment. In terms of technique, we elected to

use hand-held cameras and a camera suspension system for the shoot, which allowed us a lot more flexibility to maneuver the camera.

I understand *Mosaic Portrait* is far more challenging than your first film because it was shot in different locations. Can you talk about some of the challenges you had to face?
Logistically, shooting this film was far more difficult in part because of the much larger film crew. For the first film, there were only ten of us, but for *Mosaic Portrait*, we went up to 80 people. For

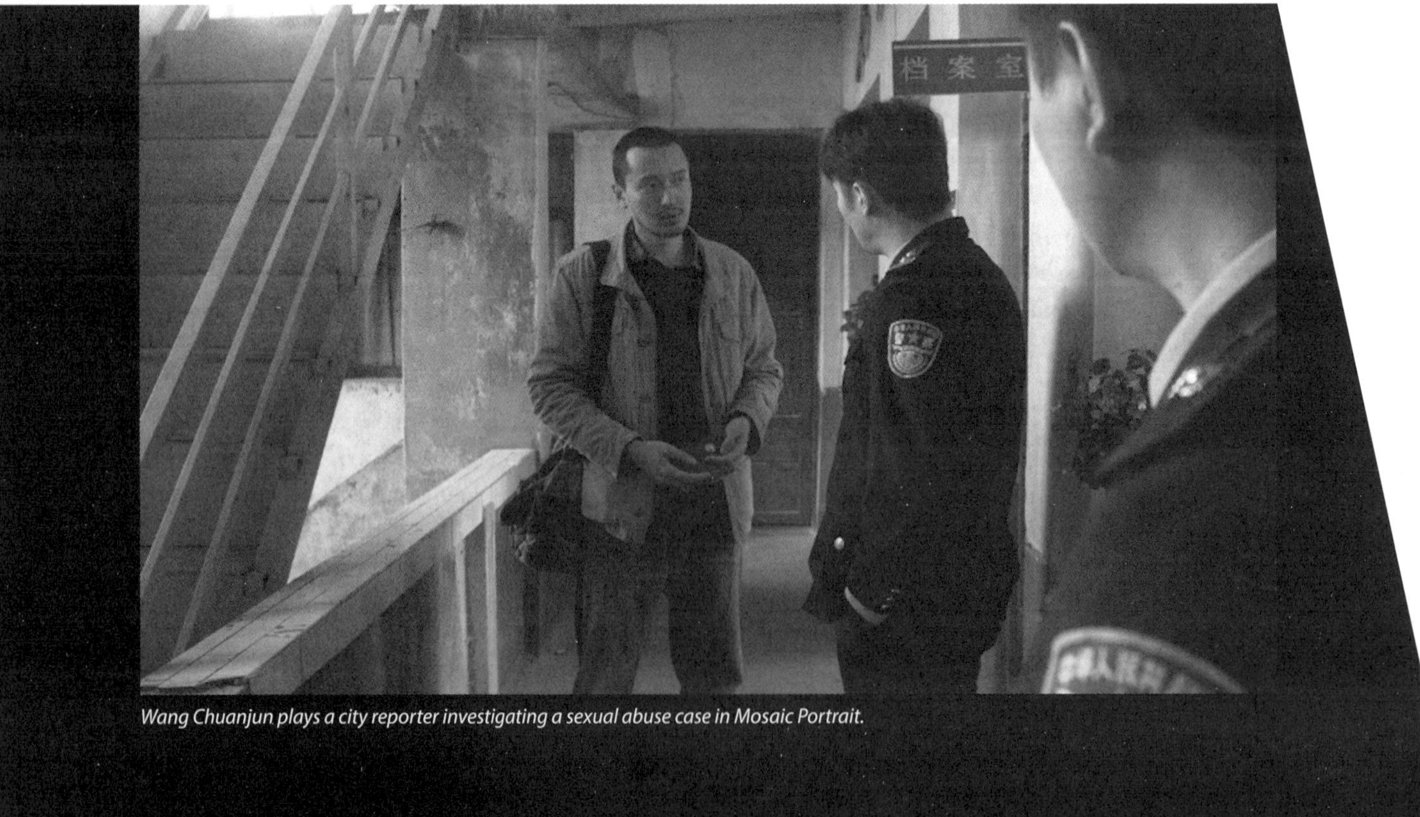
Wang Chuanjun plays a city reporter investigating a sexual abuse case in Mosaic Portrait.

a crew this size, we easily drew the attention of a huge crowd every time we got ready to shoot a street scene. We ended up having to spend a lot of time and effort trying to stop the crowds or ongoing traffic from obstructing our work. In part because of this, we spent 55 days on the shoots alone. For the first film, we only spent 21 days. So, there was a lot of pressure.

We also switched locations quite often, which made things a bit more difficult. Of course, the weather conditions in Guizhou were another factor, as fog was a constant hindrance. But then we chose Guizhou precisely because it evokes in people such a strong sense of mystery, and the atmosphere of the place suits the story very well. Then there's the language issue. I'm not from Guizhou so I don't speak the local language. I had to rely on my assistant director from Guizhou for help with everything. From that perspective, the shoot for my first film was much easier because I was very familiar with the setting and the language.

Another complication had to do with the ending, which is a segment narrated from the perspective of the young girl. For various reasons, we had to expand the last part of the film from 3 minutes to about 20 minutes, which was added to the earlier version much later. The main reason for this was to give the audience a sense of closure about the young girl's situation after her trauma. This part actually already existed at the screenplay stage, but I decided to expand it to give more balance to the film because the story is told from three different perspectives: that of the father, the reporter, and the young girl.

You mentioned elsewhere that there were a lot of things you couldn't say directly in the film because the themes are politically sensitive, and that the only way you could address them was by leaving things vague. What did you mean by that?
The first thing has to do with the real identity of the sex offender—something I merely hinted at in my original version. The second has to do with the reason why many reporters in real life often feel they can't do their job properly. I interviewed two journalists for the film. One of them said he felt very helpless doing his job because he'd seen so many cases and as a journalist, he could do little to help change the lives of the victims. Yet if you wanted to do a good job, it also meant resisting all kinds of people, including those working for the government, which is exhausting. So, one of the

journalists eventually left and took a job with Alibaba. The current Chinese system makes it impossible for journalists to take a more active role in their jobs because often, they receive orders from the top to stop their reporting. In the film, I only hinted at this practice.

You received several major film grants for the preproduction work of *Mosaic Portrait*, making it one of the most anticipated movies of recent years. Yet the film, now completed, has yet to secure a screening permit. Can you explain what happened?

I completed the screenplay for the film at the end of 2016 and started filming in October 2017. We finished all the shoots in December and submitted the film to the authorities. We spent 2018 and 2019 waiting for the final okay from the censors, but so far, the wait is not over. There was dead silence from the film bureau during the first ten months. Eventually, we received news from them, and the feedback was that "the film doesn't reflect the actual reality of the case" and that it is "overly dark and pessimistic." The authorities also didn't like the fact that I'd portrayed the police department and the school in question in a very "passive, non-cooperative way." They wanted me to change things here and there, and I am under a lot of pressure trying to work things out with them. I'm struggling to find a way to keep my original message intact without losing my chance of securing a screening permit [this time]. My last film was never approved and released in theaters, which [I feel] is really quite unfair.

What are some of the suggested changes you've received from the censors?

One suggestion is to make the age of the protagonist, the teenage girl, a bit older. In the film we set the girl's age at 14, but the authorities felt that she should be even older, preferably around the age of 16. In China, the law says when a child reaches the age of 16, she must share responsibility for her own actions when involved in a crime. I found it difficult to accept this proposal, so I ended up deleting the part that mentions her age.

The censors also urged me to add a postscript at the end of the film to clearly identify the sex offender as the elderly relative. This is the one part I didn't make clear in the original version because I was hoping the audience might come to their own conclusions. But now, it looks like I must spell things out according to the instructions [if I am to get the screening permit]. In real life, the press did report that the police had concluded that the elderly relative was the real sex offender. Yet the public could not accept this claim at the time because many felt that the aging relative was already too old and quite incapable of impregnating a girl. In the film the young girl points to her teacher as the culprit, and her father believes her and wants to prosecute the teacher. But the government couldn't accept this because to them, a teacher is considered part of the government, and in China, there's the implicit understanding that in films, it's best that people who represent the government not be portrayed as the "bad people."

My team and I have already spent [a lot of] time waiting for the permit, and something needs to be done. I know [adding the postscript] would only make the audience laugh because I trust the viewers in the know to figure out on their own who the real sex offender is. But with this demand from [the censors looming], there's really not a whole lot that I can do now.

Are you suggesting that the elderly relative might be a scapegoat in real life?
He may well be a scapegoat framed to take the blame. This is one of the possibilities I would like viewers to consider. Another suspect is the young teenage boy who travels around town with the protagonist on a motorcycle. The original point of the film is to leave lots of room for people's imagination so they can arrive at multiple conclusions on their own.

Mosaic Portrait **was screened at FIRST International Film Festival in July (2019). What kind of responses did you receive from the audience?**
At the festival, some viewers wanted to know the identity of the real rapist. When I told them that it doesn't matter because it's not the point of the film, they refused to accept this. I think many of us are just too conditioned by the habit of wanting to know about the "truth."

You wrote the screenplay in 2016, and at the time, the political climate was more relaxed. Would you say it was the relatively easy-going mood that prompted you to take on this more politically sensitive film project at the time?
Yes. In those days, I was very optimistic. I certainly didn't expect to run into so many problems. I never thought [the political issues I touched upon in the film] could create such difficulties. I cer-

tainly didn't consider all the things that could have gone wrong. My only thoughts were to get the movie out as soon as possible. Maybe I was a bit naïve.

In the end, what message do you want to bring to the audience through this film?
Shortly after I finished making *This Worldly Life*, I started reading the news in earnest in an attempt to better understand our society. I noticed a lot of the news that we read tends to be full of contradictions. Worse, often a story can swing from one extreme to the next. That's when I realized the way we understand our world has undergone great changes, which also profoundly affects the way we relate to each other.

These days, we read and digest the news very quickly, before swiftly relaying it to our friends through social media. Yet I wonder what the news-consumers might think if they realized a lot of the so-called "facts" often turn out to be totally different because there is so much that's buried beneath the surface. The so-called "truth" is very elusive because there is a lot of background stuff that's hidden. Behind the scenes there are many people with different agendas, each making it impossible for the "truth" to come out. Besides, there are always different perspectives to a story. Yet do people really have the patience or interest to follow through with the whole truth? I have my doubts. I feel many people are only interested in "the moment." They only look for the kind of answers they wish to see, or whatever catches their eye at the time.

I wanted to make the film to help us reflect on how modern people read the news and how we relate to each other. In the end, other than those who are around us, the only way we find out about others is through the explosive reports spread through the Internet. Such news is very sensational, and often full of conflicting sources. I think some of it you could even call fake news.

In the film, you also tackle the theme of the disengagement of our human relationships. Can you elaborate on that?
There's a tendency for our human relations to become more diminished in our contemporary society. In the film, we see many people having trouble getting close to one another, or finding ways to really

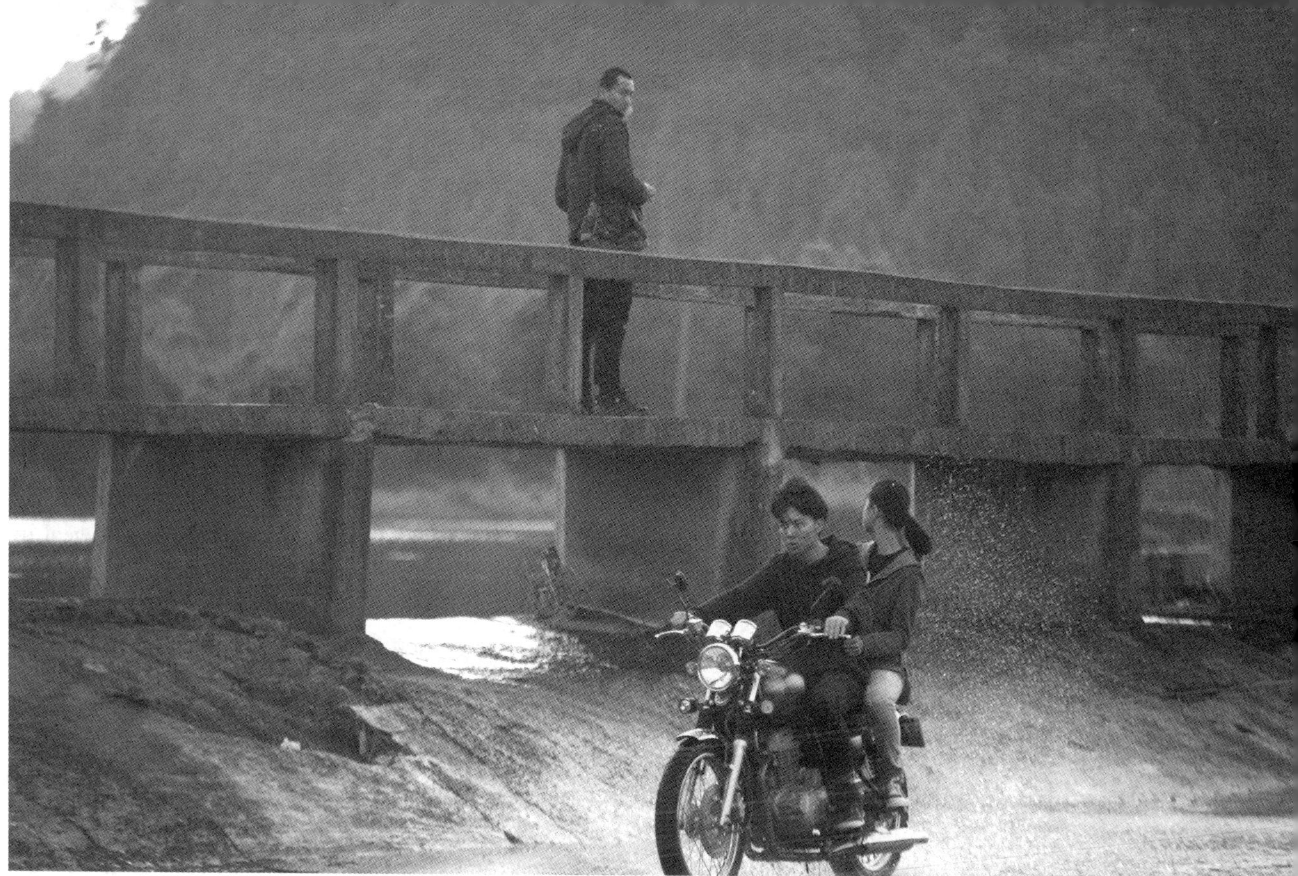

Mosaic Portrait is also a story about the relationship between a city reporter and a village girl.

communicate. This is seen in the estranged relationship between the girl and her father, and between the parents. These relationships form a sharp contrast to her much happier friendship with her gang of friends who ride together on motorcycles to steal postal packages as a form of entertainment.

The proliferation of overnight deliveries of parcels to small villages is also a manifestation of a breakdown in communication, which is quickly spreading to rural China. Face-to-face contact has become less and less common since the advent of affordable, long-distance deliveries. It takes away the pressure for many to come and visit relatives living far away. Hospitality and human relations in our society are quickly being replaced by distance and guarded personal space now. We don't want to spend the time or energy to "really get to know each other" anymore.

The city reporter character plays an important role in the film, as the rape case is seen from his urban perspective. Do you think this story would have had a very different ending had it taken place in the city?
Definitely. I found the father's decision to force his daughter to give birth to the baby particularly surreal. Such action would never have occurred in a bigger city. One of the things I want to reveal in the film is also the culture of an obliterated, closed society of a small town or third-tier city, where a family will have been living for at least three generations. Because new ideas from outside are hard to penetrate in such kinds of places, many people's sense of ethics stays unchanged from the rural past. In other words, local people are very mindful of their own image in the eyes of their neighbors.

Your film came on the heels of Vivian Qu's *Angels Wear White* and Huang Ji's *Egg and Stone*, both about rapes of under-aged girls from a female perspective. How do you think your film might complement or form a contrast to these two films, given that yours is taken from a male perspective?
I feel that in my film, I didn't make the "rape" case or the gender issue a focal point of the story. Instead, the case is merely an entry point to a larger social problem of how news is consumed and relayed in our modern world, which is all about *fast-food consumption*. This of course is not just a Chinese problem but also a global one. Yet when this issue is taken in the Chinese context, especially given the earth-shattering changes that have taken place in the country in recent decades, coupled with China's huge urban-rural divide, then the impact becomes particularly pronounced.

You have made two movies now. Do you see an emerging theme that connects both films?
I do. In both films we see the main characters feeling uncomfortable no matter where they go. They feel helpless and lost. In *This Worldly Life*, for example, you see the little monk unable to find a livelihood after returning to society. The people he knows have all changed so much from when he remembers them, and they even mock him when he tries to find a job. In *Mosaic Portrait*, the young girl feels lost both in her hometown and when she's taken to a big city. She never finds a place she

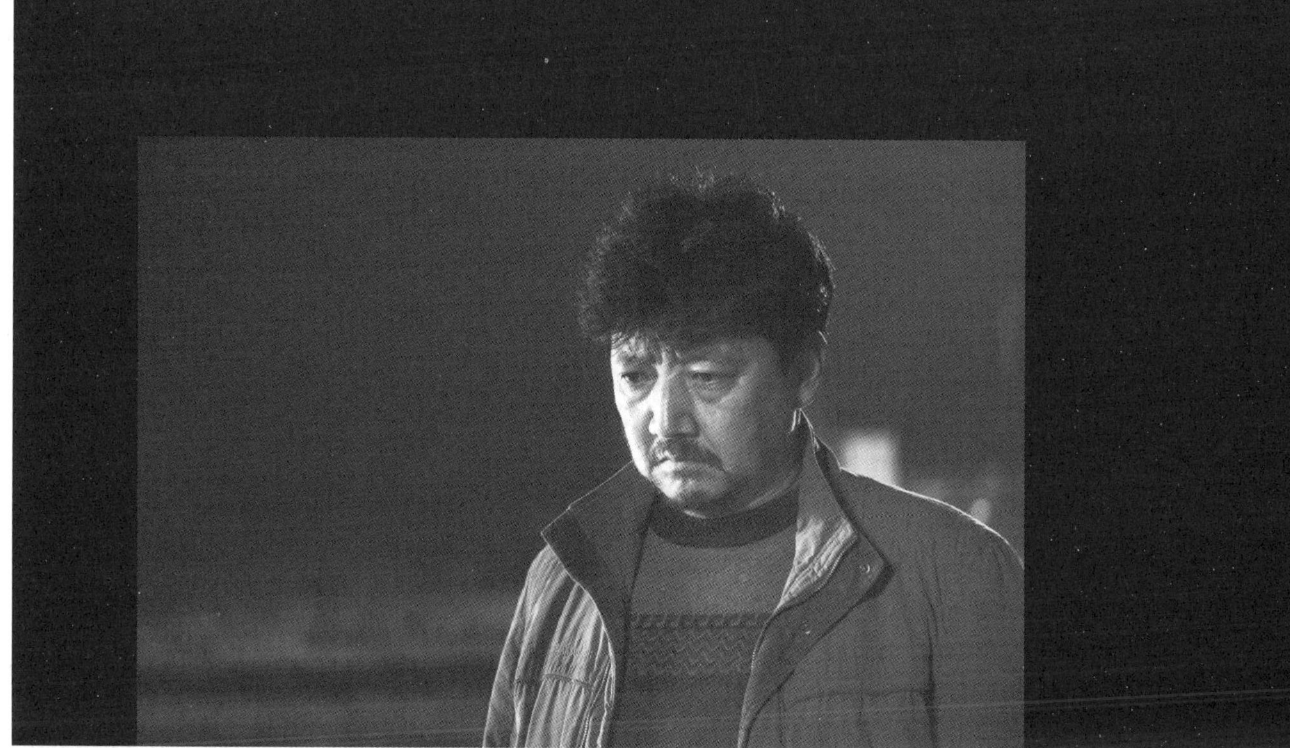

Actor Wang Yanhui plays a conservative father in *Mosaic Portrait.*

can call home. You might say this is an expression of the conflict between the individual and society. I'd say in our current Chinese society, once you've been hit by an unfortunate event, you have no legal recourse. About the only thing you can do is to accept that you've been truly unlucky. You want justice, your rights? Forget it, you won't get them. Just embrace the fact that this *is* your fate.

Your films are about ordinary people living with anxiety in today's Chinese society. Do you suppose this keen concern for ordinary people has something to do with your background, that you are not a member of the city elite who has graduated from a famous college, but someone originally from a small town?
I suppose this has something to do with it. Because I came from a smaller town, I can see things a little more clearly when I am confronted with the contrast between the well-heeled capital city folks and the parts of China where people have far fewer resources. I also feel that people who are raised in rural

183

China tend to have more space to think things through than city people because we are not overloaded with stimulation or temptations. In the village where I grew up, we didn't even have TVs.

Have you started working on a new project?
Yes, I have started writing the script for my third film. It's about a young teenager forced to go and study abroad because he lacks a proper family registration. The story involves the education structure as well as China's family registration system. Given my current difficulties (with the film bureau), I am hesitant about this new project. This story wouldn't have been very sensitive just a couple of years ago. But things have changed. Now I'm left wondering how to proceed. It poses too many challenges. I will finish writing the screenplay first. After that, I will consider my next move.

Does it make you feel privileged that you were able to find your voice through film despite your humble roots and informal training as a filmmaker?
I found my voice through film mostly because photographic equipment has become so much more affordable in recent years, allowing me to produce a film with a shoestring budget of a mere 100,000 RMB. My 40-day training at Li Xianting Film School was another factor. In that sense, people like me from more humble backgrounds now have multiple ways of making it into the film industry, and we're knocking on the door demanding that our voices be heard. Another factor is China's film market has only just started exploding, and at this critical juncture, the system is not yet firmly in place. This means that a ruling class with an absolute say in the industry has not yet been formed, leaving room for some of us coming from an informal (film) background to fight our way into the industry. I suppose I'm one of the luckier ones because of my timing. But then there will always be opportunities. What matters is whether you have the ability and foresight to grab the chance while you can.

Many of your peers are making hybrid films that are half auteur and half commercial. Even 6th generation directors have been making more commercial films in recent years. Would you consider making commercial films in the future?
For me, I'd like my films to at least hold some sort of significance for society. But I'm not willing to make movies to please the market because if you want to make money, then filmmaking perhaps is

not the best choice. To me, a film must convey the individual filmmaker's ideas and thoughts, and it needs to be an echo of the times. This should be the original intent of all filmmakers. Then again, a thoughtful film can also be exciting to watch at the same time, so the two are not mutually exclusive.

There has been a buzz about the rise of a Chinese New Wave cinema in the last few years. Some say this is the best of time for young auteur filmmakers. Do you agree?

I think there will be more and more indie filmmakers coming into the market who are not trained by the traditional institutions. With DV cameras becoming more and more affordable, you'll see more "ordinary folk" or "grassroots" types of filmmakers coming into the industry. What they bring to the table is a sense of freshness. But how independent can these films be? That's the question. I feel from the year 2001 till 2012, there was indeed a "New Wave" indie cinema created by the Post-6th Generation filmmakers. But after that, the independence of these filmmakers is increasingly compromised by the commercialization of the market. Since around the year 2015, with the Weibo and Weixin platforms becoming more commercialized, we have started seeing an increasing number of filmmakers buying "positive" reviews shortly before the release of their films as a way of boosting ratings. Of course, good ratings will translate into better box office earnings. In terms of the so-called rise of the "New Wave" art films, I don't think there have been any since 2012 because after Songzhuang [of Beijing] was dismantled as an art village, indie filmmakers have not been able to form any kind of a community to have meaningful exchanges. If you can't form a community or a group, then you can't form any "waves."

What's your view about the future of Chinese independent cinema?

I'm pretty pessimistic about the future. There are only two ways for young filmmakers to make films now: one is to respond to investors' active recruitments to become part of the commercial industry, making movies either for the Internet or the cinema circuits. But then you will become nothing but a tool in the big moneymaking machine, and it doesn't make you feel very good as a filmmaker. The other way is for you to look for investors who might be interested in your first films. I have a friend who is making his directorial debut about human relationships that are a bit out of the norm. So far, no investors are willing to invest in his film, which is forcing him to rethink the project. He is becoming very discouraged and has lost all confidence. [With the new, stricter censorship rules], even not-for-profit companies such as Blackfin Productions and Heaven Pictures are now hoping the films they support will pass censorship requirements. These days, several companies and investors may come together to invest in a single film. That way, they can minimize their losses.

There is also the option of making Internet films. These projects tend to be comedies, crime films, or sci-fi flicks—it's all about moneymaking. The quality of such films also tends to be very low, as speed is the key. Often, an Internet film has to be completed in three to five days, and the budget is capped at 1 million RMB or less. But when people become used to making low quality films for a living, they lose sight of their own original vision after a while. From observing other filmmakers, I have noticed that few are able to make thoughtful films after they have taken part in making Internet movies.

Case Study: *This Worldly Life*

In many ways, Zhai's directorial work *This Worldly Life* is reminiscent of the narrative style established by the 6th Generation film master Jia Zhangke. Shot entirely in Subei of Jiangsu Province, the film is a tale about people slowly losing their footing in their fast-changing rural environment. The former monk character, Shuangquan, starts out as a person with principles and ideals. Unable to accept his temple being relegated to a tourist site, he decides to return to his hometown Subei in Zhejiang Province to start life anew, only to find his hometown an alienating world beyond his recognition, as it has undergone seismic transformations during his absence.

Not only does Shuangquan find the many worldly habits of men disgusting, he is also shocked to find his hometown, once a quiet village, is now reduced to a large junkyard filled with debris from demolished buildings. Even his former high school has not been spared this sad fate. Worse, Shuangquan cannot find any job in the village because he has no marketable skills in the fast-changing times; his only option is to temporarily take over a dusty abandoned barbershop to earn some small change. At first, Shuangquan tries to keep his distance from the many temptations.

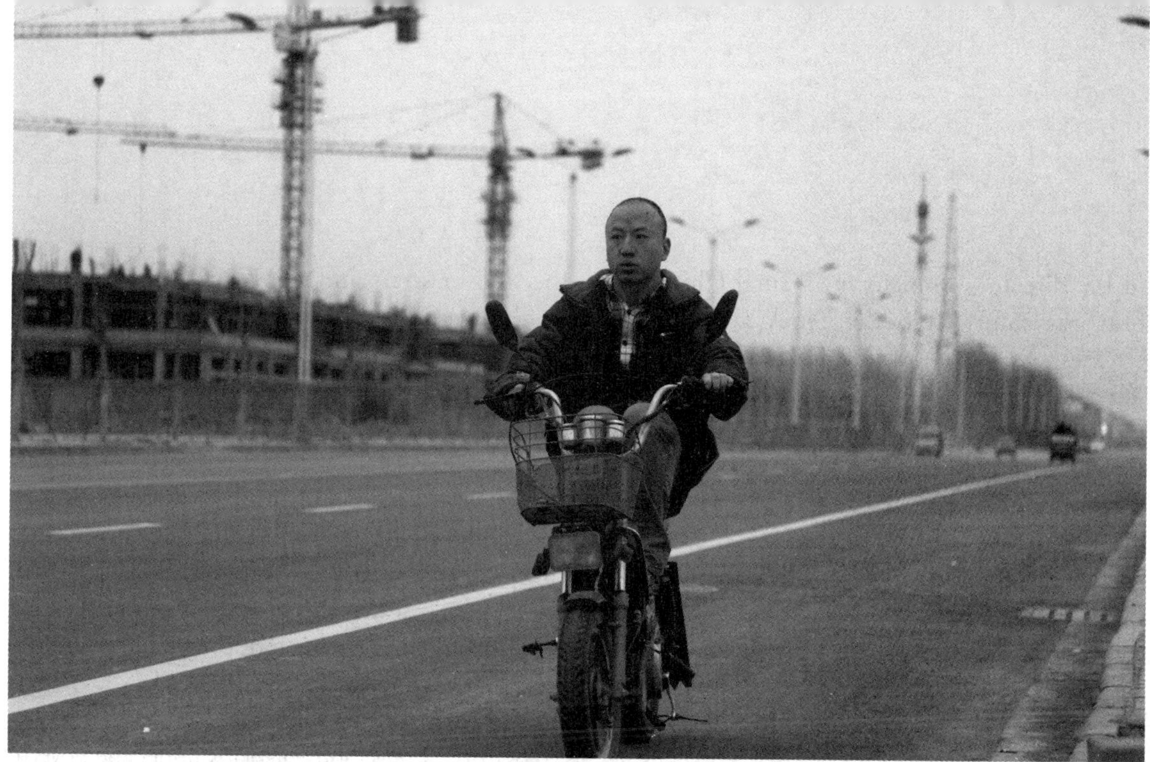

Former monk Shuangquan slowly loses his moral compass in *This Worldly Life*.

A chance meeting, however, leads him to a former classmate Lao Gou, now a small-time thug. Gou opens his eyes to a whole new world of corruption, violence and materialism. One thing leads to another, and before he knows it, Shuangquan is well on his way to becoming a gang member in his own right, breaking all of his religious vows in the process.

In some ways, Shuangquan is a character that reminds us a lot of Xiao Wu in Jia Zhangke's *Xiao Wu* (aka *Artisan Pickpocket*). Like Xiao Wu, Shaungquan finds the village folks' many new ways of maneuvering life vulgar and distasteful, as these people make earning money their absolute top goal. And both characters find themselves strangers in their own backyards, as they become quickly forsaken by society, including by the women they have feelings for. Similarly, the mood of Zhai's film also resembles *Xiao Wu*—like the latter, *This Worldly Life* is very slow-paced and is also filmed in the director's hometown in rural China. Even the shower scene and the KTV sequence in the film are reminiscent of those in *Xiao Wu*, making the film almost a cinematic tribute to Jia's work.

Yet as a work of social commentary, *This Worldly Life* tries to push the envelope further by asking more deliberate questions. One such question is: "What do you believe in?" which comes out of a little girl's mouth in a church scene. The protagonist, his beliefs shaken daily by the corrupting effects of the money worshippers around him, can't say for sure. Yet he finds himself the envy of Lao Gou, who says to him one night, "At least you have Buddha. I have no beliefs, and life is meaningless. But what else can I do, other than drifting along?" In this way, Zhai implies it is this lack of beliefs and spiritual support that allows Lao Gou and his buddies to think that it's okay to extort money and beat people up for a living; and for Juzi, Shuangquan's love interest, to believe she has no choice but to sell her body for some hard cash so that she can feel more secure in life.

Another point that Zhai tries to make pertains to the colossal rural development plans under the government's aggressive "reconstruction movement," which it pushed onto many small towns like Subei. The programs swept through rural China like a hurricane, uprooting not just old buildings and familiar structures in their path, but local people's core beliefs and traditional values. The wasteland Shuangquan first discovers when he returns to his hometown, in many ways, is a metaphor of the spiritual state of the local people. Although Zhai does not explicitly state it, there is the strong suggestion that these government programs often do not benefit individuals, no matter what the government's original intentions may be.

The Director's Take

What's an independent film?
They are films that can reflect the reality of our contemporary society. They are creative and liberated in the ideas they convey.

Why do you make films? And who is your audience?
Film is a comprehensive art that combines several art forms, which makes it more exciting than any one particular creative medium. I'm still on the road of finding my audience—those who'd appreciate my voice.

What was the first film that you saw and what were your initial thoughts?
I saw *Crouching Tiger, Hidden Dragon* in the small town where I grew up, and I remember thinking, it seemed very different from other Hong Kong *kungfu* movies that I'd seen before.

Which single movie made you realize that film is an art form?
Wong Kar-wai's *In the Mood for Love*.

What is your favorite film of all time?
Yi Yi by Edward Yang. It reflects a life philosophy that's uniquely Chinese.

Who's your favorite director of all time and why?
Edward Yang, because he cared about those who lived during his lifetime, and particularly about their spiritual life.

What in your opinion are some of the qualities that the best films all share?
The best films are always about people and life itself.

What's your best quality as an independent director?
That I care about life and the meaning of existence.

What's the title of the best Chinese film you've seen in recent years?
The Elephant Sitting Still (2018) by Hu Bo.

What is it that you most want to express through your films?
My feelings about this world.

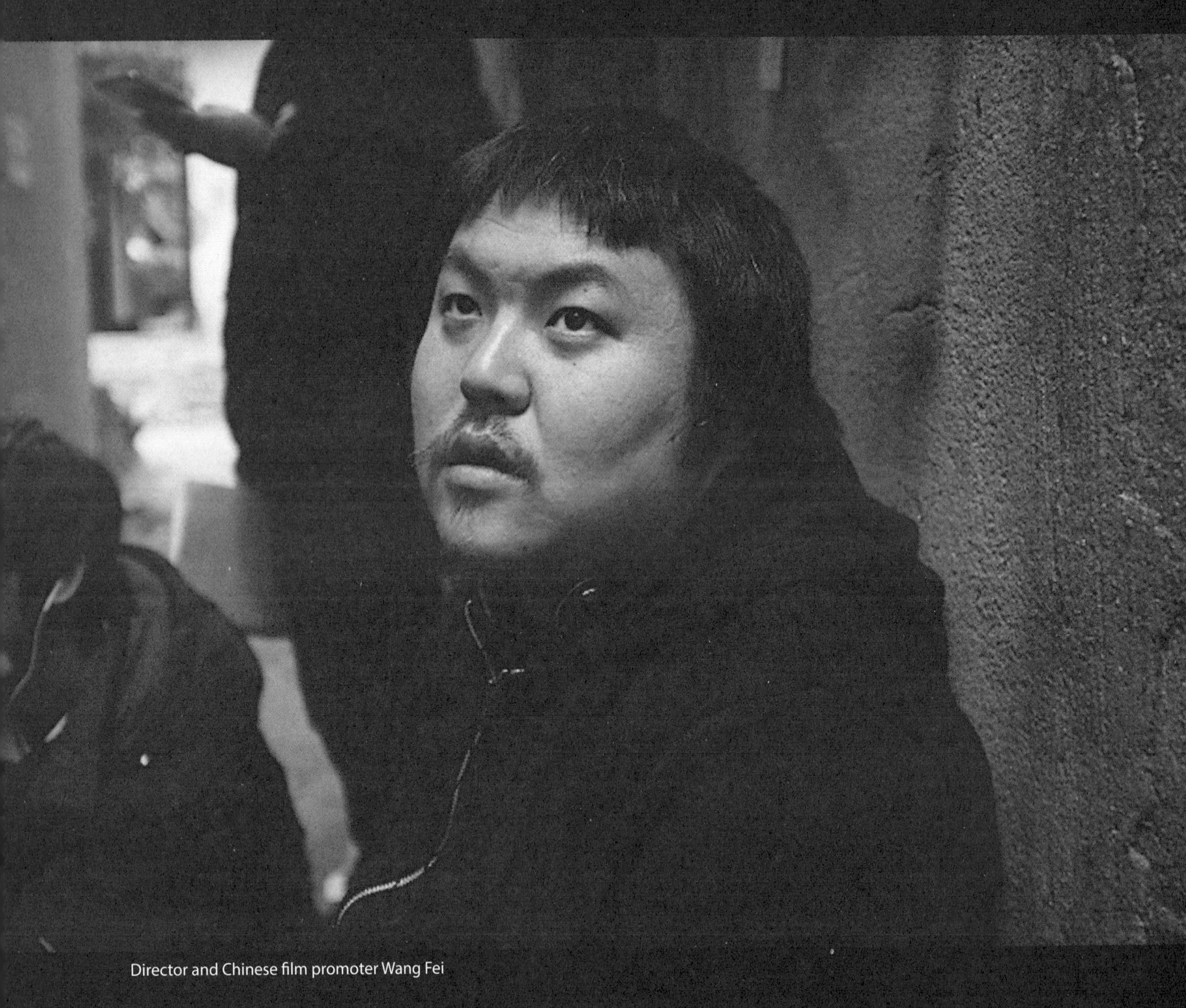

Director and Chinese film promoter Wang Fei

WANG FEI

China's 2017 Film Law and Its Implications

Introduction

WANG FEI (aka Wang Feifei), better known as a millennial co-curator for the Chinese Independent Film Festival (CIFF) and for Xining's FIRST International Film Festival, is a graduate of the Nanjing University of the Arts, with a degree in screenwriting. Between 2012 and 2018, he worked as a co-curator at the now defunct CIFF. A filmmaker in his own right, he made his directorial debut in 2017 with *From Where We've Fallen*—an urban drama of intersecting tales of apathy, greed, jealousy and infidelity among members of a new wealthy class born in contemporary capitalist China. The film premiered in the New Directors' Section at the San Sebastián Film Festival. Wang continues to work as a programmer and curator at FIRST International Film Festival.

Interview

I first met Wang Fei at a film-screening at Beijing's One-Way Street Bookstore in 2016. The following month, I sat down and had an extended talk with him about his thoughts on recent film trends with emerging directors and his interpretation of the new film law. I kept in touch with Wang until I left Beijing towards the end of 2017. In the summer of 2019, we met again during a follow-up research trip to Beijing, and we continued our conversation where we left off. The following interview was compiled from my two principal meetings with him in 2017 and 2019.

What are some of the biggest changes you've noticed in China's 2017 Film Law?
One of the more obvious changes is that the "screenplay approval" step is now changed to that of "filing of film outline." In the past, filmmakers needed to get their full script approved before shooting started. After March 2017, this step has been simplified so films dealing with non-polit-

ical or historical subjects only need to file an outline (minimum 1,000-words) on the official website. Once the outline is approved, shooting can start immediately. Those making more sensitive films on topics such as history, social unrest, religion and diplomatic relationships, however, still need to send full scripts for pre-approval.

Once the film is finished, you then need to submit it for content inspection to receive the "dragon logo." Obtaining the "dragon logo," （龙标） or content permit, is the first of two steps needed to secure a full screening permit. Many people mistake the "dragon logo" for the screening permit, but this is not the case. Once the "dragon logo" is granted, a director must then submit the film for a "technicality" inspection （技术审查）, which involves checking the quality of the sound, image, recording, lighting, etc. Only when a director has passed both content and technical inspections can he/she obtain the screening permit （公映许可证）.

Regarding the "dragon logo," another change has to do with exhibiting films overseas. Before 2017, filmmakers were able to take part in international film festivals as long as they secured a "dragon logo." Now the rules are stricter; in addition to a "dragon logo," filmmakers must also apply for an overseas participation permit.

What are some of the distinguishing features that separate 6th Generation directors from the *balinghou* filmmakers who have come of age in the last decade?
In the 80s, directors were more willing to push boundaries because in those days, the commercial sector wasn't established, and there was only the state-funded system. And those who didn't want to join the state system went underground to make renegade films. Wang Xiaoshuai, Lou Ye and Zhang Yuan were amongst the more famous underground filmmakers from that period.

Things have changed dramatically since the late 90s. These days, with China likely to become the world's largest film market, studios work very hard to attract new talent. The normal path is for a novice director to start with a small budget first film with a distinctive "auteur" style. But as soon as he or she has gained some recognition, they are immediately gobbled up by an industry hungry for a fresh voice. They will be showered with money, a large production team and a star-studded cast.

A recent example of a "successful" film by a newcomer is Bai Xue's *The Crossing* (2019). Her film, like many other recent productions by up-and-coming indie directors, is more "commercial" and far less distinctive in its auteur style, if at all. This pressure to water down individual style helps production companies more easily pass censorship. This type of film also relies heavily on big stars for success.

When the Chinese film market was smaller, filmmakers were more reliant on foreign audiences and international festivals for emotional and financial support. Winning international awards was a top priority, which helps explain why 6th Generation filmmakers in those days were rebellious and more critical of China. Since 2010, the Chinese film market has gotten much larger, changing the incentives and pushing young filmmakers to focus their energy on luring local audiences. As a result, young indie filmmakers are less willing to defy authorities (in a bid to secure a screening permit for their films).

Another big difference between 6th Generation directors and those born in the 80s, or those even younger, is that the later generations have been able to watch thousands more films than their predecessors, including many European and American films, thanks to the Internet and online film-viewing platforms. Many of these younger filmmakers are really viewers-turned-directors. Having watched such a large volume of films, they have a better understanding of film language and are more apt to understand intuitively what younger audiences want.

I noticed quite a few younger indie directors tend to lose their balance once they start making commercial films, and the quality of their works often takes a big dive. What are some of the reasons behind this?
Like I said earlier, many younger indie directors start out as "auteurs." When they shift to commercial films, especially if they face pressure to work with big stars, their works may suffer because many lack experience working with a professional, star-studded cast, and just don't know how to direct and control them. Often, the stars call the shots since they have more experience and are

juggling tight schedules. Indie directors are used to spending long periods of time working with non-professional actors and gradually mold them to fit certain roles, a very different dynamic. In working with celebrities, many lose the control they are used to that made them a success in the first place. Often, things just happen too fast for these young directors. (The commercial film craze) is rather like housing prices in China, which have exploded in recent years. The end result is that many newbie filmmakers get intimidated and let the big-stars do whatever they want to do instead of actually calling the shots as commander-in-chief. This is called the "Chinese Style of Realism." 中国式的现实主义

Another problem is that a lot of younger filmmakers lack formal training compared with more mainstream types who start early. From attending professional film schools, to working as screenwriters, to becoming assistants on the set, the process often takes ten years before they become directors. For this group, making a commercial film comes naturally because they've had time to learn the rules. Many *balinghou* directors, on the other hand, are more used to working with a smaller team, often one they have cultivated over time. The close-knit team allows them to get around hurdles their own way. Once they're absorbed into the system, however, they quickly find themselves a bit shellshocked at having to work with a mammoth team that is easily ten times the size of what they're used to, and often they don't have a lot of say in making decisions. That comes on top of the fact that commercial films are famous for squashing a director's distinctive personality. The question then becomes, can these directors adjust to these new kinds of working conditions and survive?

Some recent examples of directors tripped up by this commercial shift are Hao Jie, Bi Gan and Zhai Yixiang. It's really hard for newbie directors to balance the three forces: censorship, pressure to recoup investors' money, and self-expression. It becomes especially difficult when studio budgets are easily ten or twelve times the budget of their early films. In the end, compromise becomes the norm, and their later films often become much watered-down versions of what could have been.

Hao Jie, for one, had a lot of trouble maintaining the quality of his third production, *My Original Dream*, a commercial film. Reviews on *Douban* were consistently negative. From *Single Man* to his last film, you see a steady erosion in his personal style and early spark. In fact, one can sense that he has completely lost control of this last film.

I see a similar pattern with Li Ruijun's films. His most recent one, *Walking Past the Future*, didn't review well on *Douban*. I haven't seen the film so I can't judge, but I suspect that it might be decidedly different in style from his previous works (because in part it was made with celebrity stars and a big production team), and this may have disappointed the audience, leading to the bad reception. Other indie directors have also been lured into the commercial sector, including Xin Yukun and Zhang Dalei. How they proceed is something every indie filmmaker needs to think through carefully.

What are your observations about up-and-coming indie directors born in the late 80s or the 90s?
I've noticed that more young Chinese directors are educated overseas, especially those born in the late 80s or 90s. These directors are more adept at making films with a global vision, so I think we can expect more interesting works from this group. Judging from the short films submitted by younger directors in recent years, I see a marked difference in their themes and subject matter. They tend to have a more international perspective because many have been brought up or spent time overseas. This speaks to how these younger filmmakers are becoming increasingly assimilated into the Western world. Of course, even for those who are less well traveled, the Internet has also played a significant role in bringing changes.

One example of notable young Chinese directors is Qiu Yang. He won the Short Film Palme d'Or at Cannes in 2017 for *A Gentle Night*, the first Chinese director to do so. Qiu was raised in Australia and trained at Melbourne's Victorian College of the Arts. He has a refreshingly humble focus on his craft and his ancestral hometown of Changzhou in Jiangsu Province. Qiu has stated his clear preference for making films outside of China where he won't need to face Chinese censorship. Another example is Hu Wei, whose experimental short film *Butter Lamp* was nominated for the Academy Award for Best Live Action Short film in 2015. The film, a powerful look at Tibetans trying to preserve their heritage in the face of rapid globalization and modernization, won some 70 awards worldwide. Hu studied at the prestigious La Femis and LeFresnoy in France. Overall, my sense is that these young filmmakers with international experiences tend to be more confident than their predecessors.

Will the current chill in the Chinese film industry and extreme commercialism impede the arrival of new auteur filmmakers?

No, I think those with special talent will continue to pop up despite the changing political environment. The industrialization of Chinese cinema has attracted so many young people into the field. For every ten who want to make commercial films, there has to be at least a couple who want to make films to express themselves. And even though regular grassroots film events such as CIFF have been crushed, there are other platforms, including the Internet, overseas film festivals and smaller, salon-like café gatherings. There is also the option of attracting foreign investments and entering foreign festivals as a non-Chinese film. Even some official festivals can help nurture this young talent.

How difficult was it for CIFF to carry on as a grassroots film festival after the new film law was introduced in 2017?

We lost our official Weibo account in early 2017, which silenced much of our voice. Before the law came out, we were already trying to stay very low-key. But the new law makes the punitive measures very clear, and we'd pay a much bigger price if we continued. At its worst, this could have meant losing our jobs in the film industry. The cost became far too great.

What can young Chinese directors do in today's political climate if they still want to make indie films?

They can make films outside China and avoid releasing their works in China. They can make very low budget films and release them on the Internet. They can compromise their vision in ways they can still live with and apply for a screening permit. With effort, it's still possible to keep your core vision.

You have worked both as a director and a curator of film festivals. What advice would you give to up-and-coming indie directors?

First of all, be true to yourself and your vision. Be clear about what it is you want to express, and say it definitively. Many filmmakers entered film festivals to prove they are good at making a polished film. But such motives are not good enough, which is why their films are often rejected by CIFF and other film festivals.

Another important point: on your first two films, try to control your expenses because the lower the cost, the greater your artistic freedom. The opposite also applies. The more your film costs, the less directorial freedom you will have. There are no free lunches in this world. Yes, many indie filmmakers find investors, and many companies say they want to nurture a new generation of film directors. But be clear that there will be a price to pay. Unless it's money from a family member, there's always a catch. No one will give you free money and let you do whatever you want with it.

Many directors have complained to me about their rather unhappy experience working with investors. They faced all sorts of limitations and unexpected consequences. While you may, given your talent, think that it's only fair that you should make the film the way you want, investors think their money gives them the right to do the film their way. Several directors told me they were barred from the editing room at the final cut after falling out with investors. Some even lost their director credit on the film they worked so hard to shoot. A large investment allows you to make a film with all the latest equipment and special effects, satisfying your vanity. But in the end, it will likely come out completely different from your original vision.

AFTERWORD
Chinese Indie Cinema in the Post Covid-19 Era

During the peak of the Coronavirus pandemic in 2020, when governments throughout the world imposed strict quarantine orders and shut down cinemas, there was real fear that Covid-19 could doom the global film industry. The Chinese filmmaking community's sense of crisis was even more acute, as the authorities' lockdown orders came down swift and hard. The late January timing, at the beginning of Chinese New Year, is traditionally the biggest moneymaking opportunity for cinemas and film studios.

Many production companies with scheduled releases were thrown into a panic as moviegoers demanded refunds. Without warning, film production company Huanxi Media did the unthinkable: bypassing theaters, it went straight to online streaming with its much-anticipated road-trip hit comedy *Lost in Russia,* originally slated for a January 24 release. And it chose to stream exclusively for free on video channels owned by the Internet giant ByteDance, the company behind TikTok. The stunt, which sent shock waves through the industry, was motivated in part as a desire to springboard its new business partnership with ByteDance. Bytedance reportedly paid $91 million for the chance to acquire millions of new users.[1]

Almost immediately, 23 cinema chains and film studios in Shanghai, Nanjing and other cities charged Huanxi in a joint letter of "going against the payment and revenue model that the movie industry has cultivated over many years… with the production company totally disregarding the interests of others." In a statement, Zhejiang province's film industry also threatened to boycott future Huanxi films.[2]

The movie chains' angry reaction is understandable, with 2019 already among the industry's toughest years as it tried to recover from tax and regulatory changes that saw many shaky companies go belly up. With cinemas closed for the foreseeable future, the exhibition sector was crushed. According to research consultancy Artisan Gateway, China suffered the permanent closure of some 2,300 cinemas in the first two months of the shutdown alone. That's about 12,000 screens, or nearly 20 percent of China's theatrical release capacity[3]

▷ Will the Rise of Streaming Platforms Doom Chinese Theaters?

For a while, online debate raged over whether the direct-to-streaming model would work for other mainstream movies during the pandemic. More importantly, would streaming platforms eat the movie theaters' lunch and eliminate cinema screenings in the near future?

Some observers were quick to point out that Huanxi's move was not easily duplicated. Han Fanghang, for one, underscored in a commentary that China does not yet have a Netflix-like company pouring billions of dollars into original content. Alibaba, Tencent and newcomer ByteDance, thus far, have made little headway in production efforts. This suggests that Chinese filmmakers "will likely remain reliant on theaters for some years to come."[4]

A research director at London-based media think tank Ampere Analysis also noted that Chinese box office revenues topped $9.2 billion in 2019, while digital revenue over the same period was only $89.5 million, less than 1 percent. The director also observed that viewers in many markets are still not used to buying movies online.[5] This explains why major releases, such as Wanda's *Detective Chinatown 3* or Dante Lam's action flick *The Rescue* were postponed until the end of 2020 or early 2021, instead of following Huanxi and ByteDance's lead.

In the first couple of months of Chinese lockdown, only a handful of smaller budget films made the decision to debut directly online. Donnie Yen's low-budget action comedy *Enter the Fat Dragon*, originally scheduled for a theatrical release across China on February 14, was sold to online entertainment company iQiYi early in the shutdown through the latter's on-demand platform.[6] And Yu Miao's bank-robbery comedy *The Winners*, slated for a late February theater release, made a mid-March debut on multiple streaming platforms to include Toutiao, Watermelon Video and Douyin (China's Tiktok).[7]

▷ Impact of the Pandemic on Chinese Indie Cinema

The gradual reopening of movie theaters from late July, albeit under strict health guidelines, and the subsequent surge in box office sales, particularly during the October national and Mid-Autumn Festival holidays, initially offered cinema chains and studios a glimmer of hope. The premiers of patriotic omnibus *My People, My Home*, animated feature *Jiang Ziya: Legend of Deification*, and Peter Ho-sun Chan's *Leap*, racked in a combined $580 million in ticket sales over just eight days. This followed even though cinemas were only running at 75 percent capacity due to social distancing measures.[8]

Yet the October excitement was short-lived. According to figures provided by Beijing Endata Technology Co., Ltd., October's total box office of 6.3 billion RMB ($963 million) fell to 1.8 billion RMB ($275 million) a month later.[9] While Covid might have been part of the problem, it also speaks to a structural issue in the industry. Most major studios tend to release films at the same time—so-called 'hot' time periods like Chinese New Year and October's national day period—undercutting revenue. Given already weak finances, many worried that most theaters might not make it through 2021.[10]

Looking at recent movie trends in China, Li Yamei, Taipei Film Festival Director who's familiar with the Chinese film industry, predicted that big budget films wouldn't be affected too much by the pandemic. Rather, it's small to mid-size films that will most likely suffer. "Without visual spectacles to speak of… these films are easily replaced by the more convenient and cost-effective OTT (over-the-top media, i.e., a streaming service offered directly to viewers)," she said.[11] After the pandemic, with most people accustomed to viewing films on demand at home, it will become doubly hard to coax them back to the theaters, she added.[12]

Li nailed it on the head, begging the question: if commercial films are having a hard time drawing people back to theaters, what chance does an auteur indie film have in this new climate? *Balloon*, by famed Tibetan director Pema Tseden (*Jinpa*, 2018 and *Tharlo*, 2015), may provide a clue. The film, his most pedestrian according to the director, premiered at theaters on November 20, 2020, but lasted only eight days before being removed. Its box office was reportedly only a little over 5 million RMB (roughly $764,000). And its daily film scheduling plunged from 2.4 percent (meaning that for every 100 film screenings at a given theater chain, only 2.4 screens were showing *Balloon*) on the first day to 0.2 percent towards the end of the week despite the director's tireless publicity efforts.[13]

Wisdom Tooth, the prize-winning directorial debut by newcomer Liang Ming, suffered an even more disastrous fate. The film, which took Liang seven years to make, opened at art theaters a week after *Balloon's* premier. But it lasted only eleven days, with total box office a mere 683, 000 RMB ($104,300) and daily film scheduling for the first day reportedly just 0.3 percent.[14]

In an interview, Liang said the film was created for the big screen, including the use of high-definition equipment "so we could highlight the actors' detailed expressions and pick up the faintest sound effects." For indie films, even if they are able to squeeze into theaters, getting a proper screening slot remains extremely difficult. He said he was so disappointed with the box office he decided to put his house up for sale so he could continue his filmmaking.[15]

As critics have pointed out before, China's government-controlled film bureau typically issues one-month screening permits required to release a film in theaters. These permits are generally not extended unless strong attendance spurs the bureau into granting another month. Furthermore, if a film sees poor sales in the first week, theaters may yank it by the second week.[16] This is why artistic films often can't compete at regular theaters. This is the case even for auteur movies produced by experienced filmmakers.

Jean Su, founder and producer at Broadvision Pictures, believes production costs are not the main barrier for independent filmmakers seeking larger audiences. Rather, it is distribution. Distributors are responsible for marketing and delivering "prints" to theaters.[17] Mainstream studios typically spend millions on marketing, which smaller studios cannot afford. Su said indie filmmakers should instead seek out digital platforms given the opportunity to reach domestic and global audiences at relatively low cost. She cites the example of the US, where Netflix, Amazon and others have been touted as the "saviors of independent filmmakers."[18]
If anything, streaming services will likely play an even more important role for non-mainstream films in the post-pandemic world, given the momentum Chinese independent filmmakers have already enjoyed from digital screenings and online festivals. Zhu Rikun, an acclaimed indie film director and former artistic director with the now defunct Beijing Independent Film Festival, has organized several online screenings and discussion forums from his New York home during the pandemic. These include an online premiere of Zhao Dayong's 2019 documentary *One Says No* in late April of 2020 as a YouTube screening, followed by a Q & A Zoom session.[19]

Zhu used Facebook and fanhall.com, a pre-2012 indie distributor, exhibitor and exchange site he re-launched after years of inactivity. Fanhall provided a more targeted marketing venue, he said, adding that social media messaging tends to be too fragmented.[20]

A recent agreement between Elemeet and iQiYi could also help indie films with distribution and screening. Elemeet (dazhong dianying), a platform started in 2016 that elicits viewer interest online for niche film screenings before reserving screen time at theaters, aims to attract audiences to films routinely sidelined because of their limited blockbuster value.

Elemeet and iQiYi agreed in late November 2020 to create more screening opportunities both online and offline for young filmmakers. As outlined, both sides will collaborate in selecting quality films, evaluating them based on artistry, market potential and social influence, leveraging Elemeet's screening on-demand resources in theaters, and iQiYi's online distribution capacity.[21]

Tough Out, an award-winning documentary released in late 2020 about disadvantaged teenagers finding meaning through baseball, ultimately advancing to the international level, was the first film to benefit from the partnership. Other films scheduled for distribution under this model include fiction films *Summer Blur* and *Damp Season*, both well received at domestic and overseas film festivals.[22]

In the past, censors tended to be less vigilant about Internet screening, but experts caution that this may not continue given that Chinese censors are notoriously unpredictable at the best of times. Stanley Rosen, professor of political science at University of Southern California, said in a 2020 interview with this writer that censorship in China could be "whimsical," and "arbitrary" at times, with even approved and scheduled releases subject to last-minute cancellations.

Rosen cites Guan Hu's *The Eight Hundred* as an example. Produced by Huayi Bros. for $80 million, the action film about a ragtag band of soldiers who attempted to hold off imperial Japanese troops in 1937 was supposed to premier on July 5, 2019 but was yanked days before its scheduled release. The film, based on a true story, eventually premiered in August 2020, after cinemas reopened, becoming a commercial hit with reported box office receipts of $434 million.

Rosen said last minute cancellations has increased sharply since Beijing's propaganda department took over China's film and television oversight in March of 2018. This followed the elimination of the State Administration of Press, Publication, Radio, Film and Television (SAPPRFT), the regulatory body that oversaw media and entertainment for a generation. *The Eight Hundred* initially seemed in sync with Beijing's emphasis on patriotism ahead of the nation's 70th anniversary that October, and was granted a *longbiao* for screening. But it was later criticized for being too charitable in its depiction of China's Nationalists, who joined the Communists against the Japanese before being exiled to Taiwan in the ensuing civil war, leading to the brakes being slammed on.

Deng Yinfeng, a director interviewed by the BBC Chinese edition, added that it is increasingly hard to gauge what censors want. He pointed out that between 2018 and 2019, up to 70 percent of his filmmaker colleagues were unable to garner approval for their projects. "These films would have had no trouble making the cut a few years back, or there at least would be room for negotiation," he said. Recently in a shift in tone, "the authorities have become very merciless and blunt, telling filmmakers that they should just forget about the whole thing and do a different film," he added.[23]

In addition to *The Eight Hundred,* several other films were also pulled at the last minute in 2019, including Zhang Yimou's *One Second*, Zeng Guoxiang's *Better Days* and Lou Ye's *Saturday Fiction*, despite having received screening permits. Rosen said the reversals were difficult to understand. "If [a film had indeed missed the mark], why did the censors agree to making it in the first place?" he asked rhetorically. Independent films are likely to face growing hurdles because they tend to deal with more sensitive issues, he added.

Rita Andreetti, a director based in Italy and China and the creator of *The Observer* (2019), a portrait of the prolific Chinese documentarian Hu Jie, believes the pandemic will further erode creative freedom. This dovetails with increasingly advanced tracking of people's movements and biometrics, she said. If anything, "digital control has spread wider, and the measures have been taken in the name of public health," she added.[24]

Future Implications for Chinese Indie Filmmakers

Given all these developments, what is likely to happen to indie cinema in the post-Covid-19 era? So far, film scholar Wang Xiaolu sees relatively little impact from the pandemic. "Many of my friends haven't been working much since about two, three years ago," he said, adding that the sad state of indie film is less the result of Covid-19 than broader structural factors such as the 2017's new film law and tax and regulatory changes in 2019.[25]

While streaming can provide alternate venues for some filmmakers, those who want to stay true to their works "may gradually revert back to the production practices of the 90s to complete their films," he said.[26] The decline of movie theaters in 1990s also saw indie producers seeking new ways to survive, including more partnerships with overseas film festival organizers. "The past experience of independent filmmakers may be renewed, or at least provide us with inspiration for an alternative path," he added.[27]

In the post-Covid-19 era, with cash-rich investors in short supply, audiences less intrepid and censors more vigilant, young indie filmmakers will increasingly be forced to choose whether to reach small niche audiences or take advantage of streaming venues. Each comes with shortcomings: one unlikely to get much attention, the other forced to make artistic compromises to secure a *longbiao.*

That said, altering one's artistic creation to secure a public release is not necessarily a bad thing, Rosen argues. "Even if you have to negotiate with the censors, one can still make a very good independent film," he said, citing Diao Yinan's latest noir film *The Wild Goose Lake* as an example. "I see a real gap between a commercial film geared for the box office specifically and an independent film not made for the box office," he said. Commercial films are mostly concerned with commerce and playing politics rather than artistic values, he said. Producers don't hesitate to make use of the "little fresh meat" (an Internet buzz word in China used to describe up-and-coming young male celebrities known more for their looks than their talent) to help turn a profit, he added.

How individual young filmmakers proceed depends of course on their personal vision and what they hope to achieve. To Zhai Yixiang (see chapter 6), who has yet to hear from the authorities on the fate of *Mosaic Portrait* as of December 2020, waiting is about the only thing he *can* do right now. His prediction is that because the film is controversial (as it is a hard-hitting tale about rape, patriarchal family values and the unfairness of news reporting), it is being put "on hold" as "no one at the film bureau wants to take responsibility and get blamed for it later," he said in an email exchange.

Zhai said he has no plans of streaming the award-winning project because "several companies have invested in it." Leaving it on the Internet like he did with his previous film, *This Worldly Life,* likely means the companies will not re-coup their investment. Zhai still holds out hope that one day, he might get approval and receive a screening permit, adding that he knows of some filmmakers who saw their projects approved after years of silence.

Jiang Nengjie, director of *Miners, the Horse-keeper and Pneumoconiosis,* an independent documentary about miners suffering from a fatal lung disease, sees it differently. Subjecting his works to censors is not something he had ever entertained. "If we send it to censors, we need to edit out many parts. I'd feel humiliated by the edits as the [amended] version would no longer be my work," he was quoted as saying in the *South China Morning Post.*[28]

When Jiang's film was reviewed by Douban, a leading Chinese review site, he was surprised by the interest it garnered among enthusiasts. In response, he came up with an innovative distribution approach: he sent it to them free through download links using Douban's private messaging function. This not only attracted media attention, it also generated lots of good will with fans, many of whom sent him money for viewing the film.[29]

The 35-year-old director from Hunan said making the movie was personal for him, given that many of the subjects are relatives or friends. Jiang, who has made several documentaries over the years, helps fund his filmmaking by making wedding and corporate videos. In the past, he could put films on online video sites, but public distribution of them has become more difficult over the past few years.

Despite his "success" and innovative distribution approach, Jiang recognizes it may only work once. Baidu Cloud, the storage service where copies of his film are stored, has already erased old links to the documentary, perhaps legally required to clean up illegal or unapproved content on its site. [30]

Finding fresh ways to reach targeted audience is likely to become increasingly challenging for underground filmmakers. This is inevitable as the cat and mouse game between censors and artists in China continues.

A Guide to Seven Generations of Chinese Filmmakers

Most countries see their film history in terms of waves. In China, film experts tend to think of the generation its film directors belong to. Film professor Dai Jinhua believes this is tied to the pace and dramatic twists and turns seen in Chinese society in the last twenty years of the 20th century, causing filmmakers from different generations to have "very different historical experiences and aesthetic pursuits," allowing for relatively distinct groupings. [1]

Film insiders say the practice of generational naming grew out of 5th Generation directors who came of age in the mid-1980s. The strong collective identity of this group was due in large part to their shared experience as "sent-down youths" during the Cultural Revolution. 5th Generation directors include Chen Kaige, Zhang Yimou and Tian Zhuangzhang, a trio that sparked a film revival and put China squarely on the global film map. Once the 5th Generation were "branded," scholars looked back and defined the 4th and earlier generations in relation to the 5th Generation.

Most Chinese scholars now tend to identify six distinct generations, with a seventh one added later by some industry observers. Although some occasionally criticize this categorization approach, including the lack of clear-cut delineations, and at times, the overlapping of generations, it has remained relatively durable. Following is a rundown of their rough characteristics drawn from various Chinese and English sources. [2]

▷ 1st Generation (1905 to 1920s—the pioneers)

This generation encompasses pioneers who introduced film to China in the early 20th century, with most productions coming out of Shanghai and focused on Beijing opera, exotic romance and martial arts films. The granddaddy of Chinese film was a 1905 recording of a Beijing Opera performance, *The Battle of Dingjunshan*, by Ren Fengtai. This inspired projects over the subsequent two decades imbued with an operatic stage perspective marked by fixed camera shots, laborious descriptions of rather mundane plots and a focus on story over the actor performance. The greatest contributions during this period were Zhang Shichuan and Zheng Zhengqiu, who partnered to make China's first short silent feature *Nanfu nanqi* (*Husband and Wife in Misfortune*, 1913), followed by Zhang Shichuan making the first martial arts film, *Huoshao Hongliansi* (*Burning of the Red Lotus Temple*, 1928). Ren Pengnian also contributed with the first full-length silent feature *Yan Ruisheng* (1921). Other directors active during this period include Dan Duyü, Yang Xiaozhong and Shao Zuiweng.

▷ 2nd Generation (the 1930s and 40s—first golden period)

Trained mostly in the early Shanghai commercial cinema, 2nd Generation filmmakers produced in the 1930s and 40s some of the first truly important Chinese films. Their biggest contribution was shepherding the shift from silent films to sound with production temporarily interrupted when Japan occupied Shanghai. This group, many of them "leftists" influenced by Soviet and Hollywood film and traditional Chinese theater, developed the realist film school. They tended to focus on society and ordinary people, particularly peasants and women—symbols of the repressed and left behind. Early masterpieces during this first "golden period" include Cheng Bugao's *Spring Silkworms* (1933), Sun Yu's *The Highway* (1934), Wu Yonggang's *The Goddess* (1934) and Yuan Muzhi's *Street Angel* (1937). And they tended to evoke a more just and equal society while experimenting with innovative visual techniques and narrative structures.

After the Lianhua Company, a major Chinese production house, reestablished itself in Shanghai following the Sino-Japanese war, the city renewed its ties with leftist directors. Several key films during this period focused on disillusionment with the oppressive rule of Chiang Kai-shek's Nationalist Party as well as the Japanese war and its aftermath. These include Shen Fu's *Myriads of Lights* (1948), Zheng Junli's *Crows and Sparrows* (1949), and most importantly, Cai Chusheng's *The Spring River Flows East* (1947) and Fei Mu's *Spring in a Small Town* (1948). *The Spring River Flows East*, a two-part epic about the struggles of ordinary Chinese folks during the Sino-Japanese war, was immensely popular with its social and political references. But the crowning achievement of this period is *Spring in a Small Town*, considered by many to be the finest Chinese film ever made and among the greatest films of all time because of its mature treatment of inter-personal conflicts and the film's exceptional sense of lyricism.

▷ 3rd Generation (1949 to 1970s—the revolutionary romanticists)

A couple of key events shifted the direction of Chinese cinema during the first two decades following 1949. First, the Chinese Communist Party (CCP) nationalized all private studios. It then imprinted its stamp further by setting up studios in key locations and training people in workshops and film schools, including the Beijing Film Academy (BFA) in 1956, honing film as an effective propaganda machine. Initially, 3rd Generation filmmakers embraced socialist realism and revolutionary romanticism. Using the aesthetics of Communist cinema, they created films that showed the violent struggle and war leading up to the start of Communist China in 1949, glorifying the sacrifices of the common man and those who rose up in resistance. This morphed after 1966 into a Chinese socialist popular culture that eventually informed the aesthetic of the "model operas" during the 1966-76 Cultural Revolution.

Some of the best films during this period include Shui Hua and Wang Bin's *The White-haired Girl*, (1950) and Sang Hu's *New Year Sacrifice*, (1956), adapted from Lu Xun's novel of the same name. Others include Shui Hua's *Lin Family Shop*, (1959), inspired by Mao Dun's novel, and Xie Jin's *Women's Basketball Player No. 5* (1957)—the nation's first colored sports film. The oppression suffered by intellectuals in old China was highlighted in works such as Xie Tieli's *On the Threshold of Spring*, (1963). During the decade of the Cultural Revolution, the industry came to a near standstill, save for a few praiseworthy films such as Li Ang and Li Jun's *Sparkling Red Star*, (1974), Yu Yanfu's *Pioneers* (1974), and Chen Huaiqi and Wang Haowei's *Haixia* (1975).

The most prominent director of this era is Xie Jin, whose *The Red Detachment of Women* (1961) and *Two Stage Sisters* (1965) exemplify China's growing technical expertise. Xie was a true survivor and a chameleon of Chinese cinema. He initially made several social-realist films some categorized as part of the "Chinese Hollywood" style. Prime examples include *Two Stage Sisters* and propaganda films such as *Chunmiao* (1975)—about a village girl who became a barefoot doctor through political struggle. Then he reinvented himself in the early 1980s making "scar dramas" like the popular *Hibiscus Town (1986)*, which depicted the emotional scars left by the Cultural Revolution. He then finished the 1990s with *Opium War* (1997), a big-budget war film celebrating Chinese nationalism and Hong Kong's return in 1997.

Most 4th Generation filmmakers were trained at BFA in the 1960s, but had to wait until the Cultural Revolution ended in the late 1970s, when many were close to forty-years-old, to make their first films. This cut their careers short (most made their films in the 1980s), and they often had to compete with 5th Generation directors, many of them their own students.

Because many bore the scars of the Cultural Revolution, often enduring beatings, torture and banishment to the countryside where they were forced to do menial work, this group of filmmakers tended to focus on rural themes, including "scar dramas" involving disastrous incidents in Chinese history and the mindset of rural folk. But they were also the first generation to be formally educated at film schools. That led many to break free of the heavy reliance on overly dramatic structures that had been the hallmark of Chinese cinema, concentrating instead on film art itself. Less didactic than their predecessors, their works leaned towards sentimental humanism, and with a preference for a more humane, naturalistic style.

The best-known directors from this generation include Xie Fei, who made *Girl From Hunan* (1986) and the *Lake of Scented Souls* (1993), and Wu Yigong, director of *Evening Rain* (1980) and *My Memories of Old Beijing* (1983). Other standouts are Teng Wenji, who made *The King of Chess* (1988) and Wu Tianming, director of *Old Well* (1986) and *The King of Masks* (1996). Wu Tianming also played a key role as mentor for 5th Generation directors, helping them find hard-to-come-by opportunities to make their first films as head of Xi'an Film Studio in the 80s. The fact that this cohort was properly trained (instead of learning on the job, like many of their predecessors) helped produce the first batch of notable female directors. Among them were Zhang Nuanxin, who directed *Sha ou* (1981) and *Sacrificed Youth*, (1985); Huang Shuqin, known for *Forever Young* (1983) and *Woman, Demon, Human* (1987)—renowned as China's first feminist film; and Shi Shujun, director of *Death of a College Girl*, (1992), which helped reveal a hospital malpractice cover-up over the death of a student.

5th Generation (mid-1980s to early 1990s—China's golden cinematic revival)

This generation achieved fame as the first graduates from BFA in 1982, as schools finally reopened after the lost decade of the Cultural Revolution. This group, identified with China's cinematic revival and second golden period, is populated by many of China's biggest names, including internationally acclaimed Chen Kaige, Zhang Yimou and Tian Zhuangzhuang. *Yellow Earth* (1984), directed by Chen Kaige and photographed by Zhang Yimou, in many ways marked the beginning of the 5th Generation. Its depiction of peasant life under communism draws on Buddhist and Taoist ideas to question Maoist certainties about how society should be. Chen Kaige made his mark with *King of Children* (1987) and *Farewell My Concubine* (1993). And Zhang Yimou, destined to become an accomplished director in his own right, made *Judou* (1989), and *Raise the Red Lantern* (1991), which won plaudits from Western arthouse audiences as well as Chinese cinema-goers. Often not well appreciated, however, was how many of this generation's filmmakers owed their successes to Wu Tianming, who as head of Xi'an Film Studio in the 1980s opened many doors in a system where connections are instrumental to effectuate their first ventures.

The tough "sent-down youth" experience of this generation born mostly in the 1950s imbued them with a very strong collective identity that fueled a collaborative approach in their early films. A common theme is the weight and burden of memory and the past, especially the Cultural Revolution. Running through many of these films, and a reason they stand out, is their examination of the contradictions between reality and ideology, national culture and mass psychology.

Also distinctive was their creative use of the film language itself. In stark contrast to earlier generations, 5th Generation students were exposed to European films. With China opening, they refused to follow the established Chinese social realist art form and resolved to invent their own film language and style, which tended to be very subjective, symbolic, metaphoric and often with an emphasis on color schemes. Thus, this group ushered in the "Chinese New Wave" and started the new Chinese cinema movement with a bang that lasted almost a decade. Extremely diverse in style and subject, 5th Generation directors' films ranged from black comedy (e.g. Huang Jianxin's *The Black Cannon Incident*, 1985) to the esoteric (Chen Kaige's *Life on a String*, 1991), and the so-called "scar drama" (Tian Zhuangzhuang's *Blue Kite*, 1993), with many winning top prizes at major international film festivals.

Other notable 5th Generation directors include Wu Ziniu, Hu Mei, and Zhou Xiaowen. Although talented actor-turned director Jiang Wen was born in 1963, he was frequently lumped with this group because of his close ties with key directors and his subject matter about rural China and the Cultural Revolution. His *In the Heat of the Sun* (1994) and *Devils on the Doorstep* (2000) are both extremely well regarded domestically and internationally.

Another director often associated with this generation but was not trained at BFA is Feng Xiaogang. Feng, a highly successful commercial filmmaker known for his comedies, broke out from the normal mode by focusing on Beijing-based dramas and periodical films. He is best known for *The Dream Factory* (1997*)*, *Big Shot's Funeral* (2001), *The Banquet* (2006) and *If You Are the One* (2008).

The 5th Generation movement ended shortly after the 1989 Tiananmen crackdown. It is notable that some of the filmmakers' most critical works about the Cultural Revolution came in the early 90s. These include Chen's *Farewell My Concubine* (1993); Zhang's *To Live* (1994) and Tian's *Blue Kite*. All three movies were initially banned by authorities, and to this very day, the latter two remain outlawed. Today, the pillars of this generation continue to produce notable movies, though they are more likely to be big-budget commercial features with A-list casts without the passion and sense of purpose their earlier works were once infused with.

Still, Zhang stands out from the trio because he continues to work prolifically, producing successful, visually stunning and widely praised films, plays and operas. Zhang is also seen as a poster child of his generation for designing the closing ceremonies for the 2008 Olympics, and as the director of *The Great Wall* (2016), a historical sci-fi fantasy widely seen as a Chinese blockbuster intended for the international audience. Some of Zhang's other commercially and critically acclaimed films include *Hero* (2002), *House of Flying Daggers* (2004), *The Flowers of War* (2011) and *Coming Home* (2014).

6th Generation (1990s to 2000s, the urban generation)

Also known as the urban generation, this cohort refers to predominately narrative filmmakers who graduated in the mid-1980s from BFA and the Central Academy of Drama (CAD) in director or screenwriting programs—both part of the government film studio system. These filmmakers started their careers in the early 1990s, when most were near their 30s while China's economic reform was reducing or eliminating state subsidies for art cinema that the previous cohort thoroughly enjoyed. Worse still, their junior status in a rigid hierarchy driven by seniority and loyalty and the growing debt of many state-owned studios meant they would wait close to a decade to start their sanctioned careers. So rather than waiting, a few directors, notably Zhang Yuan, Wang Xiaoshuai and Lou Ye, started making movies underground and smuggling them abroad.

6th Generation members sought to distinguish themselves from their immediate predecessors' rural-centric, stylized epics. To the younger directors, the body of work produced by 5th Generation seemed frivolous and out of touch given that they didn't say much about what was happening in modern China. Many 6th Generation directors expressed their frustrations with a view that "my camera doesn't lie." They used long takes, hand-held cameras, natural lighting, ambient sound and documentary-like narratives. And their material focused on those at the margins of modern urban Chinese life leading to an edgy film movement. Many of these films were shot quickly and inexpensively with money from international funders.

The best-known filmmakers that emerged from this group include Zhan Yuan, who made *Beijing Bastards* (1993) and *East Palace, West Palace* (1997); Wang Xiaoshaui, who directed *Beijing Bicycle* (2001) and *Shanghai Dreams* (2005); and Lou Ye, director of *Suzhou River* (2000) and *Summer Palace* (2006). Other notable filmmakers associated with this group include Guan Hu (*Dirt*, 1992), Lu Xuechang (*The Making of Steel*, 1997), Wang Chao (*The Orphan of Anyang*, 2001) and Zhang Yang (*Shower*, 2002).

A key figure and a game-changer from this group is Jia Zhangke, director of *Xiao Wu* (1997) and *Still Life* (2006). Jia technically is not part of this cohort because he did not join the elite BFA until the early 90s, nor was he even a matriculated student there. In a bit of a rags to riches story, though, he rose from humble roots as a small-town Shanxi student. With a determination to put ordinary folks in front of his lens who lived outside the flashy city centers, he helped forge a new style that included the use of regional dialects, non-professional actors and open-ended narrative. Jia went on to win numerous international awards and become the most eye-catching star of this generation. Some of his more recent and critically acclaimed films include *A Touch of Sin* (2013) and *Mountains May Depart* (2015).

At times working underground, at times above ground, 6th Generation filmmakers have learned to live with and get around censorship. Many have seen their films banned, cut, or relegated to limited release. Lou, for example, was not allowed to make films for three years after his *Suzhou River* was banned. Today, Jia, Wang and Lou remain focused on films that express concerns about the little people left behind by China's ambitious economic reforms.

▷ 7th Generation (2000s to present, the market collaborators)

Scholars and many film industry insiders balk at adding a "7th Generation," or at least a "Post-6th Generation" designation, to China's film legacy. Some directors, notably Wang Xiaoshuai, vehemently deny there's any natural grouping citing a lack of cohesion, shared experience or visions among this class.[3] Since the 6th Generation, when many directors were trained at BFA and CAD, many new film schools and workshops have emerged, replacing the two institutes as sole training grounds for filmmakers, leading to a less cohesive, distinctive vision.

Others see certain unity in the cohort of filmmakers that has emerged since 2000. Mostly born in the 70s, these filmmakers include former actors, writers and people trained overseas. Setting them apart is a greater willingness to work with and embrace commercial realities and find a balance between their own ideas and market demand. Compared to 6th Generation filmmakers, their narrative style tends to be more westernized given that many grew up watching American and European films, although their themes and subject matter are typically Chinese. In their bid to curry favor with audiences, however, some critics say they often undercut their principles and individual style.

Two of the best-known directors from this group are Lu Chuan, director of *Kekexili: Mountain Patrol* (2004) and *City of Life and Death* (2009); and Ning Hao, director of *Crazy Stone* (2006), *Crazy Racer* (2009) and *No Man's Land* (2013). Lu and Ning, both BFA-trained, have very distinctive personal styles. They are also recognized for their daring and commercially successful takes on historical and social issues. Ning, in particularly, is recognized for achieving some of the best investment-to-return ratios among Chinese directors. Others in this generation include US trained Li Fangfang, director of *Heaven Eternal* and *Earth Everlasting* (2010); actor-turned-director Gao Peng, who made the web drama *Modern Times* (2016), and Chang Zheng, director of *Mawen's Battle* (2010).

NOTES

▷ *Introduction*

1. Jia Zhangke, 贾樟柯 Jia's Thoughts. Jia Zhangke's Film Notes 1996-2008 贾想 1996-2008: 贾樟柯电影手记 , Beijing University Press, 北京大学出版社 March 2009, p. 19.

2. Zi Chuan, "Dialogue with Xie Fei: Chinese Films Must be Reformed," *BBC British Net*, August 15, 2014. (In an interview with the BBC, Xie Fei famously said he doesn't expect much from the 5th Generation filmmakers anymore because they are already in their 60s, adding the golden period for a filmmaker is during his/her 30s and 40s—a peak production time. After that, we will begin to degenerate.) https://www.bbc.com/ukchina/simp/entertainment/2014/08/140815_ent_iv_xiefei_london

3. Julie Makinen, "Director Takes Chinese Censorship, Business Battles to Public," *Los Angeles Times*, Oct 18, 2012. https://www.latimes.com/entertainment/movies/la-xpm-2012-oct-18-la-et-mn-china-film-controversy-20121019-story.html

4. Rebecca Davis, "The Death and Revival of Independent Film in China," *Variety*, February 7, 2019. https://variety.com/2019/film/asia/china-independent-film-changing-1203131772/

5. Yin Hong, Zhan Qingsheng, 尹鸿 詹庆生 "Memorandum of the Development of Independent Film and Video in China (1999-2006)" 中国独立影像发展备忘 (1999-2006) *Aisixiang*, 爱思想 2015-12-26, http://www.aisixiang.com/data/95630-2.html

6. Ibid.

7. Yu Yaqin, 余雅琴 "The 6th Generation Directors: How to Choose Between Market and Power, To Succumb or Be Rescued?" 第六代导演：在市场于权利之间，获救还是屈服？ *Beijing News*, 新京报 July 8, 2019. http://www.bjnews.com.cn/culture/2019/07/08/600766.html

8. Yin Hong, Zhan Qingsheng, 尹鸿 詹庆生 "Memorandum of the Development of Independent Film and Video in China (1999-2006)" 中国独立影像发展备忘 (1999-2006) *Aisixiang*, 爱思想 2015-12-26, http://www.aisixiang.com/data/95630-2.html

9. Wang Xiaolu, 王小鲁 "Chinese Film is a Strict Political System," 中国电影是一个严密的政治系统 *World Art*, 世 界 艺 术 2015-06-03. https://mp.weixin.qq.com/s?__biz=MzA4NTIwNDEzOA==&mid=207029316&idx-=5&sn=03cd9a1b678e1933ac8c0b871e2463a0

10. Yin Hong, Zhan Qingsheng, 尹鸿 詹庆生 "Memorandum of the Development of Independent Film and Video in China (1999-2006)" 中国独立影像发展备忘 (1999-2006) *Aisixiang*, 爱思想 2015-12-26, http://www.aisixiang.com/data/95630-2.html

11. Ibid. The original quote: 进入新世纪以来，随着 DV 的普及以及独立制作群体的多元化，"独立"的这种社会批判色彩已经越来越淡了，许多人从事影像创作仅仅是一种职业需要或自我表达的需要。事实上，包括张元、段锦川、蒋樾、吴文光等早期独立制作人也都越来越排斥"独立"这个带着过于强烈意识形态色彩的字眼，他们并不愿将自己置于与"主流"或"意识形态""对抗"的位置上，而更愿意称自己只是一种"个人化"的创作。

12. Yu Yaqin, 余雅琴 "A New Generation of Indie Filmmakers: Escape or Discipline?" 新生代独立电影人：逃离还是规训 *Beijing News*, 新京报 July 16, 2019. http://www.bjnews.com.cn/culture/2019/07/16/603922.html

13. Lu Xinyu, 'Rethinking China's New Documentary Movement: Engagement with the Social,' p. 19. (In Chris Berry, Lu Xinyu and Lisa Rofel (eds), *The New Chinese Documentary Film Movement: For the Public Record*. Hong Kong: Hong Kong University Press, 2010.)

14. Cao Kai, 曹恺 "Raging Currents: China's Independent Film since the Millennium," 潜流汹涌：新千年已降的中国独立影像 *Aotujing DOC*, 凹凸镜 DOC 2018-3-21. https://read01.com/J0MngEP.html#.Xi2lXhd7nuw

15. Yingjin Zhang, "The Sixth Generation and Beyond: Underground and Peripheral," in Yingjin Zhang, *Chinese National Cinema*, Routledge, (New York & London, 2004), p. 289-290

16. Zhang Zhen, "Bearing Witness: Chinese Urban Cinema in the Era of 'Transformation', "in Zhang Zhen (ed), *The Urban Generation: Chinese Cinema and Society at the Turn of the Twenty-first Century (Durham: Duke University Press, 2007)*, p. 10.

17. 1) Fan Bei, 范倍 "The Growing Space of Chinese independent Film: Its Political, Social and Cultural Aspects," 中国独立电影的生长空间：政治的，社会的，文化的 *zhongguo nanfang yisu*, 中国南方艺术 2012-9-30. http://www.zgnfys.com/a/nfpl-34473.shtml ;
    2) Matthew D. Johnson et al (Eds), *China's iGeneation: Cinema and Moving Image Culture for the 21ˢᵗ Century*, (Bloomsbury Academic, 2014) p. 79.

18. Michael Berry, "Working up a Sweat in a Celluloid Sauna" in Michael Berry, *Speaking in Images: Interviews with Contemporary Chinese Filmmakers*. Columbia University Press, (2005). p. 146

19. Wang Xiaolu, 王小鲁 "Chinese Independent Film: A Dream of Twenty Years," 中国独立电影之"廿年一梦" *Economic Observer*, 经济观察网 2012-02-01. http://m.eeo.com.cn/gcj/2012/0201/220079.shtml

20. Fan Bei, 范倍 "The Growing Space of Chinese independent Film: Its Political, Social and Cultural Aspects," 中国独立电影的生长空间：政治的，社会的，文化的 *zhongguo nanfang yisu*, 中国南方艺术 2012-9-30. http://www.zgnfys.com/a/nfpl-34473.shtml

21. Paul G. Pickowicz, "Social and Political Dynamics of Underground Filmmaking in China," Paul G. Pickowicz & Yingjin Zhang (ed.) in *From Underground to Independent: Alternative Film Culture in Contemporary China*, Rowman & Littlefield Publishers, (2006), p. 3

22. Valarie Jaffee, "Bring the World to the Nation: Jia Zhangke and the Legitimation of Chinese Underground Film," *Senses of Cinema*, July 26, 2004. http://sensesofcinema.com/2004/feature-articles/chinese_underground_film/

23. Ibid.

24. Zhang Xianmin: Record of 'The Decade of Independence' Lecture," 张献民： "独立十年"讲座实录 *Mtime*, 时光网 December 31, 2010.
http://group.mtime.com/14177/discussion/1312266/ (This is a recorded lecture in 2010 about China's "independent film.")

25. According to Zhang, the term "Urban Generation" was first coined by her for a film program presented in the spring of 2001 at the Walter Reade Theater at New York's Lincoln Center for the Performing Arts, for which Zhang was a co-organizer. See Zhang Zhen, "Bearing Witness: Chinese Urban Cinema in the Era of 'Transformation'," in Zhang Zhen (ed), *The Urban Generation: Chinese Cinema and Society at the Turn of the Twenty-first Century (Durham: Duke University Press, 2007)*, p. 1

26. Ibid, p. 2.

27. Ibid, p. 6

28. Yingjin Zhang, "The Sixth Generation and beyond: underground and peripheral," in Yingjin Zhang (ed), *Chinese National Cinema*, Routledge, (New York & London, 2004), p. 290.

29. Ibid., 290

30. Zhang Zhen, "Bearing Witness: Chinese Urban Cinema in the Era of 'Transformation'," in Zhang Zhen (ed), *The Urban Generation: Chinese Cinema and Society at the Turn of the Twenty-first Century (Durham: Duke University Press, 2007)*, p. 17.

31. Ibid, p. 19.

32. Lin Xudong, 林旭东 Interview with Jia Zhangke, [A people's director who comes from the grassroots level of China], 一个来自中国基层的民间导演 *Today*, 今日 no. 2 (1999), p. 15. http://reader.epubee.com/books/mobile/51/51921a6f67af0d1b7db8974daece39ec/text00013.html

33. Ibid., p. 19

34. Zhang Zhen, "Bearing Witness: Chinese Urban Cinema in the Era of 'Transformation'," in Zhang Zhen (ed), *The Urban Generation: Chinese Cinema and Society at the Turn of the Twenty-first Century*, p. 15.

35. Ibid., p. 15.

36. Ibid., p. 16.

37. Ibid., p. 16.

38. Wei Xin, 卫昕 "Jia Zhangke: From an Auditing Student to A Teacher at The Central Academy of Drama: Opening the Era of Amateur Cinema," 贾樟柯从旁听生到中戏教师：开启业余电影时代 *Sichuan New Net* and *Chengdu Daily*, 四川新闻网 – 成都日报 September 3, 2004. http://ent.sina.com.cn/2004-09-03/0508492816.html

39. Ibid.

40. Jason McGrath, "The independent Film of Jia Zhangke," in Zhang Zhen (ed), *The Urban Generation: Chinese Cinema and Society at the Turn of the Twenty-first Century*, p. 89.

41. Chapter 4, "Investigating and Transforming Society from the Margin" in Sebastian Veg, *Minjian: The Rise and Fall of Independent Cinema*, Columbia University Press, 2019, pp. 123-163.

42. Cao Kai, 曹恺 "Raging Currents: China's Independent Film since the Millennium," 潜流汹涌：新千年已降的中国独立影像 *Aotujing DOC*, 凹凸镜 DOC 2018-3-21. https://read01.com/J0MngEP.html#.Xi2lXhd7nuw

43. Ibid.

44. Jia Zhangke, "Irrepressible Images: New Films in China from 1995", *China Perspectives*, 2010/1, p. 49. https://www.jstor.org/stable/24054379?refreqid=excelsior%3Aeabcaefb9a9bc4c66f9d-5babc6f409e5&seq=1#metadata_info_tab_contents

45. Jinying Li, "From D-Buffs to the D-Generation: Piracy, Cinema, and an Alternative Public Sphere in Urban China," *International Journal of Communication 6* (2012), p. 543 (in the article Jinying Li argues that "the collective experience of D-buffs in urban China has given rise to a vibrant cineaste culture creating cinematic forms and practices that present an alternative to the hegemony of commercial film industries and state censorship.")

46. Jia Zhangke, "Irrepressible Images: New Films in China from 1995," *China Perspectives,* 2010/1, p. 49. https://www.jstor.org/stable/24054379?refreqid=excelsior%3Aeabcaefb9a9bc4c66f9d-5babc6f409e5&seq=1#metadata_info_tab_contents

47. Ibid., p. 49.

48. Zhang Zhen, "Bearing Witness: Chinese Urban Cinema in the Era of 'Transformation'," in Zhang Zhen (ed), *The Urban Generation: Chinese Cinema and Society at the Turn of the Twenty-first Century*, p. 31.

49. Chapter 4, "Investigating and Transforming Society from the Margin" in Sebastian Veg, Minjian: The Rise and Fall of Independent Cinema, Columbia University Press, 2019, p. 123.

50. Zhang Xianmen, 张献民 "The Unease and Glory of Independent Images—For the Right Not to Fret," 独立电影的尴尬与荣耀：为了不闹心的权利 *Southern Metropolis*, 南方娱乐周刊 2014-05-15. http://ent.sina.com.cn/m/c/2014-05-15/17504142353.shtml

51. Ibid.; and Yeyu Yingmi, 业余影迷 "Farewell, 14-Year-old Independent Video Exhibition," 别了，十四岁的独立影像展 *Baidu.com*, 百度 2020-01-13 http://baijiahao.baidu.com/s?id=16556130331857757915

52. Latham, Kevin, *Pop Culture China: Media, Arts and Lifestyle*, ABC-CLIO, July 2007, pp. 184 to 186.

53. Yu Yaqin, 余雅琴 "Review of 2019 Films: The Age of Top-selling Flicks and An End to Independent Cinema," 2019 电影回顾：迷恋爆款的时代与独立电影的终结 *Beijing News,* 新京报 January 10, 2020. http://www.bjnews.com.cn/culture/2020/01/10/672448.html

54. Li Lixu, "Internal Reasons for the Reform: Serious Problems within China's Higher Education Itself," *China's Higher Education Reform 1998-2003: A Summary,* p. 14. https://files.eric.ed.gov/fulltext/EJ720523.pdf

55. "Reform in the 21ˢᵗ Century," *Education in China*, Wikipedia. https://en.wikipedia.org/wiki/Education_in_China

56. Fareed Zakaria, "The Real Challenge from China: Its People, Not Its Currency," *Time Magazine*, Oct 2010. http://content.time.com/time/magazine/article/0,9171,2024220,00.html

57. Zhang Xianmin: 张献民 "From Zhang Yimou to Guo Jingming, Some Things are the Same," 张献民：从张艺谋到郭敬明，有些东西是一致的，*Yule* 娱乐 2015-11-03. https://kknews.cc/zh-my/entertainment/gaxj98.html

58. Ministry of Education of the PRC, 2000, Issue 10, （教高厅 [2000]10 号）"Opinions on supporting several universities to establish pilot distance education colleges." 《关于支持若干所高等学校建设网络教育学院开展现代远程教育试点工作的几点意见》 http://www.moe.gov.cn/s78/A08/A08_gggs/A08_sjhj/201007/t20100729_124838.html

59. "Professor Zhou Left, But Zhou Chuanji Film School is Always Here," 周老师离开了，但周传基电影学校永远在 *Film Industry Network*, 影视工业网 2017-07-04. https://kknews.cc/education/l68x6ob.html

60. State Council, Regulation on Administration of Films, [2001] no. 342, December 2001, Article 16. SARFT, Interim Provisions on the Access Qualifications for Film Production, Distribution and Exhibition, [2003] No. 20, October 29, 2003, Article 3.

61. Lu Yang, 卢杨 "28 Director Programs in a Decade: But Who Are the Benefactors?" 十年 28 项青年导演计划到底扶持了谁？ *Beijing Business Today*, 北京商报 May 3, 2018. http://www.bbtnews.com.cn/2018/0503/239688.shtml

62. Cao Kai, 曹恺 "Film Review/Duplex Architecture—Model of History of Independent Films", 影评／复试架构 — 中国独立电影史述模型 *Drama and Film Review*, 戏剧与影视评论 May 2016 issue no. 12. http://www.artda.cn/view.php?tid=10442&cid=20

63. "Funding Sources and Distribution Strategies of Independent Films in China," 中国独立电影的资金来源与发行放映策略 *Yngangtie.com*, 高质代笔网 2017/12/13. http://www.yngangtie.com/yishu/1464.html

64. Li Wenyao, 李文瑶 "Alibaba Pictures A Plans to Work with Jia Zhanke's "Tianyi Project" to Support New Directors," 阿里影业 A 计划 携手贾樟柯‘添翼计划’扶持新导演 *Global Net*, 环球网 2016/08/05. https://tech.huanqiu.com/article/9CaKrnJWU1q

65. "2017 Survey Report on the Survival of Young Chinese Directors," 2017 年青年导演生存状态调查报告 *Global Net*, 环球网 2017-12-10. https://china.huanqiu.com/article/9CaKrnK5Zzq

66. According to *Piaofang*, Venice and Berlin int'l festivals stopped their emerging director and debuting director awards in 2013 and 2017 respectively. See Xiaoxiao," 小小 The Joy and Sorrow of New Directors," 新人导演的喜欢和忧愁 *Piaofang, maoyan.com* 票房，猫眼网 January 24, 2019. https://piaofang.maoyan.com/feed/news/52669

67. Ibid.

68. According to *Entertainment Capital*, Bi Gan's *Long Day's Journey into Night* had an investment budget of 20 million RMB ($2.8 million dollars) to start, but the film ultimately spilled over to a final budget of 50 million RMB. See Si Ta Xi, 斯塔西 "Survival of A High Investment Art Film Rescued by 16 Producers,"【地球】背后融资局：16 家出品方救场？一部高额投资艺术篇的求生之旅 *Entertainment Capital,* 娱乐资本论 January 2, 2019. https://mp.weixin.qq.com/s/AcH5lovncclfprx1Qn9PcA

69. Gabrielle Jaffe, "China's indie films and the Way of the Dragon Seal." *Los Angeles Times*, Dec. 9, 2012. https://www.latimes.com/entertainment/movies/la-xpm-2012-dec-09-la-ca-mn-china-indie-films-20121209-story.html

70. Ho Yi, "Film Censorship in China," *Taipei Times*, May 25, 2015. https://www.taipeitimes.com/News/feat/archives/2015/05/25/2003619096

71. Ibid.

72. Ibid.

73. "Our Story," FIRST International Film Festival Website https://www.firstfilm.org.cn/en/about/history/

74. Clarence Tsui, "First Film Festival Remains the Home of Challenging Chinese Cinema," *South China Morning Post*, August 3, 2017. https://www.scmp.com/magazines/post-magazine/arts-music/article/2105064/first-film-festival-remains-home-challenging

75. "Our Story," First International Film Festival Website, https://www.firstfilm.org.cn/en/about/history/

76. See "Full List of Awards" for 2015, 2016 and 2018, Taipei Golden Horse Film Festival. https://www.goldenhorse.org.tw/?r=en

77. "2018 2nd PYIFF Awards," PYIFF website, http://www.pyiffestival.com/index_en/tupian_xiangqing.aspx?id=332

78. Li Yang, "The New Filmmakers Redefining Chinese Independent Cinema," *Six Tone*, June 4, 2018. http://www.sixthtone.com/news/1002398/the-new-filmmakers-redefining-chinese-independent-cinema

79. Ibid.

80. Li Yang, 李洋 "China's New Independent Film Era is Here!" 中国的新独立电影时代到 *Sohu,* 搜狐 2018-03-18. https://www.sohu.com/a/225788069_817440

81. Zhang Xianmin made the comments during a 2017 interview with this author.

82. Yu Yaqin, 余雅琴 "A New Generation of Indie Filmmakers: Escape or Discipline?" 新生代独立电影人：逃离还是规训 *Beijing News*, 新京报 2019-07-16. http://www.bjnews.com.cn/culture/2019/07/16/603922.html

83. As we shall see in chapter 3, *Single Man* became an underground film because of its explicit portrayals of several sexually frustrated rural bachelors. But in Hao's second film *The Love Songs of Tie Dan*, the filmmaker adopted the same strategy of not making comments about historical events in the film and toned down on the sexual exploits of the main character, which helped him secure a screening permit in the end. See Yang Junlei, 杨俊蕾 "Diversity of New Youth Films and Their Cultural Significance: A Look at Some of the Productions by the Baling-hou Directors," 新青年电影的多元走向与文化意义：以 80' 后导演部分新作为例 *Film Art*, 电影艺术 1ˢᵗ issue, 2012, pp. 84-88 https://www.ixueshu.com/document/0c25e-a62490640e542e699891113a67c318947a18e7f9386.html

84. Ibid.

85. Ibid.

86. Yin Hong, Zhan Qingsheng, 尹鸿 詹庆生 "Memorandum of the Development of Independent Film and Video in China (1999-2006)" 中国独立影像发展备忘 (1999-2006) *Aisixiang,* 爱思想 2015-12-26, http://www.aisixiang.com/data/95630-2.html

87. "2017 Survey Report on the Survival of Young Chinese Directors," 2017 年青年导演生存状态调查报告 *Global Net,* 环球网 2017-12-10. https://china.huanqiu.com/article/9CaKrnK5Zzq

88. "Annual Income is Less Than 200,000 RMB? Ecological Survey of a New Generation of Young Directors," 《年收入不足 20 万？新一代青年导演生态调查》*The Paper,* 澎拜 2020-4-20 https://www.thepaper.cn/newsDetail_forward_6901281

89. "China's Female Film Directors," *Timeout Shanghai*, May 9, 2013. http://www.timeoutshanghai.com/features/Books__Film-Film_features/11712/Chinas-female-film-directors.html

90. Mei Yang, "Regional Filmmaking After Jia Zhangke: Relational Cinematic Space and Ying Liang's *The Other Half*," *Sage Journals*. August 26, 2015. https://journals.sagepub.com/doi/full/10.1177/2158244015603104

91. Elena Meyer-Clement, "Rural urbanization under Xi Jinping: From rapid community building to steady urbanization?" *Sage Journal*, September 20, 2019. https://journals.sagepub.com/doi/full/10.1177/0920203X19875931

92. Zhou Zhongmou, 周仲谋 "The Local Changes in the West and the Poetic Images of the Homesickness of the "Local People" —— On Li Ruijun's Local Film Creation," 【西部乡土变迁与 " 在地者 " 乡愁的诗意影像呈现 —— 论李睿珺的乡土电影创作】*Beijing Social Sciences*, 北京社会科学 2018, (12): 68-75. http://www.bjshkx.net/article/2018/1183/1002-3054-0-12-68.html

93. Ibid.

94. 1) Yu Yaqin, 余雅琴 "A New Generation of Indie Filmmakers: Escape or Discipline?" 新生代独立电影人：逃离还是规训 *Beijing News*, 新京报 2019-07-16. http://www.bjnews.com.cn/culture/2019/07/16/603922.

html and 2) Mei Yang, "Regional Filmmaking After Jia Zhangke: Relational Cinematic Space and Ying Liang's *The Other Half*," August 26, 2015, *Sage Journals*. https://journals.sagepub.com/doi/full/10.1177/2158244015603104

95. Yu Huadong, 于华东 "Wanda versus Dadi, Who Will Be the Ultimate King of China's Cinema Market?" 万达 vs. 大地，谁将是中国影院市场最终的王者？ *Mirror Entertainment*, 镜像娱乐 October 24, 2018. https://t.cj.sina.com.cn/articles/view/6216747334/1728c094600100dzv1

96. "Why Experts Think China's Grand Movie-making Bubble is about to Burst," *Business Standard*, June 22, 2018. https://www.business-standard.com/article/international/why-experts-think-china-s-grand-movie-making-bubble-is-about-to-burst-118062200136_1.html

97. Tang Yawen, 汤亚文 "So fast? Young people spend generously, China has surpassed the US in this market!" 这么快？！年轻人们慷慨消费，中国在这个市场已超美国 *Daily Economic News*, 每日经济新闻 2018-05-10. http://www.nbd.com.cn/articles/2018-05-10/1215847.html

98. Zhou Rui, 周蕊 "What is the Rarest Talent in Chinese Film Industry in 2017?2017 年中国电影圈最缺的是人材，青年导演计划" 风潮迭起却少了不浮躁的大环境 - *Unicorn Daily*, 独角兽日报 2017-06-26. http://news.mtime.com/2017/06/26/1570701.html

99. Ibid.

100. Zoe Li, "Noir Thriller May be a Game Changer for Chinese Cinema," *CNN*, April 2, 2014. https://www.cnn.com/2014/04/02/world/asia/china-film-black-coal-thin-ice/index.html

101. Qin Li, 秦丽 "*Black Coal, Thin Ice* Made Millions—Is it Time to Make Profitable Art-house Films?" "白日焰火" 近亿 拍有赚头的文艺片是时候了？ *Sohu Entertainment*, 搜狐娱乐 2014-04-08. https://yule.sohu.com/20140408/n397867071.shtml

102. Zoe Li, "Noir Thriller May be a Game Changer for Chinese Cinema," *CNN*, April 2, 2014. https://www.cnn.com/2014/04/02/world/asia/china-film-black-coal-thin-ice/index.html

103. Kuai Dao, 快刀 "Unveiling the Secrets of Heaven Pictures: A Company that Treats Cinema as Charity," 揭秘天画画天：把电影当慈善做三年出品 10 部电影 *Dianyingjie*, 电影界 2014-10-31. https://www.dianyingjie.com/2014/1031/1996.shtml

104. "Walking Past the Future' Became the Only Chinese Film Shortlisted in Cannes, Backed by Financial Magnate Anle Pictures?" 《路过未来》成入围戛纳的唯一中国影片，安乐影业成背后的资本推手？ *Unicorn Entertainment*, 独角兽娱乐 2017-05-23 https://www.sohu.com/a/142940320_549401

105. Ye Yuchen, 叶雨晨 "Wrath of Silence Encountered High Reputation and Low Box Office," 《暴烈无声》遭遇高口碑低票房 忻钰坤说：这是在预期之中 *YiMagazine*, April 13, 2018. https://www.cbnweek.com/articles/normal/20801

106. Ibid.

107. Piao Fang, 朴芳 "Without the Golden Horse, What's the Next Path for Young Directors and Indie Films?" 不

去金马，青年导演和独立电影接下来的路该怎么走？" Rhino Entertainment 犀牛娱乐 2019-8-11. https://36kr.com/p/5234372

108. Rebecca Davis, "China Film Festival Closes, Saying Independence Is 'Impossible'," *Variety*, January 13, 2020. https://variety.com/2020/film/news/china-independent-film-festival-censorship-1203464803/

109. Ibid.

110. Zhang Xianmin said this during a 2017 interview with this author. He also wrote about the demise of CIFF in an article. According to Zhang, in 2012, CIFF was forced to halt its 9th edition in Nanjing, after being contacted by authorities. CIFF organizers carried out a very small edition of its exhibition that year in Beijing at a bar, and continued its subsequent exhibitions more or less as an underground operation since. Zhang called 2012 the year of demolition. See Zhang Xianmin, 张献民 "China Independent Video 'Year of Demolition'," 中国独立影像 ' 强拆年 'New York Times Chinese website. 纽约时报中文网 May 16, 2013. https://cn.nytimes.com/film-tv/20130516/cc16filmfestival/

111. "The End of an Era": China Independent Video Exhibition Stops, *DW*, January 10, 2020. https://www.dw.com/zh/%E4%B8%80%E4%B8%AA%E6%97%B6%E4%BB%A3%E7%9A%84%E7%B-B%88%E7%BB%93%E4%B8%AD%E5%9B%BD%E7%8B%AC%E7%AB%8B%E5%BD%B1%E5%83%8F%E5%B1%95%E5%81%9C%E5%8A%9E/a-51955281

112. "Law of the People's Republic of China on the Promotion of Film Industry," 中华人民共和国电影产业促进法 *Xinhua News Agency*, 新华社 November 8, 2016. http://politics.people.com.cn/n1/2016/1108/c1001-28842894.html

113. The End of an Era": China Independent Video Exhibition Stops, *DW*, January 10, 2020. https://www.dw.com/zh/%E4%B8%80%E4%B8%AA%E6%97%B6%E4%BB%A3%E7%9A%84%E7%B-B%88%E7%BB%93%E4%B8%AD%E5%9B%BD%E7%8B%AC%E7%AB%8B%E5%BD%B1%E5%8-3%8F%E5%B1%95%E5%81%9C%E5%8A%9E/a-51955281

114. Rebecca Davis, "The Death and Revival of Independent Film in China," *Variety*, February 7, 2019. https://variety.com/2019/film/asia/china-independent-film-changing-1203131772/

115. Ibid.

116. Wang Xiaolu, 王小鲁 "CIFF8, Youth Art Film Screening, Preface: An Adventurous Journey," 《CIFF8 青年艺术电影展映》前言：一次冒险的旅程 *Phoenix Culture*, 凤凰网（文化）2011-10-31. http://culture.ifeng.com/huodong/special/ciff8/content-2/detail_2011_10/31/10291243_0.shtml

117. Patrick Brzeski, "China's Entertainment Industry Pays Back $17 billion in Back Taxes, Following Fan Bingbing Scandal," *Hollywood Reporter*, January 22, 2019. https://www.hollywoodreporter.com/news/fan-bing-bing-scandal-chinas-entertainment-industry-pays-back-17b-back-taxes-1178266

118. Yang Qun, 杨群 "Hot Money Retreats, China's Film and Television Industry Ushered in a Cold Winter" 热钱撤退，中国影视业迎来寒冬 *China News Weekly*, 中国新闻周刊 2019-08-22 http://www.inewsweek.cn/cover/2019-08-22/6753.shtml

119. CCI Team, "How Will the Movie Business Survive the Coronavirus?" *Content Commerce Insider*, May 7, 2020. https://contentcommerceinsider.com/blog/how-will-the-movie-business-survive-the-coronavirusnbsp

▷ **Afterword**

1. Patrick Fater, "China's 'Lost in Russia' Switches to Unprecedented Online Release in Response to Coronavirus Outbreak," *Variety*, Jan. 23, 2020. https://variety.com/2020/film/asia/coronavirus-china-lost-in-russia-online-release-1203478139/

2. Zhao Chunyu, 赵春雨 "Behind 'Lost in Russia's' Defection is the Reality that Film Industry's Ecology is 'Critically Ill,'"《囧妈》叛逃背后，电影业生态"病危" *Shangjie*, 商界 February 18, 2020. http://www.kanshangjie.com/article/167101-1.html

3. Rebecca Davis & Patrick Frater, "How China's Tech Giants Charge Ahead When Coronavirus Shut Down Cinemas," *Variety*, May 6, 2020. https://variety.com/2020/biz/features/china-entertainment-industry-internet-online-theaters-coronavirus-1234598816/

4. Han Fanghang, "'Lost in Russia' and the Search for a Chinese Netflix," *Six Tone*, February 26, 2020. https://www.sixthtone.com/news/1005239/lost-in-russia-and-the-search-for-a-chinese-netflix

5. Patrick Brzeski, "Why Global Theatrical Windows May Emerge Stronger After Covid-19," *Hollywood Reporter*, May 13, 2020. https://www.hollywoodreporter.com/news/why-global-theatrical-windows-may-emerge-stronger-covid-19-1294414

6. Yu Mengmeng, 于蒙蒙 "'Enter the Fat Dragon' Will Be Released in Advance on iQiYi on February 1," 电影《肥龙过江》提档至 2 月 1 日 以超前点映模式在爱奇艺首发上映 *China Securities Journal*, 中国证券报 January 31, 2020. http://finance.eastmoney.com/a/202001311368708012.html

7. Feng Hu, 冯虎 "Free Streaming of Da Peng and Liu Yan's New Film 'The Winners' on Douyin, Watermelon Video and Toutiao," 大鹏、柳岩新片《大赢家》3 月 20 日网络首播 西瓜、抖音、头条免费看 *Economic Daily*, 中国经济网 March 20, 2020. http://www.ce.cn/xwzx/gnsz/gdxw/202003/20/t20200320_34528484.shtml

8. Liz Shackleton, "China's Box Office: National Day Revenues Ranked as Second Highest Ever With \$580 m," *Screendaily*, 12 October, 2020 https://www.screendaily.com/news/china-box-office-national-day-revenues-rank-as-second-highest-ever-with-580m/5153936.article

9. Times Finance 时代财经 "For Movie Theaters, Winter is Not Yet Over: Movies all Releasing at Hot Periods Force Many to Expand at Losses. Survival Has Become the New Mantra," 电影院还在过冬：影片扎堆热门档，血亏扩张，"活下去"成口头禅 *Jiemian.com*, 界面 Dec. 7, 2020. https://www.jiemian.com/article/5376191.html

10. Ibid.

11. Wei Movie, 餵電影 "Film Industry in the Post-epidemic Era: Will the Film Industry Continue to Experience the Unknown, or Face an Accelerated M-shaped Distribution?"「後疫情時代／电影产业」「靠天吃飯」的影視圈將經歷未知的延續，還是 M 型化的加劇？ *The News Lens*, June 29, 2020. https://www.thenewslens.com/feature/post-covid-19/136711

12. Ibid.

13. Ha Mai, 哈麦 "Interview with Pema Tseden: 'Balloon' Suffers an Unfair Treatment, and I Feel Very Sad and Helpless," 专访万玛才旦：《气球》遭遇的排片不公挺悲哀的，很伤感很无奈 *Sohu Entertainment*, 搜狐娱乐 Nov. 27, 2020 https://m.k.sohu.com/d/499703247?channelId=3&page=1

14. Kong Xiaoping, 孔小平 "Faced with Tragic Box Office Sales, 'Wisdom Tooth' Director is Putting House for Sale," 面对票房惨状，《日光之下》导演称已把房子挂出去卖，希望能继续创作 *Yangzi Evening News*, 扬子晚报 December 9, 2020. http://www.yzwb.net/zncontent/1032771.html

15. Yi Tiao, 一条 "With First Day Box Office a Mere 90,000 Yuan, Its Director is Forced to Sell House to Save the Market, Thus Wasting a Good Movie" 首日票房 9 万，导演卖房救市，一部好片就这样被埋没了 *Sina.com*, 新浪网 Dec. 9, 2020. https://k.sina.com.cn/article_5135808743_v1321e38e701900q39w.html

16. Rebecca Davis, "The Death and Revival of Independent Film in China," *Variety*, February 7, 2019. https://variety.com/2019/film/asia/china-independent-film-changing-1203131772/

17. Angela Bao, "Declaration of Independent Films: China's Arthouse Market," *Reach Further*, September 6, 2018. https://www.eastwestbank.com/ ReachFurther/en/News/Article/Chinas-Arthouse-market-declaration-of-independent-films

18. Ibid.

19. Maya E. Rudolph, "Survival in Crisis: Talking to Chinese Independent Filmmakers During a Global Pandemic," *Filmmaker*, July 7, 2020. https://filmmakermagazine.com/109882-survival-in-crisis/#.X9Ab3V57k_W

20. Ibid.

21. Yuan Yun'er, 袁云儿 "iQiyi Teamed up with Elemeet to Solve Distribution Challenges of Art Films: Tough Out is the First to Test the Waters," 爱奇艺联手大象点映解决艺术电影发行痛点，《棒！少年》成为首部试水之作 *Beijing Daily*, 北京日报 November 19, 2020. https://ie.bjd.com.cn/5b165687a010550e5d-dc0e6a/contentApp/5b21d73be4b02439500383f1/AP5fb65a87e4b0c34aa3824d9b.html?isshare=1&contentType=0&isBjh=0

22. Ibid.

23. Ran Ran, "Chinese Film Censorship: The Struggle of the Captured Beast," *BBC News Chinese*, October 18, 2020. https://www.bbc.com/zhongwen/simp/chinese-news-49960157

24. Maya E. Rudolph, "Survival in Crisis: Talking to Chinese Independent Filmmakers During a Global Pandemic," *Filmmaker*, July 7, 2020. https://filmmakermagazine.com/109882-survival-in-crisis/#.X9Ab-

3V57k_W; https://www.dgeneratefilms.com/post/survival-in-crisis-talking-to-chinese-independent-film-makers-during-a-global-pandemic

25. Yu Yaqin and Duan Yaxin, 余雅琴 / 段雅馨 "Zhang Xianmin and Wang Xiaolu Dialogue: Movies Are an Expression of the Common Will of Mankind," 张献民对谈王小鲁：电影是对人类共同意愿的表达 , *Beijing News*, 新京报 July 8, 2020. http://www.bjnews.com.cn/culture/2020/07/08/746628.html

26. Ibid.

27. Ibid.

28. Elaine Yau, "'It's Better Than Dying of Hunger': Plight of Chinese Miners with Deadly Lung Disease Exposed in New Documentary," *South China Morning Post*, April 28, 2020. https://www.scmp.com/lifestyle/entertainment/article/3081852/its-better-dying-hunger-plight-chinese-miners-deadly-lung

29. Ibid.

30. Fu Beimeng, "Premiering in Your Inbox: China's New Indie Doc Sensation," *Sixtone*, May 4, 2020. https://www.sixthtone.com/news/1005595/premiering-in-your-inbox-chinas-new-indie-doc-sensation

▷ *Appendix*

1. Bo Jing, 驳静 "Dai Jinghua: The 6th Generation Directors Are the Only Ones Trying to Connect with Chinese Reality," 戴锦华：只有第六代导演，还在尝试与中国现实发生联系 *Sanlian Shenghuo Zhoukan*, 三联生活周刊 2019-04-15. https://www.douban.com/note/714431442/

2. See a) Filmreference.com under China; b) introduction on Chinese cinema by the British Film Institute; c) definition by Douban, a Chinese social networking service website on film, books and music; and d) Zhang Huiyu, 张慧瑜 "Disintegration and Reorganization of Chinese Film System," 中国电影体制的瓦解与重建 *Guancha*, 观 察 者 2014-08-04. http://www.filmreference.com/encyclopedia/Academy-Awards-Crime-Films/China.html; https://www2.bfi.org.uk/news-opinion/news-bfi/features/century-chinese-cinema-introduction; https://www.douban.com/group/topic/14199837/; https://www.guancha.cn/ZhangHuiZuo/2014_08_04_252862.shtml

3. Wang Xiaoshuai famously said, "In the information era… personalities are emphasized more and more, which means common, group characteristics have vanished." See "Wang Xiaoshuai: The Group of Seventh Generation Directors Will Not Appear," 王小帅："第七代导演"这个群体不会出现" *Chengdu Commercial Daily*, 四川新闻网 / 成都商报 2010-05-18. http://ent.sina.com.cn/m/c/2010-05-18/05372960835.shtml

BIBLIOGRAPHY

▷ **Books and Periodicals**

1. Berry, Chris, Lu Xinyu and Lisa Rofel (eds), *The New Chinese Documentary Film Movement: For the Public Record*. Hong Kong: Hong Kong University Press, 2010.

2. Berry, Michael. *Speaking in Images, Interview with Contemporary Chinese Filmmakers*, Columbia University Press, 2005.

3. Cao Kai, 曹恺 "Film Review/Duplex Architecture—Model of History of Independent Films", 影评 / 复试架构 — 中国独立电影史述模型 *Drama and Film Review*, 戏剧与影视评论 May 2016 issue no. 12. http://www.artda.cn/view.php?tid=10442&cid=20

4. Cornelius, Sheila & Ian Hayon Smith, *New Chinese Cinema: Challenging Representations,* London: Wallflower Press, 2002.

5. Edwards, Dan. *Independent Chinese Documentary*, Edinburgh University Press, 2015.

6. Jia Zhangke, "Irrepressible Images: New Films in China from 1995", *China Perspectives*, 2010/1

7. Jia Zhangke, 贾樟柯 Jia's Thoughts. Jia Zhangke's Film Notes 1996-2008 贾想 1996-2008: 贾樟柯电影手记 , Beijing University Press, 北京大学出版社 March 2009

8. Johnson, Matthew D. et al (Eds), *China's iGeneation: Cinema and Moving Image Culture for the 21ˢᵗ Century,* Bloomsbury Academic, 2014.

9. Latham, Kevin. *Pop Culture China: Media, Arts and Lifestyle*, ABC-CLIO, July 2007

10. Li, Jinying, "From D-Buffs to the D-Generation: Piracy, Cinema, and an Alternative Public Sphere in Urban China," *International Journal of Communication 6*, 2012.

11. Lin Xudong, 林旭东 Interview with Jia Zhangke, [A people's director who comes from the grassroots level of China], 一个来自中国基层的民间导演 *Today*, 今日 no. 2 (1999), p. 15

12. Ouyang Jianghe, 欧阳江河 Zhongguo Duli Dianying Fangtanlu, 中国独立电影访谈录 , Sichuan Literature and Art Publishing House, 四川文艺出版社 2018

13. Pickowicz, Paul and Yingjin Zhang. Ed., *From Underground to Independent: Alternative Film Culture in Contemporary China,* Rowman & Littlefield Publishers, 2006.

14. Sebastian Veg, *Minjian: The Rise and Fall of Independent Cinema*, Columbia University Press, 2019.

15. Xu Jinjing, 许金晶 Zhongguo Duli Dianying Fangtanlu, 中国独立电影访谈录 Zhejiang University Press, 浙江大学出版社 2017.

16. Yang Junlei, 杨俊蕾 "Diversity of New Youth Films and Their Cultural Significance: A Look at Some of the Productions by the Baling-hou Directors" 新青年电影的多元走向与文化意义：以 80' 后导演部分新作为例 *Chinese Academic Journal*, 1ˢᵗ issue, 2012, pp. 84-88

17. Yang, Mei. "Regional Filmmaking After Jia Zhangke: Relational Cinematic Space and Ying Liang's *The Other Half*," *Sage Journals*. August 26, 2015. https://journals.sagepub.com/doi/full/10.1177/2158244015603104

18. Zakaria, Fareed. "The Real Challenge from China: Its People, Not Its Currency," *Time Magazine*, Oct 2010.

19. Zhang, Rui. *The Cinema of Feng Xiaogang*, Hong Kong University Press (2008)

20. Zhang Zhen, ed., *The Urban Generation: Chinese Cinema and Society at the Turn of the 21ˢᵗ Century*, Duke University Press, 2007.

21. Zhang Yingjin, *Chinese National Cinema*, Routledge, 2004.

22. Zhou Zhongmou, "The Local Changes in the West and the oetic Images of the Homesickness of the "Local People" —— On Li Ruijun's Local Film Creation," *Beijing Social Sciences*, 2018, (12): pp. 68-75.

▷ Online News Sources (English)

Angela Bao, "Declaration of Independent Films: China's Arthouse Market," *Reach Further*, September 6, 2018. https://www.eastwestbank.com/ ReachFurther/en/News/Article/Chinas-Arthouse-market-declaration-of-independent-films

Brzeski, Patrick. "China's Entertainment Industry Pays Back $17 billion in Back Taxes, Following Fan Bingbing Scandal," *Hollywood Reporter*, January 22, 2019. https://www.hollywoodreporter.com/news/fan-bingbing-scandal-chinas-entertainment-industry-pays-back-17b-back-taxes-1178266

Brzeski, Patrick. "Why Global Theatrical Windows May Emerge Stronger After Covid-19," *Hollywood Reporter*, May 13, 2020. https://www.hollywoodreporter.com/news/why-global-theatrical-windows-may-emerge-stronger-covid-19-1294414

Davis, Rebecca. "The Death and Revival of Independent Film in China," *Variety*, February 7, 2019. https://variety.com/2019/film/asia/china-independent-film-changing-1203131772/

Davis, Rebecca. "China Film Festival Closes, Saying Independence Is 'Impossible'," *Variety*, January 13, 2020. https://variety.com/2020/film/news/china-independent-film-festival-censorship-1203464803/

Davis, Rebecca, & Patrick Frater, "How China's Tech Giants Charge Ahead When Coronavirus Shut Down

Cinemas," *Variety*, May 6, 2020. https://variety.com/2020/biz/features/china-entertainment-industry-internet-online-theaters-coronavirus-1234598816/

Fater, Patrick. "China's 'Lost in Russia' Switches to Unprecedented Online Release in Response to Coronavirus Outbreak," *Variety*, Jan. 23, 2020. https://variety.com/2020/film/asia/coronavirus-china-lost-in-russia-online-release-1203478139/

Fu Beimeng, "Premiering in Your Inbox: China's New Indie Doc Sensation," *Sixtone*, May 4, 2020. https://www.sixthtone.com/news/1005595/premiering-in-your-inbox-chinas-new-indie-doc-sensation

Han Fanghang, "'Lost in Russia' and the Search for a Chinese Netflix," *Six Tone*, February 26, 2020. https://www.sixthtone.com/news/1005239/lost-in-russia-and-the-search-for-a-chinese-netflix

Jaffee, Valarie. "Bring the World to the Nation: Jia Zhangke and the Legitimation of Chinese Underground Film," *Senses of Cinema*, July 2004. http://sensesofcinema.com/2004/feature-articles/chinese_underground_film/

Li Yang, "The New Filmmakers Redefining Chinese Independent Cinema," *Six Tone*, June 4, 2018. http://www.sixthtone.com/news/1002398/the-new-filmmakers-redefining-chinese-independent-cinema

Li, Zoe. "Noir Thriller May be a Game Changer for Chinese Cinema," *CNN*, April 2, 2014. https://www.cnn.com/2014/04/02/world/asia/china-film-black-coal-thin-ice/index.html

Makinen, Julie. "Director Takes Chinese Censorship, Business Battles to Public," *Los Angeles Times*, Oct 18, 2012. https://www.latimes.com/entertainment/movies/la-xpm-2012-oct-18-la-et-mn-china-film-controversy-20121019-story.html

Ran Ran, "Chinese Film Censorship: The Struggle of the Captured Beast," *BBC News Chinese*, October 18, 2020. https://www.bbc.com/zhongwen/simp/chinese-news-49960157

Rudolph, Maya E. "Survival in Crisis: Talking to Chinese Independent Filmmakers During a Global Pandemic," *Filmmaker*, July 7, 2020. https://filmmakermagazine.com/109882-survival-in-crisis/#.X9Ab-3V57k_W

Shackleton, Liz. "China's Box Office: National Day Revenues Ranked as Second Highest Ever With $580 m," *Screendaily*, 12 October, 2020 https://www.screendaily.com/news/china-box-office-national-day-revenues-rank-as-second-highest-ever-with-580m/5153936.article

Tsui, Clarence. "First Film Festival Remains the Home of Challenging Chinese Cinema," *South China Morning Post*, August 3, 2017. https://www.scmp.com/magazines/post-magazine/arts-music/article/2105064/first-film-festival-remains-home-challenging

Yau, Elaine "'It's Better Than Dying of Hunger': Plight of Chinese Miners with Deadly Lung Disease Exposed in New Documentary," *South China Morning Post*, April 28, 2020. https://www.scmp.com/lifestyle/entertainment/article/3081852/its-better-dying-hunger-plight-chinese-miners-deadly-lung

Zi Chuan, "Dialogue with Xie Fei: Chinese Films Must be Reformed," *BBC British Net*, August 15, 2014. https://www.bbc.com/ukchina/simp/entertainment/2014/08/140815_ent_iv_xiefei_london

▷ *Online News Sources (Chinese)*

- Bo Jing, 驳静 "Dai Jinghua: The 6th Generation Directors Are the Only Ones Trying to Connect with Chinese Reality," 戴锦华：只有第六代导演，还在尝试与中国现实发生联系 *Sanlian Shenghuo Zhoukan*, 三联生活周刊 2019-04-15. https://www.douban.com/note/714431442/

- Cao Kai, 曹恺 "Raging Currents: China's Independent Film since the Millennium," 潜流汹涌：新千年已降的中国独立影像 *Aotujing DOC*, 凹凸镜 DOC 2018-3-21. https://read01.com/J0MngEP.html#.Xi2lXhd7nuw

- Fan Bei, 范倍 "The Growing Space of Chinese independent Film: Its Political, Social and Cultural Aspects," 中国独立电影的生长空间：政治的，社会的，文化的 *zhongguo nanfang yisu*, 中国南方艺术 2012-9-30. http://www.zgnfys.com/a/nfpl-34473.shtml

- Feng Hu, 冯虎 "Free Streaming of Da Peng and Liu Yan's New Film 'The Winners' on Douyin, Watermelon Video and Toutiao," 大鹏、柳岩新片《大赢家》3 月 20 日网络首播 西瓜、抖音、头条免费看 *Economic Daily*, 中国经济网 March 20, 2020. http://www.ce.cn/xwzx/gnsz/gdxw/202003/20/t20200320_34528484.shtml

- Ha Mai, 哈麦 "Interview with Pema Tseden: 'Balloon' Suffers an Unfair Treatment, and I Feel Very Sad and Helpless," 专访万玛才旦：《气球》遭遇的排片不公挺悲哀的，很伤感很无奈 *Sohu Entertainment*, 搜狐娱乐 Nov. 27, 2020 https://m.k.sohu.com/d/499703247?channelId=3&page=1

- Kong Xiaoping, 孔小平 "Faced with Tragic Box Office Sales, 'Wisdom Tooth' Director is Putting House for Sale," 面对票房惨状，《日光之下》导演称已把房子挂出去卖，希望能继续创作 *Yangzi Evening News*, 扬子晚报 December 9, 2020. http://www.yzwb.net/zncontent/1032771.html

- Kuai Dao, 快刀 "Unveiling the Secrets of Heaven Pictures: A Company that Treats Cinema as Charity," 揭秘天画画天：把电影当慈善做三年出品 10 部电影 *Dianyingjie*, 电影界 2014-10-31. https://www.dianyingjie.com/2014/1031/1996.shtml

- Li Wenyao, 李文瑶 "Alibaba Pictures A Plans to Work with Jia Zhanke's "Tianyi Project" to Support New Directors," 阿里影业 A 计划 携手贾樟柯'添翼计划'扶持新导演 *Global Net*, 环球网 2016/08/05. https://tech.huanqiu.com/article/9CaKrnJWU1q

- Li Yang, 李洋 "China's New Independent Film Era is Here!" 中国的新独立电影时代到 *Sohu*, 搜狐 2018-03-18. https://www.sohu.com/a/225788069_817440

- Lu Yang, 卢杨 "28 Director Programs in a Decade: But Who Are the Benefactors?" 十年 28 项青年导演计划到底扶持了谁？ *Beijing Business Today*, 北京商报 May 3, 2018. http://www.bbtnews.com.cn/2018/0503/239688.shtml

Piao Fang, 朴芳 "Without the Golden Horse, What's the Next Path for Young Directors and Indie Films?" 不去金马，青年导演和独立电影接下来的路该怎么走？ Rhino Entertainment 犀牛娱乐 2019-8-11. https://36kr.com/p/5234372

Qin Li, 秦丽 *Black Coal, Thin Ice* Made Millions—Is it Time to Make Profitable Art-house Films?" 《白日焰火》近亿 拍有赚头的文艺片是时候了？ *Sohu Entertainment*, 搜狐娱乐 2014-04-08. https://yule.sohu.com/20140408/n397867071.shtml

Shidai Caijing 时代财经 "For Movie Theaters, Winter is Not Yet Over: Movies all Releasing at Hot Periods Force Many to Expand at Losses. Survival Has Become the New Mantra," 电影院还在过冬：影片扎堆热门档，血亏扩张，"活下去"成口头禅 *Jiemian.com*, 界面 Dec. 7, 2020. https://www.jiemian.com/article/5376191.html

Si Ta Xi, 斯塔西 "Survival of A High Investment Art Film Rescued by 16 Producers," 《地球》背后融资局：16 家出品方救场？一部高额投资艺术篇的求生之旅 *Entertainment Capital*, 娱乐资本论 January 2, 2019. https://mp.weixin.qq.com/s/AcH5lovncclfprx1Qn9PcA

Simultaneous Sound, 同期声 "List of China's First to Seventh Generation Director" 中国的第一至第七代导演一览 Douban 豆瓣 2010-09-19 https://www.douban.com/group/topic/14199837/

Tang Yawen, 汤亚文 "So fast? Young people spend generously, China has surpassed the US in this market!" 这么快？！年轻人们慷慨消费，中国在这个市场已超美国 *Daily Economic News*, 每日经济新闻 2018-05-10. http://www.nbd.com.cn/articles/2018-05-10/1215847.html

Wang Xiaolu, 王小鲁 "Chinese Independent Film: A Dream of Twenty Years," 中国独立电影之 "廿年一梦" *Economic Observer*, 经济观察网 2012-02-01. http://m.eeo.com.cn/gcj/2012/0201/220079.shtml

Wang Xiaolu, 王小鲁 "Chinese Film is a Strict Political System," 中国电影是一个严密的政治系统 *World Art*, 世界艺术 2015-06-03. https://mp.weixin.qq.com/s?__biz=MzA4NTIwNDEzOA==&mid=207029316&idx=5&sn=03cd9a1b678e1933ac8c0b871e2463a0

Wang Xiaolu, 王小鲁 "CIFF8, Youth Art Film Screening, Preface: An Adventurous Journey," 《CIFF8 青年艺术电影展映》前言：一次冒险的旅程 *Phoenix Culture*, 凤凰网（文化）2011-10-31. http://culture.ifeng.com/huodong/special/ciff8/content-2/detail_2011_10/31/10291243_0.shtml

Wei Movie, 餵電影 "Film Industry in the Post-epidemic Era: Will the Film Industry Continue to Experience the Unknown, or Face an Accelerated M-shaped Distribution?" ⌈後疫情時代／电影产业」「靠天吃飯」的影視圈將經歷未知的延續，還是 M 型化的加劇⌉ *The News Lens*, June 29, 2020. https://www.thenewslens.com/feature/post-covid-19/136711

Wei Xin, 卫昕 "Jia Zhangke: From an Auditing Student to A Teacher at The Central Academy of Drama: Opening the Era of Amateur Cinema," 贾樟柯从旁听生到中戏教师．开启业余电影时代 *Sichuan New Net* and *Chengdu Daily*, 四川新闻网 - 成都日报 September 3, 2004. http://ent.sina.com.cn/2004-09-03/0508492816.html

Xiaoxiao," 小小 The Joy and Sorrow of New Directors," 新人导演的喜欢和忧愁 *Piaofang, maoyan.com* 票房 , 猫眼网 January 24, 2019. https://piaofang.maoyan.com/feed/news/52669

Yang Qun, 杨群 "Hot Money Retreats, China's Film and Television Industry Ushered in a Cold Winter" 热钱撤退 , 中国影视业迎来寒冬 *China News Weekly,* 中国新闻周刊 2019-08-22 http://www.inewsweek.cn/cover/2019-08-22/6753.shtml

Ye Yuchen, 叶雨晨 "Wrath of Silence Encountered High Reputation and Low Box Office," 《暴烈无声》遭遇高口碑低票房 忻钰坤说：这是在预期之中 *YiMagazine*, April 13, 2018. https://www.cbnweek.com/articles/normal/20801

Yeyu Yingmi, 业余影迷 "Farewell, 14-Year-old Independent Video Exhibition," 别了，十四岁的独立影像展 *Baidu.com*, 百度 2020-01-13, http://baijiahao.baidu.com/s?id=1655613033185757915

Yi Tiao 一条 , "With First Day Box Office a Mere 90,000 Yuan, Its Director is Forced to Sell House to Save the Market, Thus Wasting a Good Movie" 首日票房 9 万，导演卖房救市，一部好片就这样被埋没了 *Sina.com*, 新浪网 Dec. 9, 2020. https://k.sina.com.cn/article_5135808743_v1321e38e701900q39w.html

Yin Hong, Zhan Qingsheng, 尹鸿 詹庆生 "Memorandum of the Development of Independent Film and Video in China (1999-2006)" 中国独立影像发展备忘 (1999-2006) *Aisixiang,* 爱思想 2015-12-26, http://www.aisixiang.com/data/95630-2.html

Yu Huadong, 于华东 "Wanda versus Dadi, Who Will Be the Ultimate King of China's Cinema Market?" 万达 vs. 大地，谁将是中国影院市场最终的王者？ *Mirror Entertainment*, 镜像娱乐 October 24, 2018. https://t.cj.sina.com.cn/articles/view/6216747334/1728c094600100dzv1

Yu Mengmeng, 于蒙蒙 "'Enter the Fat Dragon' Will Be Released in Advance on iQiYi on February 1," 电影《肥龙过江》提档至 2 月 1 日 以超前点映模式在爱奇艺首发上映 *China Securities Journal,* 中国证券报 January 31, 2020. http://finance.eastmoney.com/a/202001311368708012.html

Yu Yaqin, 余雅琴 "The Sixth Generation Directors: How to Choose Between Market and Power, To Succumb or Be Rescued?" 第六代导演：在市场于权利之间，获救还是屈服？ *Beijing News*, 新京报 July 8, 2019. http://www.bjnews.com.cn/culture/2019/07/08/600766.html

Yu Yaqin, 余雅琴 "A New Generation of Indie Filmmakers: Escape or Discipline?" 新生代独立电影人：逃离还是规训 *Beijing News*, 新京报 July 16, 2019. http://www.bjnews.com.cn/culture/2019/07/16/603922.html

Yu Yaqin, 余雅琴 "Review of 2019 Films: The Age of Top-selling Flicks and An End to Independent Cinema," 2019 电影回顾：迷恋爆款的时代与独立电影的终结 *Beijing News,* 新京报 January 10, 2020. http://www.bjnews.com.cn/culture/2020/01/10/672448.html

Yu Yaqin and Duan Yaxin, 余雅琴 / 段雅馨 "Zhang Xianmin and Wang Xiaolu Dialogue: Movies Are an Expression of the Common Will of Mankind," 张献民对谈王小鲁：电影是对人类共同意愿的表达 , *Beijing News*, 新京报 July 8, 2020. http://www.bjnews.com.cn/culture/2020/07/08/746628.html

Yuan Yun'er, 袁云儿 "iQiyi Teamed up with Elemeet to Solve Distribution Challenges of Art Films: Tough Out is the First to Test the Waters," 爱奇艺联手大象点映解决艺术电影发行痛点，《棒！少年》成为首部试水之作 *Beijing Daily*, 北京日报 November 19, 2020.
https://ie.bjd.com.cn/5b165687a010550e5ddc0e6a/contentApp/5b21d73be4b02439500383f1/AP5f-b65a87e4b0c34aa3824d9b.html?isshare=1&contentType=0&isBjh=0

Zhang Huiyu, 张慧瑜 "Disintegration and Reorganization of Chinese Film System," 中国电影体制的瓦解与重建 *Guancha*, 观察者 2014-08-04.
https://www.guancha.cn/ZhangHuiZuo/2014_08_04_252862.shtml

Zhang Xianmin: Record of 'The Decade of Independence' Lecture," 张献民："独立十年"讲座实录 *Mtime*, 时光网 December 31, 2010 http://group.mtime.com/14177/discussion/1312266/

Zhang Xianmin, 张献民 "China Independent Video 'Year of Demolition'," 中国独立影像'强拆年'New York Times Chinese website. 纽约时报中文网 May 16, 2013. https://cn.nytimes.com/film-tv/20130516/cc16filmfestival/

Zhang Xianmen, 张献民 "The Unease and Glory of Independent Images—For the Right Not to Fret," 独立电影的尴尬与荣耀：为了不闹心的权利 *Southern Metropolis*, 南方娱乐周刊 2014-05-15. http://ent.sina.com.cn/m/c/2014-05-15/17504142353.shtml

Zhang Xianmin: 张献民 "From Zhang Yimou to Guo Jingming, Some Things are the Same," 张献民：从张艺谋到郭敬明，有些东西是一致的, *Yule* 娱乐 2015-11-03. https://kknews.cc/zh-my/entertainment/gaxj98.html

Zhao Chunyu, 赵春雨 "Behind 'Lost in Russia's' Defection is the Reality that Film Industry's Ecology is 'Critically Ill'," 《囧妈》叛逃背后，电影业生态"病危" *Shangjie*, 商界 February 18, 2020. http://www.kanshangjie.com/article/167101-1.html

Zhou Rui, 周蕊 "What is the Rarest Talent in Chinese Film Industry in 2017? 2017 年中国电影圈最缺的是人材，青年导演计划"风潮迭起却少了不浮躁的大环境 - *Unicorn Daily*, 独角兽日报 2017-06-26. http://news.mtime.com/2017/06/26/1570701.html

Zhou Zhongmou, 周仲谋 "The Local Changes in the West and the Poetic Images of the Homesickness of the "Local People" —— On Li Ruijun's Local Film Creation," 西部乡土变迁与"在地者"乡愁的诗意影像呈现 —— 论李睿珺的乡土电影创作 *Beijing Social Sciences*, 北京社会科学 2018, (12): 68-75. http://www.bjshkx.net/article/2018/1183/1002-3054-0-12-68.html

"2017 Survey Report on the Survival of Young Chinese Directors," 2017 年青年导演生存状态调查报告 *Global Net*, 环球网 2017-12-10. https://china.huanqiu.com/article/9CaKrnK5Zzq

"Annual Income is Less Than 200,000 RMB? Ecological Survey of a New Generation of Young Directors," 《年收入不足 20 万？新一代青年导演生态 调查》 *The Paper*, 澎拜 2020-4-20 https://www.thepaper.cn/newsDetail_forward_6901281

"'Walking Past the Future' Became the Only Chinese Film Shortlisted in Cannes, Backed by Financial Magnate Anle Pictures?" 《路过未来》成入围戛纳的唯一中国影片，安乐影业成背后的资本推手？ *Unicorn Entertainment*，独角兽娱乐 2017-05-23 https://www.sohu.com/a/142940320_549401

"Wang Xiaoshuai: The Group of Seventh Generation Directors Will Not Appear," 王小帅："第七代导演"这个群体不会出现" *Chengdu Commercial Daily*, 四川新闻网 / 成都商报　2010-05-18. http://ent.sina.com.cn/m/c/2010-05-18/05372960835.shtml

▷ Reports and Statements by Governments and Non-government organizations:

Elena Meyer-Clement, "Rural urbanization under Xi Jinping: From rapid community building to steady urbanization?" *Sage Journal*, September 20, 2019. https://journals.sagepub.com/doi/full/10.1177/0920203X19875931

Li Lixu, "Internal Reasons for the Reform: Serious Problems within China's Higher Education Itself," *China's Higher Education Reform 1998-2003: A Summary*, p. 14. https://files.eric.ed.gov/fulltext/EJ720523.pdf

"2018 2nd PYIFF Awards," PYIFF website, http://www.pyiffestival.com/index_en/tupian_xiangqing.aspx?id=332

British Film Institute, introduction of Chinese cinema
https://www2.bfi.org.uk/news-opinion/news-bfi/features/century-chinese-cinema-introduction

Filmreference.com, under China
http://www.filmreference.com/encyclopedia/Academy-Awards-Crime-Films/China.html;

"Full List of Awards" for 2015, 2016 and 2018, Taipei Golden Horse Film Festival. https://www.goldenhorse.org.tw/?r=en

"Funding Sources and Distribution Strategies of Independent Films in China," 中国独立电影的资金来源与发行放映策略 *Yngangtie.com*, 高质代笔网 2017/12/13. http://www.yngangtie.com/yishu/1464.html

Ministry of Education of the PRC, 2000, Issue 10, （教高厅 [2000]10 号）"Opinions on supporting several universities to establish pilot distance education colleges." 《关于支持若干所高等学校建设网络教育学院开展现代远程教育试点工作的几点意见》 http://www.moe.gov.cn/s78/A08/A08_gggs/A08_sjhj/201007/t20100729_124838.html

"Our Story," FIRST International Film Festival Website https://www.firstfilm.org.cn/en/about/history/

"Professor Zhou Left, But Zhou Chuanji Film School is Always Here," 周老师离开了，但周传基电影学校永远在 *Film Industry Network*, 影视工业网 2017-07-04. https://kknews.cc/education/l68x6ob.html

"Reform in the 21ˢᵗ Century," *Education in China*, Wikipedia. https://en.wikipedia.org/wiki/Education_in_China

State Council, Regulation on Administration of Films, [2001] no. 342, December 2001, Article 16. SARFT, Interim Provisions on the Access Qualifications for Film Production, Distribution and Exhibition, [2003] No. 20, October 29, 2003, Article 3.

INDEX

C

D

ABOUT THE AUTHOR

Karen Ma is a US-based independent film scholar and movie critic specializing in Chinese cinema. Ma was raised in Hong Kong and Japan, educated in the US and was a former Chinese culture and film lecturer for several years at The Beijing Center of Chinese Studies, China. Her film reviews and China-related articles have appeared in *The New York Times,* NPR, *The Japan Times, The Asahi Evening News, South China Morning Post* and the online *VCinema* and *dGenerate Films,* among others. A longtime film enthusiast, Ma has worked, edited and judged at several China-related film festivals, including the China-based Chinese Independent Film Festival (2016) and the 5th DC Chinese Film Festival (2020).

Ma has an undergraduate degree from Tokyo's Sophia University and an M.A. in Chinese literature from the University of Washington, Seattle. She is the author of *Excess Baggage* (China Books, 2013), a novel about a Chinese family's struggle to make its way in Tokyo.